OUT

OF

FOCUS

Why Gen Z's Mental Health Crisis Is More Complex Than You Think

Aly Vredenburgh

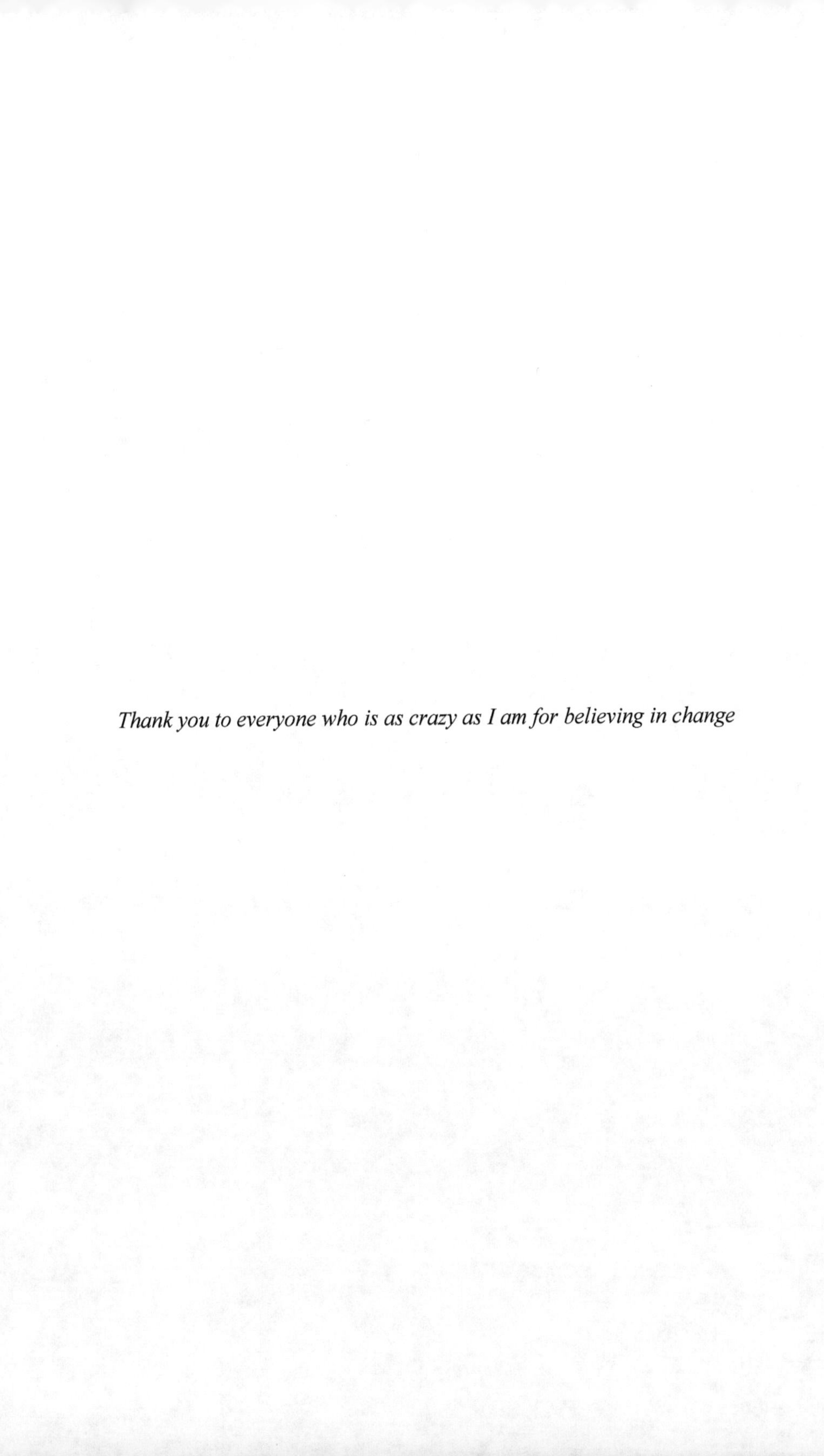

CONTENTS

Part 1

How the System is Failing

Introduction: Why Mental Health Matters

The humanity we all share is more important than the mental illnesses we may not.
— Elyn R. Saks

The first time I was failed, I was 15 years old and had been sexually assaulted by a classmate. After that incident, I started self-harming, withdrawing, and was bullied by both classmates and teachers. The first time I entered the mental healthcare system was when I was hospitalized months later for a suicide attempt. During my three days at the hospital, I was put on heavy doses of antipsychotics, subjected to group situations with others who had much scarier stories than my own, and exposed to adults who told me I was broken and needed to be fixed.

As an adult, I do not view my experience as unique, but I do see where I was failed by our many systems and institutions, including our medical and educational ones. When I went to a trusted school nurse about being bullied by other students, I was told to ignore it. When I self-harmed in front of a teacher, they ignored it. After being hospitalized, parents no longer let their kids near me because I was suddenly "dangerous." The medications gave me cystic acne, caused weight gain, and numbed my existence. I ask myself, *had someone listened to me, saw the abuse I received, intervened, and given me trauma counseling to process the assault, could I have avoided hospitalization?* If I was successful in my attempt at 15, I would have been another statistic.

In an episode of the podcast *The Happiness Lab*, Dr. Laurie Santos, a Yale professor, was interviewed about her experience working with students at her prestigious university. The statistics she highlights from a national poll of college students (ages 18-25) should startle anyone: 40 percent of students reported being too depressed to function; 60 percent reported being very anxious; 50 percent of students said they were very lonely; and 10 percent had seriously considered suicide recently. I think, by now, most of us recognize there is a mental health crisis because the rates of depression, anxiety, and suicide in our youth are alarmingly high.[1,2] The question is: what is the cause?

Mental health is the core indicator of a robust society. Yet, we are in a crisis, one centered on my generation: Generation Z (born between 1997 and 2012). Currently, more than 50 million people (roughly 1 in 5)[3] are experiencing mental illness in the US. Almost a third of all adults struggling with a mental illness reported that they were not able to receive the treatment they needed, with almost half reporting that they were unable to receive necessary care because of prohibitive costs.[4] According to the National Alliance on Mental Illness, suicide is the second-leading cause of death among people aged 10 to 14 and 25 to 34.[5] Our youth are being failed, but there is opportunity to change the way America addresses it. While this book addresses the American system, many other countries are facing the same systemic issues and mental health crisis among their young adults.

When my parents were kids, mental illness was considered rare. Data suggest that the rates of depression and anxiety have increased over 100 percent in youth since the 1980's. Gen Z has faced a unique array of intersectional factors that have led to this crisis, and news outlets have published story after story about the alarming rates of suicide, unemployment, and disability. But blame continues to be placed most prominently on social media and the technological revolution: from NYU's Jonathan Haidt's, *The Anxious Generation*,[6] to NPR's, *Body Electric* series,[7] many researchers and experts agree social media is causing serious harm to mental health. While these professionals make a valid point, they are ignoring other factors that I aim to address. From my perspective, blaming social media alone is irresponsible because it excludes important interrelated factors that contribute to this crisis.

It is no secret that many members of my generation are considered the "snowflake generation," because we are poorly adjusted, and very sensitive, but it seems as though we were set up to fail. Not only are we fighting an impending climate crisis, a housing crisis, inflation crisis, the unfeasible rise in cost of living, and the inability to pay for necessities, but we are also living through an unprecedented mental health crisis. I come from a generation of defunded arts programs, defunded music programs, and an exhausting competition for jobs, college admission, careers, and beauty culture. And when I dig deeper, I find that social media is just one among many causal factors of this epidemic. The Declaration of Independence states that we have an "unalienable right to the pursuit of happiness,"[8] yet we shamefully leave those of us with disability behind. For some reason, this topic continues to be neglected from our discourse, and the failure to confront it is devastating families across our country—and the urgency of the mental illness crisis should not be taken lightly. The consequences of untreated, or insufficiently treated, mental illness are far-reaching and demand consideration. Beyond the individual, families, communities, and societal productivity are greatly impacted by our failed system. Neglected mental health conditions can lead to significant disability, unemployment, substance abuse, homelessness, incarceration, and suicide. In terms of economic impact alone, the US bears a burden exceeding 282 billion dollars annually due to the costs associated with untreated mental illness.[9] Taken together, mental illness is a crisis that needs to be addressed differently.

What is unique about mental health is that it's a universal concern. It impacts you whether you are rich or poor, conservative or liberal, religious, degreed or not. It affects individuals regardless of race, gender, class, and sexual orientations (although some groups may have stressors that increase the probability of being afflicted, which I discuss in Chapter 10). It is a state of being that impacts us all. Many of us may feel that we are responsible for our own mental health, but it is important to recognize that our systems and institutions created the root causes of our mental health crisis of increased rates of anxiety and depression. There is an array of intersectional systemic issues that are continuously overlooked by our leaders, even the ones advocating for change. Over and over, we are told we need more workers, more hospitals, and to make care affordable. Yes, we do. But what if the reason we are supremely understaffed in mental healthcare has been due to the alarming rates of increasing mental illness? And what if this increase is beyond what has ever been discussed in one treatise? I believe we aren't the problem; the system is. And until we view this crisis holistically, the changes made will only bandage a growing, festering epidemic of mental illness.

Systems Thinking

You might be wondering how mental health can be viewed from a systems level. To fully engage with this book, I invite you to delve into systems thinking with me. In simplest terms, it involves examining the various elements and relationships that can influence a desired outcome. From a holistic viewpoint, this theory considers the entire system, its diverse subsystems, and the repetitive patterns and interconnections that emerge among those subsystems. Systems thinkers recognize the interconnectedness of everything. Trees, for instance, rely on carbon dioxide, water, and sunlight to flourish. In turn, humans depend on food and oxygen produced by trees, as well as the wood to construct and heat their homes.

A systems thinker views the world as a dynamic and interdependent web of relationships and feedback loops. There are two main types of feedback loops: reinforcing loops, which amplify trends, and balancing loops, which maintain equilibrium. In psychology, experts examine how feedback loops influence one or more symptoms of someone experiencing an illness. For instance, consider a person's emotions leading up to a significant event: anxiety or fear may have a detrimental effect on the person's experience/action relative to the event, while confidence may produce the opposite outcome. A person might create an equilibrium loop by not attending the event and isolating themselves; in this case, nothing goes "wrong," but.... in turn, the person could create a reinforcing loop by attending the event, and in the case that something goes wrong it would reinforce their beliefs that were causing their anxiety in the first place. Lastly, a systems thinker perceives causality as a dynamic and ever-evolving process that enables deeper comprehension of feedback loops, agency, connections, and relationships.

The American mental healthcare system comprises a network of providers, facilities, pharmaceutical companies, and support services aimed at addressing mental health needs (see Figure 1). While mental healthcare has made considerable progress, especially in the destigmatization of some forms of mental illness, significant challenges persist. Identifying and understanding these systemic failures is essential for implementing meaningful reforms. All of these, and more, will be explored in depth in the subsequent chapters.

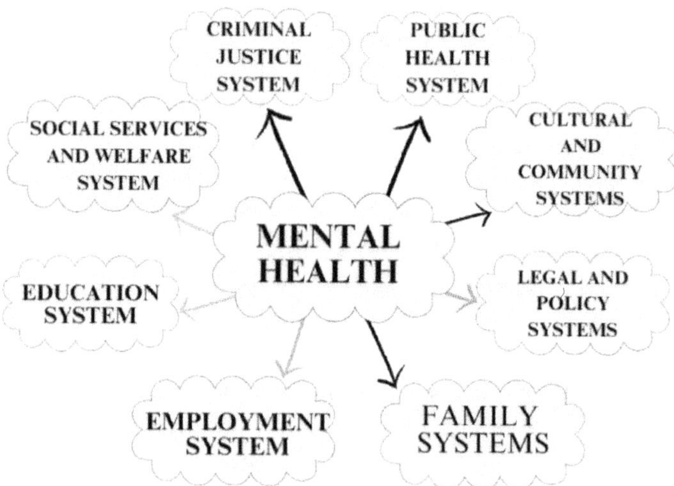

Figure 1. Our mental health system

What This Book Will Do

I created this book with two motives in mind: to educate our world about the root causes of the Gen Z mental health crisis, and to motivate solutions. I begin by sharing the stories of my generation to help immerse you into our world. Leveraging research, real stories, and personal experience, I will discuss the intersectional factors contributing to our mental health struggles, from systemic issues (like economic instability, public policy, and educational shortcomings) to societal shifts in parenting and nutritional deficiencies stemming from modern farming practices. The chapters ahead explore specific dimensions of systemic failures, including access barriers, stigma, inadequate resources, emotional neglect, media, and the loneliness epidemic. Grounding the discussion in empirical evidence, I will provide a comprehensive and objective examination of the systemic failures within the mental healthcare system, as well as external factors that impact an individual's mental health, and then offer potential solutions in the final two chapters. By critically examining the interacting failures of our system, I seek to contribute to the discourse surrounding mental health reform and inspire meaningful change.

Chapter 1: Our Stories

Names have been changed for privacy

Telling a story has power. Hardwired into our social biology is our need for storytelling to understand each other. I have devoted this chapter to diverse members of Gen Z to tell their stories—so you can hear us, learn from us, and understand more about what it's like to be us. Our struggles are real, and we deserve to be heard. Our stories call for systemic change in how our society approaches mental health. The following section is a collection of real accounts submitted by anonymous Gen Zers about their mental health journeys and their experiences with mental illness.

<u>James, Male, Born 1999</u>

D.A.R.E. To Resist Drugs AND Violence to Keep Kids Off Drugs

As I sit here typing out my trauma, I feel the coarseness of regret hidden deep within my throat—a sensation akin to swallowing sandpaper. The regret doesn't stem from using my voice; rather, it stems from how I used it. I yelled, not just once, but twice. I screamed so loudly that I can't even recall what I said. When you black out from rage, it's like seeing the darkest shade of red. When I shouted at him, I almost couldn't recognize whose voice it was. It sounded cold and malicious— like the voice of someone threatening to hurt another person, a tone my voice had never taken before.

When I put my hand over his mouth to silence him, it felt as though I were outside my own body, playing a character, fulfilling the overly aggressive nature of a dramatic role. The truth is, I didn't try to silence him to hurt him; rather, I wanted to stop him from hurting me. Each word felt like a bullet, each interruption like a knife. This entire event happened today around 5:00 p.m. while I was trying to drive my father to a nearby Target.

Pops is the kind of Gen Xer who's useless with an iPhone, much like many in his generation. He loses it multiple times a day, like a retriever chasing its tail, only to forget about it, then remember the chase again—a humorous and endearing trait in a pet, but painfully cyclical in a parent. I'm not saying my dad is my pet; I'm not trying to dehumanize him by suggesting he's a dog. He simply has a brain that works linguistically in a quirky manner, akin to a bad pickup line. Imaginary someone says, "Can't spell 'pet 'without P-E-T." Even more imaginary someone responds, "Can't spell 'parent 'without P-E-T either." Now you understand. I have a linguistic brain that forces connections between words that share even a hint of synonymity. Intrusive thoughts really do win after all, don't they?

Anyway, I was just getting to the part where I talk about my drug-addicted father and how that impacts my ever-changing mental health. I can laugh through the tears, and now I can type through them too.

To be honest, my father's battle with addiction and mental health significantly impacted my life from ages 0 to 25. I'm currently 25 years old. The part that really messes me up is that I've used my father's faults as an excuse to cover up my own.

"I drank an entire fifth of vodka last night because my dad's an alcoholic. I did an entire eight ball of cocaine because my dad's an addict. I got into a physical altercation that derailed my entire graduate education because I almost fought my dad today."

The worst part about having a drug-addicted father is being hypocritical when you criticize him while failing to mention your own habits. He's homeless and addicted to crystal meth. I'm a festival goer who likes to roll with my friends. He's an addict who stays in a crappy apartment and gets higher than his hosts. I'm the guy who shows up with ethically sourced and reliably safe cocaine to party with my very successful friends on the 31st floor of some East Village apartment building.

The worst part? I left him there. I pulled and told him to get out. I abandoned him on the street to save myself from the embarrassment of bringing my vulnerability into a house full of friends and roommates...those who don't know what's really going on in my life...those who will see me today, share a laugh, and assume I'm doing great…those who will see me tonight at the club and ask for drugs, mistaking me for a dealer.

I left him there on the streets, because I couldn't take it anymore. I was wearing a D.A.R.E. shirt when I did it—you know, the non-profit organization/program Drug Abuse Resistance Education, from the '90s with the Tony the Tiger meets Daren the Lion rip-off. The irony of the shirt is that it says, "D.A.R.E. to resist drugs *and* violence to keep kids off drugs." Thankfully, the shirt doesn't say anything about almost succumbing to domestic violence and pushing your father further into drugs.

Today, I was a coward.

Tonight, I am a hypocrite.

Tomorrow, I wake up a son who is hungover, regretful, and even closer to following in my father's footsteps.

Maria, Female, Born 2004

When I woke up this morning, I really wished I hadn't. I feel like every day is the same, and I just want it to end. It's been two years now since I left home. I've lived paycheck to paycheck with stress at the end of every month, worried I will be homeless.

I grew up kind of in the middle of nowhere, and my parents, even though they love me, were never really there. They both worked and because they were divorced, I hardly saw either of them. In a lot of ways, I feel like I raised myself.

I'm twenty years old now, but I feel like if my life continues on this path, I'll never get to live the life I always dreamed of as a kid. I can't afford college, and I don't want loans. My job pays a little more than minimum wage, but it's not enough. I will never own a home, and dating really sucks, so will I ever find love? Will I ever raise a family someday?

I don't know if I'm depressed, I just don't think I want to live this way anymore. I never feel happy. It's just a perpetual state of stress, loneliness, and anxiety. And I have some friends at work, but they don't understand me. It feels like they don't care about me. It kind of feels like no one cares, honestly. All I know is I don't want this life anymore.

Ethan, Male, Born 2001

I'm not sure how much of a story this is, but it's mine. As a kid, do you remember being innocent, not paying attention to your surroundings, just being in your own world? That was me until I was nineteen. I thought the world was good and didn't understand how people could have bad intentions. No matter what happened—good or bad—I saw it all the same, as nothing to be upset about. Little did I know that one of the best gifts a person can receive is pure innocence. Life is wild…crazy…beautiful…but if you let it, chaotic. And in that chaos, one can experience self-decimation.

When I was nineteen, my stepfather of nine years decided to emancipate himself from his guilt and told my mother he had slept with another woman. She was crushed, heartbroken. She thought she could trust this man who had helped support her and raise her two kids. His reason? After she got sick in 2011 and could no longer work after a few years, he was beaten down and tired of caring for her and the rest of the family without financial help. I understood his pain. He wasn't built to handle such stress. I forgive him for leaving, but not for betraying my mother. I haven't forgiven him to this day, which is sad because I want to.

After he admitted his wrongdoing, my mother knew she no longer wanted to be with him. It was final. She was crushed. The only problem was we weren't sure what to do or where to go at that moment. Unfortunately, he was so consumed with guilt (which embarrassed him) and the fact that she wouldn't take him back (even though he begged her not to leave), that he decided to make the decision for us. He gave us three days to pack our bags and leave, threatening to call the cops. My mother's name wasn't on the lease. That left us with three days to say goodbye to our neighbors, our friends, and all the memories. He didn't care where we ended up, just that we were gone on that third day.

My mother went on Craigslist and found an RV on someone's property with enough space for just her, her things, and not much else. My brother had previously moved out two years prior, not by choice, but because the same man kicked him out at the age of seventeen for being too much to handle. He rented a room from a family two cities away. As for me, I was homeless for two weeks, sleeping in my car until my aunt reached out. Her husband had passed away, leaving her alone with their dog, Mugsy, and because of it, she was able to offer me a place to stay. I slept on her couch as I kept her company through her pain. About a month in, my brother decided to leave his place and joined me in the same living room on another couch. That is where we both remained for nine months, right when the pandemic started. Luckily, I still had my job at that time, working at a hotel. It didn't pay much, but it helped.

At first, my brother and I were fine sharing the same space. But soon, about a month in, as the back pain set in from the couches and blow-up air mattresses, we started clashing and bumping heads—over the shower, the bathroom, sleep schedules, when to turn off the TV, who would get the stove. And we didn't have much space to store food. Yet somehow, we made it work, even though it made me want to pull my hair out.

And through all this, the person I was dating at the time, who I confided in so deeply, saw the change in my life and in me. I became more irritable, unstable, sad. Depression washed over me for the first time. And being a happy-go-lucky kid beforehand, this almost completely altered me—how I viewed the world. I let it affect our relationship. And because I was no longer the same person she met, she decided to leave me. I didn't blame her. This furthered my depression. Alone and nervous about what was next to come, I was lost.

After those nine months, my aunt's lease had ended, and we all had to move. Luckily, by that time, my brother and I had saved up enough to get a cheap, run-down apartment of our own together. Even with no credit and having run low on resources, at least we had a place to call home. We felt like we were finally getting somewhere on our own. But then, I became addicted to marijuana.

Growing up, after school when I arrived home, I would often smell "sage" as I walked through the door. My mom was quite literally burning sage. She would say it was to ward off negativity and bad spirits. Little did I know, it had another purpose: to mask the smell of weed. You could say that I was always around it, but I never knew about it or what it was because she hid it so well. Yet, it was only a matter of time before I knew what it was. For years, when I smelled it at random times, whether from a passing car or neighbors, I thought it was sage. It wasn't until hanging with friends that I learned what that smell really was and finally correlated the two. At eighteen, in my last year of high school, I tried the substance for the first time. For the next year, it was recreational and random that I smoked. But when everything with my ex-stepfather happened, and depression kicked in, I leaned on the substance for more than just recreation.

Every morning, every night, every hour, every meal, every time I left the apartment, at work, I was high or had to be high. I was high so often for the following five years that it became my new normal. The brain fog, forgetfulness, lack of motivation, laziness, laying around, and doing nothing after work became my life. I had constant eye bags. The substance helped me suppress things and, in a way, at the time, made life "easier." On average, I'd spend $400 a month on the substance. It was sucking away any savings I had. But it was okay as long as I was high.

The mental pain and exhaustion never fully went away, even though I told myself it had. Frankly, I was lying to myself. Smoking didn't really help. And it took a long time to realize. It wasn't just recreational anymore. I knew I wanted to stop but couldn't't. It was like I was stuck in a loop of wanting to quit, knowing what it was doing to me, and then going right back to it. It was draining. My savior had become my oppressor.

After that fifth year, to move on and regain that motivation to move up in life, I decided to stop—just cold turkey. It wasn't easy, if I'm being honest. I had terrible night sweats and would wake up in what felt like puddles for weeks. My appetite wasn't there and caused me to eat less. And I'd have mood swings or be more irritable. But waiting long enough made the outcome far more valuable. My head became clear again. I'd be less nervous around people, the daily eye bags went away, my skin felt healthier. I felt all around better and more motivated. Right now, I am currently on this path towards a greater life, including career-wise, because I've found a much better job. I just can't wait to see where it brings me, to see what limits I can push. If anyone out there is struggling (mentally, physically, anything at all), fight. Don't give up. It's easier said than done, I know. But I know that deep down inside every person, there is a fighter.

It's not much. But that's my story. Others have it worse. But we all have our struggles. And that's okay. It helps us become us—a version of us that wouldn't exist without it. It's about a single moment and what you do with it.

<u>Ashley, Female, Born 1998</u>

My story starts amid chaos. I was born into a world filled with love, but it was overshadowed by my mother's undiagnosed schizophrenia. We didn't receive that diagnosis until I was five, which led to a domino effect of challenges—more than most families see in a lifetime. I remember countless nights crying, not understanding what was going on in our home. My older sister would hold me and tell me everything was going to be okay. We lost our home, our possessions, and eventually, our family split apart as my dad took my sister and me to seek refuge with my older brother. It was a turn of events no one could have predicted. My dad did a great job trying to make us focus on the positive, but even then, anxiety became a familiar friend at such a young age.

When I was just seven, I found myself sitting in a counselor's office, trying to make sense of the instability at home. I felt lost, isolated, and often lonely. Life was anything but steady, especially when my mom wasn't taking her medication. We bounced around between different relatives. I can't quite remember why we left my brother's place; all I know is I ended up at my aunt's. My mom ended up in the hospital, and my dad was doing his best to work two jobs to financially support my sister and me, all while trying to find us a stable home. Since I was so young, I couldn't make out the exact emotions I felt, but I was confused. My dad always did his best to make things fun and happy. I tend to remember those memories best. I'm sure my mind blocked out the hardest memories to protect me.

As I grew older, I faced more than my fair share of trauma—assaults, a near-death experience from some freak accident, you name it. It's the kind of stuff that could create a book series. And it's left me grappling with anxiety, depression, and OCD...but don't worry, I have been in therapy on and off since the second grade to keep myself sane. The unstable home environment followed me into adulthood, as I became a caregiver to my mom.

Through it all, I've learned some hard lessons. With those lessons, I found ways to cope with my emotions by recognizing the importance of self-awareness and honest communication. Being thrust into the role of caregiver for my mom at such a young age messed with my head, making friendships a bit of a minefield. It often led me to accept poor behavior from those in my life, brushing it off because they needed someone. I'd take it upon myself and have the mindset of "if I don't help them, then who will?" I'd often put others first at the cost of my own boundaries.

But here's the thing: I refuse to let my past dictate my future. Sure, life threw me some curveballs, but I'm determined to swing back. I've learned to set boundaries, prioritize self-care, and understand that seeking validation from others is a dead-end road. True acceptance comes from within, and that's something I'm thankful to say I have finally accomplished. What's happened to me isn't my fault, and I can't control what's happened or what will happen. All I can do is control my reactions to the things that happen and how I choose to move forward.

Shoutout to my therapist…and to all the people out there who are willing to have open, honest conversations about trauma and mental health.

<u>Nick, Male, Born 2000</u>

One of the lowest points in my life (and the earliest that I remember) was in middle school. Growing up is tough and learning how to make friends seemed to be one of the hardest things for me. I remember trying to be part of different groups of friends and constantly being told "Why are you here?" Looking back at it now, it might have been a childish curiosity that had no malicious intent behind it. But as a kid, I wanted so badly to be accepted so it felt like a harsh rejection.

People bullied me badly because I was "weird." One time, I thought these kids were being nice to me and wanted to be my friend. It turned out they only wanted to laugh at me and not with me. When I wanted to leave one of them started being rough with me. I didn't know what to do other than play along. One of the other boys put his arm around my neck and pretended to wrestle me. I started panicking and tapped his arm to tell him to stop but he just laughed. I started to see black and was about to pass out—and I would've, but the girl that was there made him stop. That left an impression on me.

I vividly remember crying in the shower that night wondering why nobody liked me. I thought, *every time I say what's on my mind, people don't like it.* I decided to not say anything anymore.

After that I joined groups as a silent observer, and it worked. I was accepted that way and I slowly made more friends. This stuck with me until high school where I began breaking out of my shell. On the one hand, I feel this has helped me learn how to push past the uncomfortable fear of rejection. On the other hand, the negative thoughts never went away.

Another one of the lowest points in my life was when I was drinking very heavily almost every day. I had built my tolerance so high that only some of the strongest liquor you could buy would give me the buzz I wanted. The turning point for me was when I woke up one morning and was told by my girlfriend the mess that I left. I was ashamed and determined to do something about it. I tried doing it on my own, but I gave into my desires repeatedly. It felt like alcohol had taken control of me. I hated who I had become. After a few failed attempts to stop myself, I had decided to seek professional help.

I am very fortunate that my job not only provides healthcare but also does not take money from my check to pay for it. (I have many friends who cannot say the same.) After a couple loops through the system, I had landed on the therapy I needed. I don't know anyone my age whose healthcare is as good as mine, I know they would all benefit from it.

Therapy helped me realize that I had anxiety. I learned that everyone has cognitive distortions but for some it can become an endless loop. My loop was where I felt like I was *never enough* or that *I had failed in life.* I feared disappointing my family and friends. Alcohol numbed those feelings. Therapy helped me recognize when I was having these thoughts and how to cope with them. I realized that I was projecting the negative image I had of myself into the minds of others and assumed they must have thought all these negative things about me. I believe this is due to the bullying and feelings of isolation that I went through in middle school.

I had been keeping my alcohol abuse a secret from my family and friends. The only person who really witnessed the worst of it was my girlfriend. It was hard to tell them what I had been going through, and they only found out when I told them I was going to therapy. My friends were very supportive and respected my sobriety. I broke down in front of my parents when I told them. They have always been brutally honest and told me that they were disappointed but happy that I was seeking professional help. I'm not the only one in my family that struggled with drugs.

When you grow up in an environment where people don't talk about their feelings, you're destined to be emotionally ignorant. If I felt angry, I was wrong. If I was sad, I had to suck it up. Be happy or be quiet. That seemed like the only acceptable way of being in my family. Of course this was all a facade. When I grew up and learned about how my parents and extended family grew up, I felt like I was meeting new people. My parents shut down my emotions because they thought I would make the same mistakes they did. To this day my extended family seems incapable of having a serious conversation without it blowing up or being ignored. Now I see it was just the blind leading the blind.

I still struggle with anxiety. I am still learning about the landscape of my emotions, and I hope to pass my knowledge onto my future children. As I am writing this, I'm six months sober. I feel like I'm in control again.

<u>Sam, Female, Born 2003</u>

Growing up, I always felt out of place, like I didn't quite fit in. Even as a young child, I knew I was different. While my friends stuck to playing with dolls or trucks, I was drawn to both, puzzled by why society insisted on separating them by gender.

My parents, though loving, had traditional views. They tried to shape me into the son they thought they had, not realizing that inside, I was struggling to become the person I knew I was meant to be. By my teenage years, this internal conflict became unbearable, leaving me overwhelmed with confusion, depression, and anxiety.

When I finally found the courage to come out as transgender, my parents were taken aback. Their initial support was clouded by confusion and fear. They thought sending me to a place that could "fix" me would help, which is how I ended up being treated by the troubled teen industry. The first facility I went to was a nightmare. Called a therapeutic boarding school, it felt more like a prison. The staff lacked training in transgender issues and used outdated and harmful approaches to mental health. They emphasized discipline over understanding and acceptance. Every day was a fight to maintain my identity and sanity.

Isolation was the hardest part. They separated me from the others, claiming it was for my safety, but it only worsened my sense of being an outsider. The therapy sessions focused on trying to "fix" my gender identity rather than addressing my mental health issues.

One particularly difficult night, I felt like giving up. Alone and crying in my room, I thought about the future and the person I wanted to become. I knew I had to keep fighting, not just for myself, but for others who felt as lost and alone as I did.

Eventually, my parents realized the facility wasn't helping me. They found a therapist who specialized in working with transgender youth. With the right support, I began to heal, starting hormone therapy and taking steps towards living as my true self.

Looking back, I see how far I've come. My identity is something to be celebrated, not fixed.

<u>Erin, Female, Born 2007</u>

I've known I was gay since I was little. Other girls liked boys and I didn't. Other girls liked Barbie's and I hated them. I never felt like I fit in until I met a few people like me in high school who made me feel like it was safe to be myself. I joined the Gay Straight Alliance club at my school, and it was one space I felt like being myself wasn't an abomination.

Every Sunday growing up I was dragged week after week to church where I'd hear the words echo across the walls "marriage is between a man and a woman," and other homophobic sh*t.

My mom is so controlling, and I only realized that recently. I literally couldn't choose my own clothes until this last year after having a summer job. My mom has always forced her ideas onto me like wearing feminine clothes and walking with the "lord."

The first time I started having suicidal thoughts I remember vividly. I was on my way to summer camp a few years ago, run by my church. I tried to sit next to a classmate, and she told me she didn't want a "homo" next to her. Well, she didn't say that, she looked at me like that though. I sat alone staring out the window on the long drive to some random campground feeling so alone. Thoughts raced through my mind like *what would happen if I just disappeared?*

Every time I tell my mom I don't want to go to church, or that I want to wear something else, she tells me she knows best. I'm tired of being controlled and minimized. I dream of my escape. I can't afford college, and neither can my parents afford to help me but the loans feel worth getting the hell out of here. It's my only source of motivation right now. The depression is hard to fight. I just want to be myself; I just want real friends; I just want a family that loves the real me.

I'm too afraid of seeking help honestly, because when I told my mom I was depressed she literally looked at me and told me that it was going against God to feel this weak and told me to pray. The only thing I pray for is a better world. I don't like this one.

<u>Summary</u>

James, Maria, Ethan, Ashley, Nick, Sam and Erin bravely share with us their thoughts, emotions, and tribulations. Each of their stories presents important issues that I explore in-depth throughout this book. For example, Maria discusses her trouble with affordable living, describing her life as a twilight zone scenario. Her inability to provide for her basic needs leaves her feeling chronically stressed and anxious, while her lack of connection with peers has made her isolated. Her wish not to live illustrates how heartbreaking, tired, and hopeless she among many others feels in conjunction with American economic and social systems. I discuss the impact of loneliness in Chapter 13 and how individualism has isolated us in Chapter 19. I further discuss the impact of our capitalist system and the relatively unbearable expense of colleges in the U.S. in Chapters 11 and 17.

Ashley's story illuminates the struggle and hardships that come when parents are not available for their children, a topic I cover in Chapter 12. Ashley's experience also highlights the potential efficacy of therapy, which I examine further in Chapter 6. Sam's story demonstrates the detrimental effects of the troubled teen industry, which I delve into in Chapter 7. Sam also emphasizes a subject I investigate deeper into in Chapter 10, that is, the potential challenges faced by many in the transgender community. Erin's story illustrates why parental invalidation is so harmful, which I discussed in Chapter 12. In Ethan's story, we hear about how he coped with his unstable home life, his tragic moments of homelessness, and his battle with substance abuse. James's and Nick's story also illustrates how drugs are often a coping mechanism for Gen Z. In Chapter 8, I discuss how the drug epidemic has swept over our generation and its effects on mental health.

Each of these unique stories plays into a greater picture: how systemic injustices that have led to our mental health crisis. While some of us have improved, like Ashley, and Sam, others, like Maria, James, and Erin lack the resources and/or support systems to make progress. The good news is there is hope, and I explain in chapter's 20-21 how we can transform our systems for better mental health outcomes for everyone

Chapter 2: The History that Laid the Groundwork of Mental Health Treatment in America

Madness is the false punishment of a false solution, but by its own virtue it brings to light the real problem, which can then be truly resolved.
— Michel Foucault

It is essential to understand how and why we got to where we are. Let's start by looking through history to understand the foundation of our failed system. The discourse around mental health, though amplified in recent years, is not a new conversation. The following section briefly covers the evolution of treatment starting from before the Middle Ages to our contemporary landscape.

The Evolution of Mental Health Treatment Across Centuries

One of the earliest recorded attempts at mental health treatment comes from the Middle Ages, a time known for the plague and feudal society in Western Europe. People struggling with mental illness found themselves ostracized and labeled as demon-possessed or witches.[1] The solutions of the time included exorcisms, malnutrition, and imprisonment—but these were often cruel attempts to expel perceived "demonry" of the afflicted. Long before the Middle Ages, however, historians have identified an ancient practice called trephination, which might give us a glimpse into the earliest days of mental illness treatments. Invented approximately 7,000 years ago, trephination involved removing part of the skull and was likely used to relieve not only headaches, but also mental illnesses and perceived cases of demonic possession.[2] By the 1600s, bleeding, purging, and even vomiting were considered remedies to restore equilibrium and heal physical and mental illnesses.[3]

Isolation was the main treatment for mental illness during the Middle Ages and laid the groundwork for the proliferation of mental asylums over time. While these institutions purportedly served as treatment centers, they often removed patients from the view of their families and communities and instead forced patients into a kind of societal exile.[4] Overcrowding and poor sanitation plagued asylums, leading to movements advocating for improved care quality and heightened awareness. Medical practitioners of the time relied on physical methods, often employing tactics such as ice water baths and restraints in their pursuit of treating mental disorders.[5] As we emerge from the COVID-19 lockdown, we have come to see how detrimental isolation can be to mental health. Gen Z were especially impacted by isolation, no longer able to foster essential in-person social connection during their formative years.[6] Thus, the medieval tactic of isolation as a treatment for mental illness was likely to worsen, rather than improve, an individual's mental maladies.

Jumping forward a few hundred years, the introduction of insulin coma therapy in 1927 created a new wave in psychiatric medical intervention. Basically, physicians deliberately induced low blood sugar comas, believing that fluctuations in insulin levels could alter brain function.[7] Although this treatment persisted until the 1960s, it came with many risks, including prolonged comas and mortality rates ranging from 1 to 10 percent[8] This new wave also included Metrazol therapy—a contentious treatment that involves the induction of seizures using a stimulant medication. Despite its dangers and adverse effects (such as fractured bones and torn muscles), Metrazol therapy paved the way for the development of electroconvulsive therapy, which is still used in certain cases to treat severe depression, mania, and catatonia.[9]

A fairly new treatment, called transcranial magnetic stimulation (TMS) is a procedure that uses magnetic fields to stimulate nerve cells in the brain to improve symptoms of major depression, and it is essentially the evolved version of Metrazol therapy. It is called a "noninvasive" procedure because it does not require surgery. However, speaking from experience, I have found that TMS can cause seizures. I tried it a few years ago, (before discovering the root cause of my depression was undiagnosed Celiac Disease), and woke up on the floor, not knowing where I was or how I got there. Still, the provider at the time received zero penalty from the FDA report I sent. Furthermore, advertisements across the nation purport TMS to be the next big wave in psychiatric care.[10] The truth is much more complicated than shocking peoples' brains expecting depression to vanish.

Around the same time period that Metrazol therapy and insulin comas emerged, the mid-twentieth century witnessed the controversial rise of lobotomies—a now-obsolete treatment that won the Nobel Prize in Physiology and Medicine in 1949.[11] Designed to disrupt brain circuits, lobotomies were prescribed in severe psychiatric cases, involving the surgical cutting or removal of connections between the prefrontal cortex and frontal lobes.[12] While some patients experienced symptom improvement, the procedure introduced additional impairments. Lobotomies gradually fell out of favor after the creation of the first psychiatric medications in the 1950s.

Surgery to treat psychiatric disorders is still practiced but differs greatly from a classical lobotomy. Now, doctors can precisely map the malfunctioning parts of the brain by imaging techniques like computed tomography (CT) scans, magnetic resonance imaging (MRI) scans, electroencephalograms (EEG), and other sophisticated methods.[13] The current techniques are called stereotactic neurosurgery[14] and are used to treat mental health disorders such as schizophrenia, OCD, and depression.[15] A licensed neurosurgeon now performs the procedures, and the side effects are reportedly more predictable.[16]

A final turning point in mental health treatment comes from the work of Sigmund Freud. Before his research, little information on therapy existed, although some historians believe that talk-based interventions may have taken place in Ancient Greece.[17] Yet Freud coined the term psychotherapy, and many of the concepts of his research and work are present in today's modern therapeutic landscape. Alongside apprentices such as Alfred Adler, Otto Rank, Karl Abraham, Snador Ferenczi, and Carl Jung, Freud's work led to the development of psychoanalysis and psychodynamic therapy.[18]

Mental Health Treatment Today

The founding of the Diagnostic and Statistical Manual of Mental Disorders (DSM) can be traced back to the early twentieth century, when attempts to classify psychopathology led to the first Statistical Manual for the use of "Institutions for the Insane."[19] This precursor to the DSM series, published in 1918, featured 22 diagnostic categories, reflecting a biologically-oriented classification approach. It emphasized the physiological and medical aspects of mental disorders, prioritizing observable symptoms and physical causes over psychological or social factors. In 1952, the DSM-I was officially released, comprising 102 diagnostic categories.[20] Despite its limited impact on psychiatric practice, the DSM-I set the stage for standardized categorizations and influenced the trajectory of psychiatric diagnosis and treatment approaches. Subsequent editions added more disorder categories and incorporated empirical and neuroscientific data. Despite its benefits, the DSM has faced criticism for the potential for medical professionals to over-diagnose patients, for the pharmaceutical industry to overextend influence, and for normal behaviors to become medicalized. In addition, because the DSM-V continues to emphasize biological data, neuroethical debates have ensued about the potential consequences.[21] The DSM's evolution reflects changing values and assumptions within psychiatry, underscoring the need for flexibility and awareness of biases. The DSM-VI is expected in 2025.[22]

Alongside modern efforts at diagnosis through the DSM-V, there are a range of new treatments, such as TMS, psychoactive/psychotropic medications (first developed in the 1950s),[23] Eye Movement Desensitization and Reprocessing (EMDR), psychedelic therapy (ketamine and psilocybin), and support groups. Currently, Cognitive Behavioral Therapy (CBT) stands as the gold standard of treatment.[24] While CBT has recently come under fire,[25] available data about CBT still suggests that it is the best option because it treats a wide array of mental illnesses and is widely accessible.[26] Also, researchers found that CBT can improve brain function by changing brain activity over time.[27]

In addition to therapy, ketamine has stood out as a highly effective treatment for suicidal depression—with one double blind study finding that half of people who received ketamine treatment experienced reduced depression within just two days.[28] Leading experts agree that in the coming years, the integration of machine learning, deep neural networks, and multimodal biomedical artificial intelligence (AI) is set to revolutionize clinical research across various domains.[29] This includes enhancing drug discovery processes, interpreting medical images, optimizing electronic health record systems, streamlining workflows, and ultimately, promoting advancements in public health.[30]

Conclusion

The evolution of mental health treatment across centuries is a testament to humanity's evolving understanding of mental illness. Given that mental healthcare has a long history of exploitation, stigmatization, pharmaceutical influence, and reliance on the DSM-5 it is evident that while there have been many advancements in the field, there is still a long way to go towards holistic, prevention-centered care. It is clear we need to rethink our approach. Nonetheless, the comprehensive understanding of mental disorders continues to evolve with scientific and research developments, as mental health professionals gain new insights. But to emphasize my point: the key to advancing treatment is to take a step back and examine the systemic root causes of mental illness, which have clearly been overlooked. How does mental illness interrelate with medical conditions, the environment, and our social systems?

Chapter 3: The Harm of Stigma

I try to be strong not only for other people but also myself, but sometimes there are weaknesses in strength and that's okay; and it's okay not to be okay; and I've taught myself that.
– SIMONE BILES

Throughout my life, I have noticed that people have treated me differently when I've shared my struggles with depression. In college, I heard a lot of "stop playing the victim," or, "you have everything, you are acting entitled." But, entitled to what? Entitled to biological needs? Entitled to happiness?

One moment I will never forget is when I was running a volunteer-based nonprofit and spent a week working overtime, single-handedly organizing a very demanding event. I explained to my fellow volunteer colleagues that I was feeling very burnt out, and during this time, I was grieving the death of my best friend. I was struggling with suicidal ideation, and I needed help. Instead of offering me compassion, I was criticized for being "unprofessional." Yet, we were a small unpaid organization of friends. I saw how stigma could even pervade a non-profit whose goal was to support de-escalation policies for safer policing of citizens in a mental health crisis.

When I think about stigma, I remember my experiences, but I also think of all the hundreds of shows and movies that portray mentally ill people as dangerous and violent. As a teenager, the movie *Split*—depicting a man with multiple personalities whose evil alter ego kidnaps and murders little girls—haunts my mind with graphic images of scary violence. Or *The Joker*, the Marvel thriller about a man who has a mental illness that makes him struggle socially and laugh uncontrollably, until he loses his marbles and starts killing everyone who ever wronged him. And even more recently, the Netflix Series *Baby Reindeer* that chronicles a story about a man who was stalked by a mentally ill woman who becomes violent and lets her delusions and frantic emails overcome the wannabe comedian's life. Even though people with mental illness are far more likely to be victims of violence, and very unlikely to be violent, the media still chooses to portray mental illness poorly. Researchers conducted a study about the *Joker* film and found that "viewing it was associated with higher levels of prejudice toward those with mental illness," potentially exacerbating self-stigma and causing delays in seeking help.[1]

Stigma often arises from a lack of understanding or fear, intensified by inaccurate portrayals in the media. Despite public acceptance of the medical nature of mental health disorders and the necessity for treatment, negative depictions persist.[2] Researchers distinguish between various forms of stigma:

> **Public Stigma:** Involves the negative or discriminatory attitudes others harbor toward mental illness.[3]
>
> **Self-Stigma:** Encompasses the negative attitudes, including internalized shame, that people with mental illness may harbor about their own condition.[4]
>
> **Structural/Institutional Stigma:** Systemic issues involving government and private organization policies that intentionally or unintentionally restrict opportunities for those with mental illness. Examples include reduced funding for mental illness research and fewer mental health services relative to other healthcare.[5]

People with severe mental illness face a double burden. On the one hand, they struggle to manage the symptoms and disabilities arising from their condition. On the other, they confront the impact of public, self, and structural stigma, fueled by misconceptions surrounding their mental illness.[6] Approximately 54 percent of people experiencing mental illness remain untreated.[7] Stigma not only directly affects people struggling with mental illness but also impacts their family members. The issue of mental health stigma is particularly pronounced in diverse racial and ethnic communities, acting as a substantial barrier to accessing mental health services.[8] Cultural values, such as strong family bonds, emotional restraint, and avoidance of shame, can hinder seeking professional help in certain communities. Similarly, distrust of the mental healthcare system poses a barrier for some groups, including certain ethnic communities that were historically subjected to horrific medical "testing."[9] Stereotypes and prejudices associated with mental illness, such as viewing people as dangerous or incompetent, contribute to discrimination—which can lead to adverse consequences, such as employers refraining from hiring Gen Z who disclose mental illness or landlords refusing to rent to people with mental illness.[10]

Stigma and discrimination play a role in worsening symptoms and diminishing the likelihood of seeking treatment. Many hesitate to seek assistance because of apprehensions about differential treatment and the potential jeopardy to their status, employment and livelihood. A recent comprehensive research review[11] revealed that self-stigma has adverse effects on the recovery from severe mental illnesses. These effects look like:

- reduced hope
- lower self-esteem
- increased psychiatric symptoms
- difficulties with social relationships
- reduced likelihood of staying with treatment
- more difficulties at work

A 2017 study that spanned two years and involved over 200 people with a mental illness diagnosis found a correlation between greater self-stigma and poorer recovery after one and two years.[12] A 2016 study by Zurich University underscored the universal nature of mental health stigma by showing how there is no country, society, or culture where those with mental illness are afforded the same societal value as those without.[13] The data tell a compelling story about how damaging, complicated, and impactful stigma is. When I personally experienced stigma for depression, I felt isolated, lonely, and my symptoms worsened.

The healthcare system may also offer a lower standard of care because of stigma, perpetuating unintended losses of opportunity. This, too, was part of my experience. Over a period of ten years, I sought diagnosis and treatment for a variety of confusing symptoms including persistent physical pain, which were all attributed to depression. It was not until I was in my mid-twenties that I learned I had two serious physical medical conditions that had affected my mental health because they were left untreated my whole life up until a year ago. Discovering my real medical diagnosis explained why antidepressants did not work for me.

Workplace Stigma

Mental illness is the single greatest cause of worker disability worldwide.[14] Many people remain silent and choose not to seek help due to fear of others' perceptions. The American Psychiatric Association's 2019 national poll highlighted the persistent challenge of mental health stigma in the workplace. [15] Approximately half of the workforce expressed apprehension about discussing mental health matters at their jobs, with over one-third expressing concerns about potential retaliation or job loss if they were to seek mental healthcare.[16] One in four workers also admitted uncertainty about where to turn for mental health assistance, emphasizing the need for increased awareness and accessibility.[17]

Stigma can negatively impact our economy. My generation has experienced the highest job loss rate due to mental health struggles, and as someone who was fired for my disability only hours after disclosing it, I understand why staying in silence is attractive. Something must be said about older generations laying strong judgment on us. "Gen Zers are lazy and waste all their money on coffee," is a common sentiment shared by older generations. But the truth is, we are subjected to a multitude of burdens that only heighten mental illness. How are we supposed to work when over half of our generation is depressed, anxious, and lonely? How are we supposed to work when we know we have little to work *for*? We can't afford houses anymore. We are watching big industries poison the planet and placing the burden on our shoulders as if we are the cause of the climate crisis. We are disconnected.

Conclusion

The fact that mental illness is the single greatest cause of worker disability worldwide indicates a need to change our approach to how we view and treat mental illness in America. There is a correlation between greater stigma and poor recovery outcomes which highlights the importance of immediate action. The narrative of laziness and irresponsibility often attributed to Gen Z fails to acknowledge the complex web of challenges we face—from housing unaffordability to existential concerns about the future of our planet. Our mental health crisis is so much more complex than people realize, and stigma only makes it worse.

Chapter 4: Inadequate Resources and Access

There is a crack in everything, that's how the light gets in.
— Leonard Cohen

My first experience with getting treatment was after it was already too late. At fifteen, I had tried to take my own life. I was struggling with social isolation, severe depression, an eating disorder, and the effects of a sexual assault and bullying by my perpetrator—unable to walk down the halls of my school without boys coughing words of profanity at me. I went home every day asking to change schools. But my parents, the Boomers that they are, did not understand how growing up as a member of Gen Z had new complications that were unfamiliar to them. For me, my first exposure to mental healthcare was in the emergency room. From there I was sent to the only adolescent mental health hospital in the county, an hour away from my family. Because it was so overcrowded, I was forced to share the room with another girl who was struggling. I quickly learned there are many barriers to effective mental healthcare.

Emergency Rooms Have Become a New Treatment Center

It turns out that I was not alone in my experience. A new study by the U.S. Centers for Disease Control and Prevention (CDC) reveals that the average number of emergency room visits by children and adolescents seeking treatment for mental health issues exceeded 1 million annually from 2018-2021.[1] This research builds on previous studies highlighting the rise in mental health disorders among youth, including suicide attempts.[2] Mood disorders, anxiety disorders, and behavioral/emotional disorders were the most commonly treated conditions. Emergency visits were notably higher among adolescents aged 12-17 compared to younger children, and girls were more likely than boys to seek emergency treatment for mental health disorders.[3]

Our Mental Healthcare Systems are Fragmented

A panel of experts from the University of Pennsylvania's Leonard Davis Institute of Health Economics (LDI) concluded that our mental health system is deteriorating more rapidly than it is improving. Rachel M. Werner, MD, noted that over 75 percent of US counties lack a mental health prescriber, resulting in wait times for treatment that can stretch from weeks to months.[4] This situation is particularly dire for Gen Z.[5] The lack of coordination between healthcare providers leads to patients falling through the cracks, significantly impacting treatment outcomes and patient experiences.[6] In other words, experts agree the current system is failing due to its fragmentation.

The mental healthcare system is highly fragmented, causing harm to both patients and providers. In California for example, mental health services for Medicaid (Medi-Cal) enrollees are divided between non-specialty mental health services provided by Medi-Cal health plans and specialty mental health services provided by County Mental Health Plans.[7] This division complicates the delivery and access to mental health services, often leading to patients receiving inadequate care or experiencing detrimental delays. The lack of coordination between these entities means that many patients do not get the comprehensive care they need, as services are disjointed, and responsibilities are unclear.

Because the system is often difficult to navigate, patients can be left confused about where to seek help, resulting in untreated or poorly managed mental health conditions. The fragmentation also significantly impacts mental healthcare providers, because they face increased administrative burdens and longer working hours due to the need to navigate multiple systems and meet various bureaucratic requirements. The divided nature of service provision often means that providers cannot spend enough time with each patient, leading to mental exhaustion and a diminished ability to offer compassionate care. This stressful environment can drive many professionals out of the field, adding to the shortage of mental healthcare workers and further straining the system.

<u>Support Services are Severely Lacking</u>

I have had several troubling experiences with therapists who were very unprofessional to me. For example, I walked into a session with my service dog and the therapist jumped on her table and screamed. "How dare you bring your dog, get out! Session over!" Perhaps she needed some therapy before becoming a therapist. And, if you ask around, you might hear many more stories like mine. In fact, BetterHelp, a new online therapy platform came under fire recently for having "sketchy" therapists who have even been reported to use the bathroom while on video during sessions.[8] This seems indictive of a low standard of care.

The quality of available mental healthcare is subpar at best, and the rate of advancement lags behind the treatment of other medical conditions. Concerningly, less than half of patients with government-funded insurance receive sufficient follow-up after mental health hospitalization.[9] This rings true to my experience, as I have rarely received follow up from therapists or my psychiatrists. Some argue the ongoing deficiency in mental healthcare quality is attributed, at least in part, to the absence of systematic approaches for evaluating quality. Until recently, our systems had no measures in place to show improvement or levels of patient satisfaction, and the new measures that do exist still need improvement.[10]

<u>Mental Healthcare Costs Too Much</u>

Another major issue is cost. Without insurance, a person experiencing mental illness may forego treatment, because out-of-pocket costs for therapy and pharmaceuticals are unaffordable for a majority of people. The average cost of psychotherapy in the US ranges from $100 to $200 per session[11] (depending on the state). What's worse, about half of people indicate that cost is a barrier preventing them from pursuing a treatment, and this increases to 74 percent among those who lack insurance.[12] Furthermore, 61 percent of those without insurance indicated that they had to discontinue a treatment because they could no longer afford it.[13] This comes at a time when 70 percent of American's report struggling to afford food.[14] For most of the country, then, mental health is an added, deprioritized financial burden.

<u>We have a Considerable Shortage of Mental Healthcare Providers</u>

Access to timely healthcare is severely hindered by an insufficient number of behavioral health professionals.[15] A historical lack of investment in behavioral healthcare by insurance programs (such as Medicaid and Medicare) has intensified this issue, resulting in inadequate coverage and low reimbursement rates. In 2021, less than half of people with mental illnesses could access timely care, and those with substance use disorders faced even greater challenges.[16] Medicaid beneficiaries, and to a lesser extent Medicare recipients, struggle to find providers due to low reimbursement rates. In some states, like Oregon, more than half of mental health providers listed in Medicaid directories don't actually serve Medicaid enrollees.[17] This poses significant challenges to equitable access, given that Medicaid is the largest payer of behavioral health services in the US.

Certain demographic groups are disproportionately affected by therapist shortages. For example, rural areas, as well as economically distressed cities, often lack behavioral healthcare providers. Likewise, according to the University of Michigan's School of Public Health, in 2018 over half of US counties had no practicing psychiatrist.[18] None. Counties outside metropolitan areas had one-third of the number of psychiatrists and half the number of psychologists compared to metropolitan areas.[19] Experts estimate that we would need over 8,000 additional professionals for bare minimum adequate mental healthcare coverage.[20] Underserved groups (including people of color, non-English speakers, and LGBTQIA+ communities) often face difficulties in finding effective services. The behavioral health workforce's demographics often do not reflect those of the populations they serve. For instance, although nearly one-third of the US identifies as Black or Hispanic, a mere one-tenth of active psychiatrists identify as these demographic groups.[21] This disparity restricts the availability of culturally and linguistically suitable care. By lacking a workforce that represents the populations they serve, our practicing workers are lacking key cultural competencies that are necessary to reduce disparities and discriminations.

What Does the Workforce Look Like?

The behavioral health workforce can be broken down into a few key categories with diverse roles and specializations:

Licensed Providers: Licensed providers encompass a range of professionals with specialized training sanctioned by state and professional boards. This category includes psychiatrists, psychologists, clinical social workers, marriage and family therapists, primary care physicians, and nurse practitioners.[22] While some licensed providers have prescribing privileges, all offer psychotherapy and contribute clinical oversight within care teams. Although these services are typically covered by health insurance, including Medicaid and Medicare, accessibility may be hindered by low reimbursement rates. Furthermore, reimbursement policies often fail to adequately address the needs of underserved areas and promote diversity within the workforce.[23]

Clinical Supporters: Clinical supporters are specialized professionals dedicated to prevention and recovery efforts, working closely alongside the licensed providers listed above, to facilitate clinical care. This group encompasses various roles, such as social workers, occupational therapists, certified addiction counselors, nurses, certified peer specialists, and recovery coaches. Their roles emphasize education, care coordination, advocacy, and the provision of social support.[24] Despite their vital contributions, and that many of these positions do require licenses, reimbursement for these services typically falls below that of licensed providers.[25]

Community Care Workers: Community care workers operate within nonclinical environments such as community centers and social service agencies, where they engage with individuals in need. Their responsibilities mirror those of clinical supporters, with examples including peer support specialists and community health workers. While some community care workers may be volunteers, others are compensated or participate in behavioral health volunteer programs.[26] However, these services typically rely on grant funding and are not covered by insurance, resulting in restricted availability and obstacles to accessing them.[27]

Frontline Workers: Frontline workers encompass an array of professionals in areas such as law enforcement, correctional staff, teachers, emergency medical personnel, and social service providers, who find themselves offering behavioral health support due to shortages within the formal behavioral health workforce.[28] Often operating with limited training and support, these frontline workers cannot always refer people in crisis to appropriate resources. Additionally, the services they provide are typically not reimbursed by insurance, necessitating a reliance on grant-funded initiatives to sustain their efforts, or simply pulling them away from the other work they're paid to do.[29]

Despite the diversity of roles, each category faces challenges, such as low reimbursement rates, limited availability in underserved areas, and disparities in accessing care. The challenges on these providers contribute to ongoing issues in the behavioral health landscape.

The System Causes Worker Burnout

Physician burnout poses a significant threat to our healthcare system. Burnout is projected to cost the healthcare system at least $4.6 billion each year.[30] Dr. Khullar, professor of health policy and economics at Weill Cornell Medical College, found that three key forces that drive physician burnout: (1) the overwhelming pressure to provide care to too many patients in too little time with insufficient resources; (2) the requirement to engage in tasks perceived as repetitive, irrelevant, or counterproductive; and (3) the inability to address patients 'medical or social needs effectively.[31]

The design of the healthcare system has in part caused physician burnout, adversely affecting both patient care and the medical workforce. More than half of US physicians report burnout symptoms, which are nearly double the rate of the general working population[32] and with not enough new clinicians to fill the gap, the accessibility gap widens. Further, with a nearly 20 percent increase in demand for mental health services, patients face substantial delays in receiving essential care.[33] Additionally, burnout deteriorates the quality of care that mental health professionals can offer.[34] Longer working hours, increased caseloads, and minimal time to rest between appointments leaves providers mentally exhausted and less effective in their roles, and yet this has become the norm in healthcare settings.[35]

Workers are expected to abide by these unsustainable practices, harming everyone as a result. It is perplexing how we continue to expect those who hold our lives in their hands to accept such substandard working conditions. Our systems have failed to implement the necessary changes to provide healthcare workers with the balance they need to treat patients effectively, and healthcare professionals cannot be expected to deliver the highest standard of care if their own basic needs are not being met.

Astrology and Manifestation Responses are on the Rise

One thing that history teaches us is that during times of great crisis, opportunists find a way to monetize our misery and take advantage of vulnerable populations. Have you noticed a huge shift in discourse since 2020? It seems like everyone I talk to says, "I am going to manifest," and goes on to describe their goal. Others tend to use the "oh, you're a Pisces…oh gosh girl, no wonder you're struggling. The Pisces moon is…" and so on. It is no coincidence there is an increase in this language.

Astrology, tarot card reading, and other spiritual practices have become popular within Gen Z[36] and reflect a growing market that caters to those who may be skeptical of traditional therapy or unable to afford extended treatment. For many, these practices serve as accessible substitutes or supplements to therapy, offering explanations and instilling faith in the future. In rural areas, where therapy and medication are scarce, local astrologers and psychics become emotional anchors during distress. Astrology and tarot cards, focusing on future guidance, provide comfort and a sense of control, especially for those facing anxiety or limited healthcare access. The universal appeal of these practices has expanded through technology, with mobile apps and social media outlets offering daily readings akin to therapy. However, studies reveal that dependence on astrology can worsen mental health outcomes, fostering a fatalistic view and a sense of helplessness.[37] As these practices gain popularity, questions arise about their efficacy in treating mental illness and whether they are quick fixes for systemic healthcare shortcomings.

We've all come across fitness magazines that make unrealistic promises of achieving a "smaller waist" or a "six-pack in just two weeks." And most of us bypass the magazine cover, knowing those claims are misleading. Such quick-fix schemes are designed to encourage "clicks" or ensure the magazines continue selling and sustain the multibillion-dollar health and fitness industry. But, somehow, many of us are buying into a new type of clickbait form of astrology and manifestation.

With platforms like Twitter and trendy horoscope apps like Co-Star readily available, along with a wealth of online information, tarot, horoscopes, and birth charts have become more accessible than ever before. Sari Chait, a clinical psychologist and owner of the Behavioral Health and Wellness Center in Newport, Massachusetts, explains that during times of stress or negativity, people often seek to understand the 'why' behind their experiences.[38] She notes that astrology and tarot readings can offer a framework for this understanding, even if it is not based on empirical evidence.

The integration of tarot and astrology with mental health advice is on the rise, reflecting a larger trend of therapeutic guidance through alternative means, which has even been concerningly promoted by therapists. While astrology is loosely rooted in astronomy, it diverges from scientific principles by offering predictions or observations rather than testable conclusions. An interactive checklist from the University of California, Berkeley highlights key scientific characteristics, such as testability, reliance on scientific evidence, and engagement with the scientific community, are not included in astrology.[39] Some argue there are benefits to astrology—for instance, a sense of spirituality and a sense of calm and peace from positive readings. And the popularity of this trend signals that the blind faith in this practice is resonant for many. But at what cost, particularly for those who need genuine mental healthcare?

In a similar mode, the cult of manifestation has garnered significant relevance lately—with the uptick revealing itself during the pandemic. This makes sense, given that people often turn to spiritual practices in times of uncertainty. As explained by a *Medium* op-ed writer "The love and light movement is a scam. And it has many followers, duped into wearing pink-colored glasses and snorting affirmation glitter three times a day."[40] Some high-profile celebrities, including Cara Delevingne, Oprah Winfrey, Ariana Grande, and Lady Gaga, have joined the movement—and they are convincing others that they can achieve their dreams, simply by thinking hard enough.

The exorbitant prices charged for questionable wisdom should raise concerns about the underlying intentions behind these "law of attraction" practices. Many opportunists have found a business in selling their services to desperate people who may require professional care not an astrologist's reading, that may cost them upwards of $100 to $150 an hour.[41] For example, Regan Hillyer, who is featured in magazines like Forbes, claims to be an "entrepreneur," and purports to have an eight-figure business helping people "manifest wealth." Can you see the problem with this? We do not manifest wealth—wealth is created through a variety of approaches, most effectively being born into a wealthy family, and hard work, not daily affirmations and whatever else these people are selling.

The question is, do manifestation and astrology practices cause harm? Neuroscientists and psychiatrists caution that excessive introspection through modes of astrology and manifestation can lead to anxiety disorders.[42] The concept of manifestation has increasingly taken on the characteristics of a cult, particularly in certain wellness and self-help circles. Prominent figures like Dr. Joe Dispenza promote manifesting as a transformative practice, promising life-changing outcomes through visualization and positive thinking.[43] This trend often relies on blending scientific language with spiritual and/or pseudoscientific ideas, creating a narrative that attracts devoted followers seeking quick fixes or miraculous solutions to life's challenges. The allure of manifestation as a pathway to wealth, health, and happiness can lead to fervent belief and a sense of belonging among adherents. However, this fervor can also create a cult-like environment where skepticism is discouraged, and followers may be exploited emotionally and financially under the guise of self-improvement and empowerment.

Another opponent, Dr. Therese, a licensed clinical psychologist, argues that manifestation culture is harmful in a few ways.[44] For one, it oversimplifies life by emphasizing positive thinking and individual actions without considering external factors and systemic barriers that can impact success. This approach can lead to feelings of guilt, shame, and inadequacy when desired outcomes are not achieved, perpetuating the false notion that failure stems from inadequate manifestation efforts. Notwithstanding the reality of these structural barriers, this approach also undermines the importance of hard work by suggesting that positive thinking alone is sufficient for success. Therese also argues that manifestation exhibits confirmation bias. This one-sided perspective fails to acknowledge the complexities and realities of life, especially for those who have experienced trauma or systemic challenges beyond their control. Manifestation potentially undermines critical thinking and genuine mental health support, substituting empowerment with false promises and unrealistic expectations.

Essentially, while there are numerous claims online about manifestation and astrology being "helpful," or even" magical," these practices could cause more harm than good. Yet due to our systemic failure in providing enough access to trained professionals, many Gen Z members have turned to these "gurus" in the hopes of a quick fix.

While it might be fun to make a vision board or have positive thinking towards big goals, without the work, actionable steps, and motivation to achieve those goals, magic won't bring your dreams to fruition,[45] as explained by psychotherapist Dr. Cohen as follows,

> "Conspiracy theories thrive on cognitive biases—mental shortcuts that allow us to make sense of the world around us. One such bias is the 'proportionality bias, 'which leads people to believe that significant events must have substantial causes. Hence, some individuals find it hard to accept that monumental occurrences could result from simple, mundane causes. This bias can fuel belief in conspiracy theories that propose grand, elaborate explanations for significant events."[46]

So not only do these practices prey on people financially, but they also fall victim to cognitive biases that can make people more susceptible to conspiracies. All in all, this uptick in spiritual healing signals a clear need for more comprehensive access to quality mental health professionals without barriers. Astrology and manifestation are undoubtably fun hobbies and can be a great activity socially, but they should not replace professional care.

<u>Conclusion</u>

Given that Gen Z increasingly must rely on emergency rooms for immediate mental health assistance, and half of Americans report that cost is a barrier to mental health treatment, the lack of access and affordability of care become undeniable. The shortage of mental healthcare workers aggravates the situation further, particularly in rural areas and underserved communities. These factors combine to produce a difficult landscape for Gen Z to access services. When we create a desperate situation, we also feed into a system that exploits us—where opportunists can scam us into believing in magic. So many of us are stuck in a system that was poorly designed, shamefully leaving those of us with disability behind, and creating new disabilities through the failure to restructure our system to meet our most basic needs.

Chapter 5: Failure in Early Intervention & Misdiagnosis

The early adolescence years are crucial for a child's cognitive,
emotional and social development.
-Patty Mills

Growing up, I struggled on and off with severe fatigue, joint pain, digestive issues, acne, and dizziness. I saw doctors often; each time being dismissed as either depressed or just being dramatic. As you can imagine, my childhood felt very invalidating. Fast-forwarding to 2021, I got COVID. And it was bad; I was sick for three weeks, to the point of not being able to leave my bed for longer than five minutes. After recovering from the major symptoms, I realized that I was still not getting better. I went to my doctor and asked if I had "long COVID." My doctor at the time told me, "Long COVID does not exist." After a year of unhelpful appointments with this doctor, I switched insurance and saw another doctor. It took many months of me being pushed along to specialist after specialist, dismissed over and over, to eventually find one doctor who listened to me.

But unlike in my childhood (where I did not have the agency to seek justice for my health), as an adult, I had the determination to find answers to my life's pains. And I would not accept long COVID as my only answer, since I had felt sick on and off my whole life. Finally, I was disabled enough to believe my health deserved priority in my life. At the time, my mom helped me, as I was too disabled most days to leave my home but strong enough to request help. We developed a plan; she got me up, drove me, sat in on appointments, and strongly advocated for me when I was too weak or sick to fight. I wrote down every symptom, even ones that seemed unrelated. Finally, after seeing ten different specialists, armed with my list, I got answers. I had been living my whole life with two chronic diseases: postural orthostatic tachycardia syndrome (POTS) and celiac disease—both of which can cause symptoms of depression. Within months of treating these two diseases, I felt healthier and happier than I could ever remember. With clarity and my chronic pain diminished, I finally have my life back. Yet, I wondered after my experience how my story compares to the stories of so many others. How many people are dismissed by our healthcare system, with undiagnosed and untreated medical conditions that present as psychiatric symptoms? How many people never find answers? What are the consequences of misdiagnosis?

The interplay of our physical and mental healthcare systems can create a dynamic of cause and effect. Many physical health conditions such as autoimmune and autonomic diseases as well as food intolerances, can lead to mental health struggles that can be due (in large part) to the lack of appropriate medical diagnosis. Early intervention, both for physical and mental health, is of immense importance because problems often escalate if not addressed early, and seeking assistance at the earliest opportunity can significantly diminish the intensity and duration of necessary treatment. While some symptoms may fade away on their own, mental health conditions typically worsen over time, underscoring the crucial nature of early intervention.

Consider, for instance, a high school student grappling with initial symptoms of depression. Early engagement in therapy or medication can prove beneficial, preventing the escalation of symptoms into a major depressive episode. Similarly, a young person with anxiety faces the risk of experiencing more severe symptoms without timely intervention, as well as the development of additional mental health challenges, such as substance abuse or suicidal thoughts. We need a redesign and enhancement of our current prevention and early intervention services for everyone, especially youth. A screening test at one's primary care doctor is arguably not enough to reach early intervention. Moreover, how many people seek their primary care provider each year versus the number of people who silently struggle? How many people struggle with chronic disease and live for a lifetime with both chronic pain and mental illness that might have been alleviated with proper treatment?

Early Intervention is Difficult

Most people with mental illness start exhibiting obvious symptoms by age 14.[1] The issue is that parents, teachers, and other adults do not always have the training or knowledge to identify these symptoms. And because as a society we love to blame teens for being "hormonal," the chances of early intervention diminish. Though some schools are now screening students for certain mental health conditions, what happens when they do discover an issue? What does the referral process and coordination of care look like? Imagine a scenario where a teen gets referred to an effective therapist or psychiatrist, but the parent refuses or cannot, provide their child with transportation to receive care? What if the parents cannot afford the treatment, even with insurance? Our teens are in crisis, and yet authoritative services, interventions, and abilities to remove obvious barriers still do not provide a full, spectrum solution needed to respond to this crisis.

Under/Over-diagnosis

One harmful form of misdiagnosis is the over-diagnosis or under-diagnosis of mental illness. For example, bipolar disorder is often misdiagnosed—40 percent of these patients are initially diagnosed with unipolar depression.[2] The delay in prescribing mood stabilizers among patients with bipolar disorder has been linked to elevated healthcare expenses, heightened rates of suicide attempts, and increased utilization of hospital services.[3] Lifetime risk of suicide attempts in patients with this disorder is between 25 and 50 percent compared to 15 percent in patients with unipolar depression.[4] Additionally, this disorder is often misdiagnosed, especially in women and people on the autism spectrum, as many of the presenting symptoms of being on the spectrum can appear similar to this mood disorder.[5] Similarly, obsessive-compulsive disorder (OCD) is largely misdiagnosed, and sufferers can go undiagnosed for ten or more years.[6] This is a huge problem, because the misdiagnosis of OCD causes suffering that could include development of psychosis and suicidality.[7]

The DSM-5's rigid, yet vague parameters for diagnosis set it up for scrutiny. Some may ask, why do we even need labels? The DSM-5 has faced criticism, particularly for its diagnostic criteria. Critics argue that the revised criteria have expanded psychiatric diagnosis into areas of normal-range distress and everyday problems, potentially leading to unnecessary and harmful treatments. Concerns have been expressed about the "false positives problem" of mislabeling normal conditions as mental disorders, impacting psychiatric epidemiology, which heavily relies on DSM criteria in community studies.[8] The DSM-5 task force in charge of updating the mental health diagnostic manual wanted to revise the way mental health conditions were categorized: they proposed using a system based on the "severity of symptoms" rather than traditional categories.[9] This approach, which aimed to reduce issues like multiple diagnoses per person or vague diagnoses, is now facing criticism because it didn't clearly explain what counts as a mental health disorder. In other words, the proposed changes in the DSM-5 have led to mistakes in labeling normal experiences as mental health issues. False positives are a legitimate problem, and the consequences of attaching lifelong labels to our youth with disorders have real implications like interfering from accurate diagnosis and tailored interventions, unnecessary treatments, and unnecessary stigma and costs associated with treatments. My experience is a case and point: in college I struggled with severe fatigue, whole body pain, and other symptoms. Instead of getting my proper diagnosis, I was funneled through our psychiatric system and put on anti-depressants that didn't work for me and caused painful side effects. So, while some people are being underdiagnosed, being over-diagnosed carries problems too.

Though these are just a few examples of misdiagnosis, but the numerous disorders that are over or under diagnosed have serious detriment to all of us who are left without valid answers.

Overlooked Health Conditions

Neglecting physical health can have a profound impact on mental wellbeing. For example, chronic illnesses, pain, or discomfort can contribute to stress, anxiety, and depression. Some physical diseases have direct effects on the brain and its functioning. Certain infections, hormonal imbalances, or neurological disorders can influence mood, cognition, and behavior. Ignoring these underlying physical conditions may lead to the development or worsening of mental health issues. Autoimmune diseases that are misdiagnosed, or overlooked completely, can lead to mental health struggles as well. Likewise, autonomic conditions, researchers are learning, are becoming increasingly more common, yet the treatments have not caught up, and often go undiagnosed. Many of us have food intolerances, if not food allergies, yet our medical model does not emphasize their importance. Overlooking physical diseases means delayed or inadequate treatment. This can result in the progression of the illness, leading to more severe symptoms and complications. Moreover, physical and mental health are closely interconnected: the longer someone experiences physical health challenges, the greater the likelihood of developing mental health issues.[10]

Medical gaslighting, (especially for women, people of color, and the LGBTIA+ community) is extremely problematic, because it under-diagnoses physical illness as mental illness. Somehow there is more research and medical attention towards erectile dysfunction than for many chronically disabling diseases.[11,12] Women are four times more likely to have autoimmune diseases,[13] yet conditions that afflict groups outside of cis White men are chronically under-diagnosed. Gaslighting in medical settings is evident, often manifesting as the dismissive statement, "It's all in your head." A glaring example is the treatment disparity of heart attacks, where women's symptoms are disproportionately attributed to mental issues compared to men.[14] Despite claims that women's heart attack symptoms are "strange and unpredictable," the symptoms look relatively the same.[15] Instances of medical gaslighting are rampant on social media, highlighting cases where women have faced life-threatening delays in cancer diagnosis or have had their severe pain downplayed as anxiety or postpartum depression by doctors. Not only is it demeaning for doctors to further stigmatize mental health struggles as "making sh*t up," it also paints a clear picture of the medical negligence we face.

I believe my story is the perfect case in point. I struggled with lifelong chronic pain and was dismissed as "making it up" or being mentally unwell. But since receiving my diagnosis and treatment, I have been in remission from depression because I am now well aware that the cause of my pain is real. I am not being dramatic or attention-seeking. My medical providers now recognize that the many years is struggled with depression was in large part due to the chronic pain I experienced caused by undiagnosed celiac disease and POTS.

Conclusion

Early intervention at first emergence of symptoms, typically in early teens, is critical in mitigating the potentially devastation of untreated mental illness. The importance of timely support and treatment cannot be overstated due to its effectiveness. The challenges inherent in implementing effective early intervention strategies illustrate a need for a comprehensive overhauling of existing systems. The cost of late intervention is undeniable. Medical gaslighting further perpetuates a culture of neglect. Misdiagnosis, whether through over or under diagnosis, also compounds the problem, depriving us of the personalized support and treatment we desperately need. Essentially, the intersection of physical health and mental illness evidences the need for a holistic approach to care—one that addresses the intricate interplay between mind and body. All of this should show how important it is that our systems recognize the harm in not truly hearing people and relying on our highly medicalized model.

Chapter 6: Overemphasis on Medication

Writing prescriptions is easy, but understanding people is hard.
- Franz Kafka, from The Country Doctor

Pretty much every encounter I have had with a psychiatrist has looked the same: they would ask me what medication I wanted and then prescribe a starter dose of the new drug 'de jour' to see how it affected my brain chemistry. Their expectation that I would have already chosen a medication myself always confused me. Aren't they supposed to be experts? Shouldn't they be the ones who know what is best? My first experience with pharmaceuticals started when I was 15; I quickly developed strange side effects including shaking, brain shocks, and headaches. Since then, I played a game of "let's try that one" and bounced on and off pretty much every name brand drug for depression treatment. Every single medication had a drawback for me. One of them made my legs and hands go numb randomly, while another caused me to lose all emotion and feel like a walking zombie. My side effects were apparently normal according to my frantic Google searches.

The shocking part was discovering that my undiagnosed celiac disease was the culprit all along and that a gluten-free diet was enough to ward my depressive thoughts off into remission. Sadly, other people have experienced much worse outcomes from taking medication, like serotonin syndrome, suicidal ideation, and even permanent movement disorders such as Tardive dyskinesia. And while medications can be very helpful, especially after underlying medical causation has been ruled out, the "tough pill to swallow" is the notion that it is unrealistic to expect people to wash away bills, debt, loneliness, undiagnosed diseases, grief, comparison culture, or job loss—with a pill.

Medication has become the first line of defense against mental illness.[1] The increase in prescribing rates evidences this: between 1990 and 2008, there was an astounding 400 percent increase in use of psychiatric medication.[2] Opponents of pharmaceutical interventions, like Harvard's Dr. Kirsch, have argued that placebo interventions have actually been more effective in the treatment of anxiety and depression,[3] perhaps because there are no adverse side effects. Millions of people are using medication, but their recovery rates look like those who never used medication at all.[4] Research has also found that psychotherapy alone is often more effective than medication.[5]

Many experts now find that long-term use of psychiatric medications is causing our society "net harm."[6,7] In recent decades, psychiatric medication has become the cornerstone of mental health treatment, raising concerns about the over-reliance on pharmacological interventions. The increasing trend of prioritizing pills as the primary treatment modality warrants a closer examination. Despite a growing body of evidence supporting the efficacy of psychotherapeutic approaches, a significant proportion of mental health professionals resort to medications as the first line of treatment.

I must mention that there is no shame in taking medication. There were points in my life when taking medication, despite side effects, was extremely helpful: I do not know if I would have survived the grief of my best friend's passing without medication, honestly. However, acknowledging the influence of pharmaceutical industry practices on prescribing patterns, and understanding the limitations and potential risks associated with medication-based interventions is crucial. Why should we drug ourselves if we don't have to?

Is Big Pharma to Blame?

At this point, I think most people are aware of "Big Pharma" and its influence on our healthcare system, but many of us don't know how or why. In one year, the top ten pharmaceutical companies amassed over $112 billion in profits, yet we, as Americans, still endure the highest prescription drug prices globally.[8] If you are wondering why: follow the money. The pharmaceutical industry holds immense political sway in America. Amidst a Congress comprising over 500 people, the pharma industry boasts over 1,800 well-compensated lobbyists on Capitol Hill, including former leaders of both the Democratic and Republican parties.[9] Last year alone, these drug companies spent over $375 million on lobbying efforts directed at Congress,[10] and over the past quarter-century, the pharmaceutical industry has funneled substantial campaign contributions to politicians across party lines, encompassing nearly every member of Congress.[11] To add fuel to the fire, they also spend billions on direct-to-consumer television and print advertising.[12] The outcome of this extraordinary political influence, is that the US pharmaceutical companies operate without important oversight that many other countries have. One exception to note is that in 2022, the Biden Administration enacted the Inflation Reduction Act, which may help in some areas in terms of drug pricing (but as of now, it covers only ten medications).[13] Basically, the US big pharma can often establish prices at any level for any rationale they desire—and they do so with impunity.

The pervasive influence of the pharmaceutical industry on psychiatric treatment practices cannot, and should not, be ignored. Marketing strategies, financial incentives, and industry-sponsored research have contributed to the overprescription of medications.[14] Psychiatrists and healthcare providers may succumb to external pressures, consciously or unconsciously favoring medication-based solutions over alternative treatments.[15] One study revealed a correlation between industry-sponsored activities and increased prescribing of psychotropic medications,[16] highlighting the need for transparency in disclosing potential conflicts of interest within the medical community. There is a long history concerning the formation of modern psychiatry and its relationship to large pharmaceutical companies. Though I cannot cover this history in detail here, I want to highlight one example to illustrate how the system is currently failing.

In 2013, there was federal Open Payments legislation aimed to bring transparency to the relationship between pharmaceutical companies and physicians by requiring the disclosure of direct payments.[17] The expectation was that making these payments public would deter medical school faculty from authoring ghostwritten papers on clinical trial results and prevent them from receiving compensation for promotional talks related to newly approved drugs.[18] Recently published 2020 payment records by the Centers for Medicare and

Medicaid Services reveal a seven-year history of accessible payment data.[19] An investigation by Mad in America (MIA) suggests that while the legislation has reduced the involvement of academic psychiatrists in certain activities, the influence of pharmaceutical money remains pervasive in all aspects of drug development.[20] Since emerging, the psychopharmacology service industry has relied on academic psychiatrists to consult/author reports for drug trials, review results to increase drug awareness, and market the drugs to prescribers. The Open Payments legislation has unveiled the financial influence in an unprecedented way, showcasing the commercial involvement in clinical trial design, result manipulation, and drug promotion.

Let's use Trintellix as an example. MIA identified 62 US psychiatrists who received direct payments from pharmaceutical companies "totaling $1 million or more from 2014 through 2020."[21] The top earner was Stephen Stahl, at $8.6 million, with $6.6 million coming from Takeda, the company that brought the antidepressant Brintellix to market in 2013.[22] Stahl, a UCSD adjunct professor who had to leave his job at Stanford for plagiarizing a book chapter, has been one of the heaviest pushers for the drug now called Trintellix.[23] I have had my own experience with Trintellix. When I was 20, I was referred to a specialist who was supposed to be a pharma expert (and also happened to be associated with a school that rhymes with UCSD). She immediately started me on a "free" sample of Trintellix. When I ran out, I commented how expensive it was and that my insurance would not cover it because it was not on its preferred drug list, so she provided another free sample. After the third free sample, I ended up with no intended effect and had some side effects that I complained about. She said that was all she had to prescribe, and said I had to go see someone else for treatment if I wanted a different medication!

If you look at the actual research about this medication, from invention to pill, many concerns arise. Upon initial review, the drug's three short-term trials appear to support the efficacy of vortioxetine (Trintellix).[24] However, concerns arise regarding the placebo groups composed of drug-withdrawn patients and a design feature that downplays adverse events.[25] The studies' protocol instructed investigators to ask patients a general question, "How do you feel?" instead of inquiring about specific antidepressant-associated side effects, potentially leading to unreported adverse reactions.[26] In US trials, three out of five found <u>no drug benefit</u>, which brings to question the claim of efficacy.[27] *Patient Drug News* echoes concerns, emphasizing "little benefit" and "significant risks," while the FDA disallowed claims of cognitive benefits because of insufficient supporting data.[28] Post-market adverse events reported to the FDA revealed a problematic drug: including 45 deaths, adverse behavioral changes, sexual dysfunction, and eating disorders.[29] That should be important for people to know…right?

Although the $340 million disbursed to psychiatrists by pharmaceutical companies between 2014 and 2020 [30] may have represented substantial earnings for individual practitioners, it constitutes a relatively minor expenditure for these Big Pharma companies. These payments contribute to constructing a narrative, seemingly grounded in the scientific rigor of "double-blind, placebo-controlled, randomized trials," portraying drugs as safe and effective when, in reality, more research (without sources of potential bias) is needed.

<u>Limitations and Risks</u>

Psychiatric medications, while beneficial for many, are not without limitations. Side effects, dependency issues, and the challenge of finding the right medication pose inherent risks to patients. In addition, there is evidence suggesting that the long-term efficacy of certain psychiatric medications may be limited, as their effectiveness may diminish.[31] The STAR*D trial, the largest antidepressant study ever conducted, demonstrated that a large proportion of people with major depressive disorder did not achieve remission even after multiple medication trials.[32] In other words, the STAR*D trial showed us how ineffective these medications often are.

Many argue that a legitimate path towards healing starts with ensuring that basic needs are being met. For example, providers should look at patients holistically and ask questions like: does this person have a support system, affordable housing, employment, a network of friends, community engagement, and an active health-minded lifestyle? Why are we pushing pills before addressing these greater systemic issues like lack of community? Well, it is probably because it is much easier to prescribe medication than remedy the systemic societal problems discussed in this book.

Psychiatrists acknowledge the potential importance of psychiatric drugs in stabilizing and saving the lives of suicidal teens when appropriately prescribed.[33] However, concerns arise as these medications are often dispensed too readily, serving as a convenient alternative to therapy, especially for families facing financial constraints or a lack of interest. Despite being designed for short-term use, psychiatric drugs are sometimes prescribed for extended periods, leading to severe side effects such as psychotic episodes, suicidal behavior, weight gain, and interference with reproductive development.[34] A recent study, published in *Frontiers in Psychiatry,* highlights these risks, finding that many psychiatric drugs prescribed to adolescents lack FDA approval for children under 18, and their combination, often untested for safety or long-term effects on the developing brain, raises additional concerns.[35] Yet, doctors have the prescribing power to use their own discretion, and there has been a surge in combination prescriptions, particularly among low-income children. [36] Moreover, 85 percent of Medicaid-enrolled children on antipsychotic drugs were also prescribed a second medication. This in turn also disproportionately affects disabled and foster care youth.[37]

It is important to consider that there is still a paramount concern regarding the limited efficacy of psych medications, with studies suggesting only modest benefits, at best, for major drug classes like antidepressants—and there is limited research about the impact of these drugs on youth.[38] And as highlighted above, much of the research on these medications, themselves, is heavily influenced by large pharmaceutical companies.

Conclusion

The overemphasis on psychiatric medication for mental health treatment has raised significant concerns, especially for our generation. Personal experiences I've had with psychiatrists reveal a trend of prioritizing medication without sufficient consideration for individual needs or expert guidance in evaluating underlying medical causation. Because the pharmaceutical industry has pervasive influence on psychiatric practices—with financial incentives and industry-sponsored research contributing to the overprescription of medications—we must take a critical look at the role we allow big Pharma to play in our healthcare. Psychiatric medications, while valuable in specific cases, are not without risks. The complexity of mental health conditions necessitates a comprehensive approach, considering basic needs and addressing underlying medical and systemic issues before resorting to pharmacological interventions. In other words, psychiatrists and doctors need to stop drugging us without evaluating the complete picture—and I mean the whole damn picture.

Chapter 7: Policing, Prisons, and Hospitals

Some of these children do need help, but is this the right type of help?
Over the years counselors have been charged with sexual abuse, physical
abuse, and predatory behavior.
-Kenneth R. Rosen

It feels wrong to me, in my present introspection, that I did not recognize the impact of our policing system until I was forced to read *Crime and Inequality* by Ruth Peterson, for an undergraduate sociology class.[1] As a child, the relationship between mental illness and policing looked to me like unhoused people pacing the streets talking to themselves, hissing at passersby, or peeing on the sidewalk. And then those same people would eventually be arrested for some petty crime like jaywalking—to get them out of the public eye. Yet the relationship between our policing system and mental health exists within a gray area, and is incredibly complicated, sometimes corrupt, and highly stigmatized. Some police departments have adopted crisis response teams (CRTs), but these teams operate within and train through the police system.

Last year, an investigation in the *Journal of the American Academy of Psychiatry and the Law* concluded that police crisis intervention teams have only slightly helped reduce arrests of people with a mental illness and only modestly kept them out of the criminal justice system.[2] Dr. Reneé Binder, who directs the Psychiatry and Law Program at the University of California, San Francisco, highlights that the study also concluded that CRTs have failed in a fundamental goal: to de-escalate and reduce violence to citizens and police alike.[3] According to Binder, "It hasn't shown any consistent reduction in the risk of mortality or death during emergency police interactions."[4] In other words, for the departments that have adopted a CRT, they have not considerably decreased the number of people who are killed or injured.

Many times, when someone is in crisis, the police are the first to respond.[5] The critical issue is that police are arguably not adequately trained in how to respond to and de-escalate a mental health crisis. Also, the culture of policing tends to have a high level of stigmatization towards mental disability.[6] As much as 50 percent of our prison population struggles with some type of mental illness, and a high percentage of those in prison are people who fell into addiction. At least 1 in 4 people fatally shot by police had a serious mental illness.[7] Between 6 to 10 percent of all police contacts with the public involve persons with serious mental illnesses.[8] The police have a lot of power, and they are also highly tied to those of us struggling with our mental health. Why are we policing people who should be receiving mental healthcare? Jailing people to address mental health issues is proven to be ineffective.[9] Yet the US continues to heavily invest in prisons and jails and other forms of detainment, confining individuals who would benefit more from community-based treatment.

Roughly 40 percent of people in state prisons met the criteria for a substance use disorder in the year preceding their admission[10] and 20 percent of prisoners were convicted of crimes related to drug acquisition or obtaining money for drugs.[11] Unfortunately, once incarcerated, there is limited assistance provided.[12] And many people with substance use disorders do not receive necessary treatment while behind bars.[13] Since Gen Z has a high rate of mental health struggles and substance abuse, this predisposes us to negative interactions with the law enforcement system.

Police Culture is Not "Mental Health Friendly"

It is well documented that police culture in general has a negative attitude towards mental illness.[14] Ironically, this stigma has translated to officers avoiding seeking treatment themselves, even after being put into traumatic situations. Officers who disclose struggles with mental health have had their careers destroyed as a result. Given this information, it is evident that such strong negative attitudes and high rates of stigma have an impact on police discretion while in the field. This is a concern because it directly impacts how officers interact with members of the public who are struggling with a mental illness.

Mental illness is a disability as defined by the Americans with Disabilities Act (ADA). Yet, when people who are in a mental health crisis encounter the police, they are not given the type of accommodations and support that they need for their health. This happens daily with our unhoused populations. Police culture tends to criminalize people in crisis, instead of offering helpful support. And there is little training for police about how to interact with disabled people in a way that complies with the ADA. According to the Congressional Research Service, our police are allowed to comply with the ADA on a case-by-case basis.[15] Essentially, police will determine at the scene in the moment whether they will choose to follow the ADA. In some cases, this might make sense if the officer is being shot at or their life is in danger, but in general this means that under current law, police have the discretion to discriminate against people with disabilities and face no repercussions. Many police departments have adopted new training (i.e. de-escalation training) and have sought to give officers the time and space to address mental crises without using undue force. But it is important to question whether police are given too much discretion.

The Troubled Teen Industry

The first time I realized there existed a troubled teen industry (TTI) was in a documentary called *This is Paris*. This film highlights the Paris Hilton's experience as she speaks out about her time at Provo Canyon School, a youth treatment center in Utah. Since then, she has released more information documenting her horrific experience—including abuse, neglect, and sexual assault. I had known these centers existed, though, because as a depressed teen, these expensive "treatment centers" were offered as a potential solution to my "problem" in the form of a pamphlet handed to my parents.

The troubled teen industry refers to a sector composed of privately-run programs and facilities that offer interventions and services aimed at addressing behavioral, emotional, and psychological challenges faced by adolescents and young adults.[16] These programs typically target youths struggling with issues such as substance abuse, delinquency, mental health disorders, academic difficulties, and familial conflicts—issues that fall within the gray area of hospitalization and our prison system. [17] Examples of interventions within this industry include therapeutic boarding schools, wilderness therapy programs, residential treatment centers, boot camps, and therapeutic ranches.[18] While some programs in the troubled teen industry may adhere to recognized therapeutic approaches and ethical standards, others have faced criticism and controversy. Criticisms have emerged regarding the lack of regulation, inconsistent treatment quality, allegations of abuse, and the exploitation of vulnerable youth. Despite these criticisms, the troubled teen industry continues to operate, serving as a resource (that is often pushed by healthcare providers) for families seeking support for their adolescents in crisis.

Hilton's story is one that should worry everyone. At 16, she was abruptly confronted with the unwelcome intrusion of two men privately hired by her parents, wielding handcuffs and offering a blunt choice: "the easy way or the hard way." [19] Across four different facilities, Paris endured a relentless barrage of physical and psychological torment at the hands of those entrusted with her care.[20] From choking and slapping to invasive surveillance and forced medication devoid of diagnosis, according to her account, her existence became a crucible of suffering. As she recalls in her op-ed, "At one Utah facility, I was locked in solitary confinement in a room where the walls were covered in scratch marks and blood stains."[21] For Paris Hilton, and the countless survivors who share her anguish, the quest for justice is not merely a matter of politics—it is a fundamental imperative rooted in the sanctity of human dignity. According to the non-profit Unsilenced,

> "These programs market themselves to parents, therapists, state and judicial agencies, and insurance companies as providers of therapeutic treatment for almost every problem. These programs will often claim to treat or be experts in an impossibly diverse and broad myriad of mental health diagnoses and behavioral issues. In the absence of a mental health diagnosis, the programs will often attempt to pathologize normal teenage behavior such as talking back, breaking rules at home, internet addiction, normal sexuality, homosexuality, etc., and treat teenagerhood as a problem that needs to be solved."[22]

Further, Unsilenced reports that these programs cost a range of $5,000 to $30,000 per month with no set duration for how long "patients" stay.[23] And, beyond the exorbitant cost, the TTI exploits vulnerable youth by accessing public funds and accommodating a range of victims including migrant children, foster children, juvenile justice system participants, and children with special education needs or Individualized Education Programs (IEPs).[24] What's more, as was the case in Paris's story, these programs will often recommend youth escort services or "legal kidnapping." Due to little or no government regulation or oversight, companies often send strangers to forcefully seize, handcuff, and transport children from their beds in the middle of the night. In many cases, as highlighted by countless accounts of survivors, these methods have resulted in permanent trauma for the child.

This abuse is documented by many researchers. According to Olivia Stoll, "these programs deliver a mix of maltreatment such as physical, verbal, and sexual abuse, isolation, forced hard labor, chemical sedation, sleep and food deprivation, attack therapy, aversion therapy, etc."[25] This abuse is intensified by the program's function as a "total institution" where the children live under total authority of the program.[26] In modeling programs as total institutions, teens are forbidden to freely leave the programs for months or even years.[27] What's more, once kids arrive to the programs already traumatized by forceful extraction from their homes, the child is further distressed as part of the intake process by having their belongings confiscated—followed by a forced strip search and/or cavity search.[28] Essentially, kids are forced into a prison-like system where they are expected to endure abuse without retaliation, and live with little knowledge of when they will be free—all with very little evidence that they will recover from mental health struggles in treatment.

To exemplify the horrors of the TTI, according to Jamie Mater, a graduate student at the University of New Hampshire, most programs utilize antiquated "points and levels-based systems that force the child to earn basic privileges," and survivors have shared that these systems are often punitive attempts to correct behavior.[29] At many of these institutions, regardless of diagnosis, children are expected to adhere to the same set of stringent rules or be "harshly punished."[30] Some of the punishments and abuses that have been reported in TTI programs include but are not limited to:

> "…food and/or sleep deprivation, use of isolation/solitary confinement rooms, being forced to eat bodily fluids, emotional, physical, and sexual abuse, dangerous use of physical, chemical, or mechanical restraint methods, the punitive use of restraints, forced and excessive exercise, military methods of discipline, forced labor, restricted social interaction or social ostracization, exposure to harsh elements like extreme heat, snow, or rain, use of attack therapy, group

> attack therapy, aversion therapy, conversion therapy, sexual
> shaming and/or forced sexualized behavior/sexual abuse as a
> part of 'treatment, 'and even peer hierarchies where children
> are responsible for punishing and restraining each other."[31]

And while these punishments, (masked as treatments) themselves are enough to make anyone anxious and depressed, another concern is about in-program deaths and lack of accountability of program leadership documenting such occurrences. Program deaths are not officially tracked by a single authority, but *Unsilenced* found that over 350 children have died while in these facilities, and further reports that thousands more have passed away due to suicide after leaving the programs.[32] This information calls attention to how destructive, damaging, and horrific the TTI industry truly is.

Beyond abusive practices, these programs have come under fire for their failure to deliver evidence-based treatment. Scared Straight programs date back to the 1970s, and are known for their confrontational approach to "benefit" at-risk youth,[33] yet, a study found that juveniles participating in these programs committed 28 percent more crimes compared to non-participants.[34] Mark Lipsey from the Vanderbilt Institute for Public Policy Studies also asserts that Scared Straight programs simply "do not work."[35] Though the efficacy of these programs is not substantiated with reputable data, programs continue to operate nationwide, partly fueled by the popularity of the A&E television series "Beyond Scared Straight," and "Dr. Phil."[36] Therefore this industry requires careful intervention, innovation, and substantial change. These programs operate within a gray area of schooling, hospitalization, mental healthcare, and our policing system, yet they are failing and traumatizing thousands of kids every year and will continue to unless something is done.

Conclusion

By allowing policing as a form of mental healthcare to endure, we are perpetuating a system that compounds mental illness. Therefore, now more than ever, one of the critical intersections we must examine is the interaction between mental health crises and law enforcement. The current reliance on police as first responders to mental health crises highlights systemic shortcomings and raises important questions about the role of policing in addressing mental health issues. The fact that the "troubled teen industry" programs, which are a form of "policing" our children, such as the one Paris Hilton was part of, exist, hints to a deeper issue within our nation. Policing mental illness does not work. It is time to rethink this.

Chapter 8: The Drug Epidemic

It's hard to grasp the full scope and scale of the opioid crisis we're in the midst of. The numbers are staggering. Almost half-a-million Americans have died in the last 15 years from an overdose, and the majority of those involve opioids. On average, 91 Americans are still dying every single day.
-William Brangham

I grew up in a middle-class suburban neighborhood in an upscale beach town in California, and my exposure to drugs probably came later than many. The first time I learned about the concept of drugs was while walking home from elementary school when I asked my mom why a certain house always smelled like "skunk." My mom reluctantly explained to me that certain people smoke something called "marijuana" that causes them to be high. At such a young age, I didn't quite understand what any of that meant. By middle school, I witnessed classmates leave school to smoke weed with older kids. And by the time I was in high school, I had the mishap of dating a boy whose nickname was "Reefy." At 18, I had given into peer pressure, and I tried weed. I was fortunate, because I reacted to it terribly. I was anxious, I hallucinated, and my brain felt like it was spinning in circles. I absolutely hated it and have not used it again since. I consider myself lucky as I watched many others experience something different.

The big weed industry took a strong hold on my generation. Although there are many users who seem to have limited negative outcomes, many aren't as lucky. Pot is one drug that became widely accessible and popularized during my childhood, but so did many other substances. The following chapter will highlight the drug crisis that shaped Gen Z, and why it threatens future generations.

<u>The Fentanyl Crisis</u>

The opioid/fentanyl crisis is the most severe drug epidemic in U.S. history. Many experts attribute the origins of the opioid epidemic to the overprescription of legal pain medications during the 1990s.[1] However, the crisis has escalated in recent years due to the influx of inexpensive heroin, fentanyl, and other synthetic opioids supplied by foreign drug cartels. Since 2013, synthetic opioids—particularly fentanyl—have been responsible for a sharp increase in overdose deaths.

According to the CDC, the number of people who died from a drug overdose in 2021 was over six times the number in 1999. The number of drug overdose deaths increased more than 16 percent from 2020 to 2021.[2] Over 75 percent of the nearly 107,000 drug overdose deaths in 2021 involved an opioid.[3] Over 1,500 Americans succumb to opioid-related fatalities each week. In recent times, the epidemic has been predominantly fueled by fentanyl, an exceedingly potent synthetic opioid. 77.1% of overdose deaths in US teens were due to fentanyl.[4] According to UCLA Health,

> "The increase is not due to more illicit drug use – which has in fact fallen over the years; for example, excluding cannabis, the rate of any illicit drug use among just 12th graders had fallen from about 21% to 8% in the 20 years since 2002. Instead, the increase is the result of drugs becoming deadlier due to fentanyl, which is increasingly found in counterfeit oxycodone, benzodiazepines and other prescription pills that fall into the hands of adolescents."[5]

Initially developed as an intravenous anesthetic in the 1960s, fentanyl served as a crucial medication in healthcare settings.[6] However, its illicit production and distribution have posed an unprecedented threat to public health. In 2022, Anne Milgram, the head of the U.S. Drug Enforcement Administration (DEA), described fentanyl as the most lethal drug menace the nation has ever faced.[7] Moreover, the crisis has been further complicated by the emergence of new combinations of synthetic opioids. Chemicals like xylazine, commonly used in horse tranquilizers, and other novel opioids, are reported to possess even higher potency levels than pure fentanyl. Given this historical background, it is clear Gen Z essentially was born into an impending drug crisis unlike any other generation.

These drugs are being marketed and sold to youth via social media (making the drug widely accessible).[8] Fentanyl is frequently found in counterfeit pills that are made to look like legitimate prescription medications such as OxyContin, Xanax, or Adderall.[9] Experts are warning that youth with mental health struggles are at highest risk in being implicated in this crisis because they seek these counterfeit pills to trying to self-medicate.[10] Because the distribution channels of opioids are so sophisticated, law enforcement have struggled to keep up.[11] By making counterfeit pills so easily accessible to teens, it is no wonder many who are struggling may turn to what seems like a "quick fix." Unfortunately, by failing to provide youth with a stigma free, easily accessible mental health care, many young people have resorted to a devastating alternative.

Weed is Everywhere, but is there Risk?

Statistics reveal a concerning trend of cannabis use among Gen Z—indicating the presence of a weed epidemic: usage rates in children and young adults have reached an all-time high. And today's weed is much more potent in THC than what our Gen X/Boomer parents smoked.[12] 8.3 percent of eighth graders, 19.5 percent of 10th graders, and 30.7 percent of 12th graders reported using cannabis within the past year.[13] Cannabis use among youth can negatively impact brain development, academic performance, and mental health. The normalization and accessibility of cannabis in today's society may magnify the issue, making it even more challenging to address than in previous generations.

Many people see no issue with cannabis. In fact, many users purport an array of benefits to using the substance. But the truth is, there is no clear answer to whether its use is beneficial or not. Some data support positive aspects of the substance. For example, in a comprehensive review conducted in 2017, encompassing over 10,000 scientific studies, it was concluded that cannabis and cannabinoids, the active compounds in cannabis, demonstrate efficacy in alleviating chronic pain.[14] Specifically, medicinal cannabis shows promise in mitigating neuropathic pain, which originates from nerve-related sources. Likewise, a study published in the New England Journal of Medicine found cannabis to help reduce seizures for those with epilepsy.[15]

Conversely, research has also found concerning data about the drug. The use of marijuana, especially when initiated during teenage years or earlier, poses significant risks to brain health. The CDC reports that THC can interfere with brain development, potentially leading to impairments in cognitive functions such as processing, memory, and learning.[16] Additionally, marijuana use has been associated with mental health issues, including depression, social anxiety, and temporary psychosis characterized by hallucinations, paranoia, and a distorted sense of reality.[17] Long-term use may even elevate the risk of developing enduring mental disorders like schizophrenia, particularly among those who start using marijuana frequently at a young age.[18] Also concerning is that weed has been shown to shorten rapid eye movement (REM) sleep—which, as most argue, is incredibly important for health and wellbeing.[19] Lack of REM sleep, especially over time for habitual users, can cause fatigue, mood problems, decreased motivation, weight gain, and is correlated with increased cancer risk.[20] Children who begin using marijuana before the age of 18 face an elevated likelihood of developing marijuana use disorder, highlighting the increased potential for addiction and dependency associated with early initiation of use.[21] To add further, according to research conducted at Columbia University, teenagers who engage in recreational cannabis use are two to four times more likely to experience psychiatric disorders, such as depression and suicidal thoughts, compared to teenagers who abstain from cannabis use altogether.[22] The study reveals that even occasional cannabis use among teens increases their susceptibility to engaging in problematic behaviors. These behaviors include achieving poor grades, skipping school, and encountering legal issues, all of which could lead to detrimental long-term effects hindering youths from reaching their full potential in adulthood.[23, 24]

Another concern is that many teens and young adults are driving while high. Driving while under the influence of marijuana is dangerous, as it impairs essential driving skills, including reaction time, coordination, and concentration. This not only jeopardizes the safety of the individual but also puts others on the road at risk. In fact, the National Institute on Alcohol Abuse and Alcoholism found that the proportion of crash deaths involving cannabis increased significantly, more than doubling from 9 percent in 2000 to 21.5 percent in 2018. Similarly, the percentage of deaths involving both cannabis and alcohol also more than doubled, rising from 4.8 percent to 10.3 percent over the same period.[25]

Critics of my argument will attempt to cite research about the "benefits of weed." This is part of the problem. The weed industry has employed a sneaky, yet highly successful marketing scheme that MIT expert Dr. Caputi calls "research as marketing"—where the companies use weak, low power, corrupted "research" to tout the benefits of their product.[26] This method has created a network of propaganda that has produced a wealth of misleading information on the subject. For instance, Aurora, a prominent marijuana company, referenced an industry-funded study in a blog post to assert that "Medical cannabis patients report using CBD for a variety of purposes, including alleviating symptoms of PTSD, anxiety, and pain."[27,28] This statement might lead consumers to believe that there is scientific evidence supporting the effectiveness of CBD in treating these conditions. However, sound research advises against using CBD for mental health.[29] As consumers we are accustomed to believing there are regulations on health claims imposed by pharmaceutical firms, therefore we may assume that claims made by marijuana companies are under the same scrutiny—when in reality, these companies utilize loopholes to spread false information and unscientific research.[30] It is important to note that a lot of the research is correlational (saying that something is related to something else), but does not support causal inferences (which makes it weak in comparison to double blind controlled studies).

In pointing this out, I am not trying to demonize weed—but it is important for habitual young users who are now participating at the highest rates in history to recognize the potential risks to their mental health. And we as consumers have a right to know that these large corporations are spreading misleading information and touting it as "verified research."

Conclusion

The crisis, epitomized by the increased use of opioids, has brought devastation across communities, claiming thousands of lives annually[31] yet drugs continue to harm our youth. Almost 22 teens die every week from Fentanyl.[32] The normalization and widespread availability of cannabis has contributed to a concerning amount of youth using the drug at record highs. The fact that 8.3 percent of eighth graders are using it is frightening. Because of the risks associated with cannabis, especially in use for those under 25, signal the need for young users need to be informed of the real dangers and more genuine precautions to be taken by our nation's leadership.

Chapter 9: The Rise of ASD & ADHD

I didn't let ADHD prevent me from achieving my goals, and neither should you.
-Howie Mandel

In the thick of my chronic illness, I was misdiagnosed with "level one" autism spectrum disorder (ASD). During this time, chronic pain from my undiagnosed physical disease made me present with many of the same symptoms as someone with autism. Like many trauma survivors, I struggled with eye contact. And like many people with chronic pain, I had severe brain fog from undiagnosed celiac disease. And the constant headaches and stabbing abdominal pain consistently made conversations and being verbal a struggle for me. Other autistic symptoms also rang true for me, such as struggling to make and keep friends; I often needed to cancel plans last minute due to my symptoms. Likewise, I hate having my skin touched—common in both people with autism and chronic pain. After discovering and receiving effective treatment for the medical conditions I did not know I had, I went back to get reevaluated for a full psych workup. Not only did the new results find that I am not autistic, but that I also did not have ADHD as I was diagnosed with in the past.

These misdiagnoses, however, bring up a lot of questions and concerns for me about what the field of psychology does when it mislabels patients. Part of me is angered, because I lived for a year thinking I was autistic. Yet another part of me remembers feeling validated when I was diagnosed. The diagnosis, before finding out about having chronic disease, brought me a ton of relief. I felt so seen, heard, and understood. Finally, I had a reason for why I felt like I was so misunderstood my whole life, and why I struggled with isolation at certain points. Interestingly, both ADHD and ASD have seen a stark rise in diagnosis since the time my generation was born—the late 1990s. In fact, ADHD diagnosis alone has doubled just between 2007 and 2017.[1]

My experience makes me wonder about the thousands of other women who are diagnosed with autism as adults. Do they feel relief too? Even though I am not autistic, I believe that there are so many people living with autism that struggle with many of the things I did when I was diagnosed. When I shared my diagnosis, many people treated me differently (some people completely unfriended me), my healthcare providers told me they had nothing to offer for it, and my therapist at the time told me to "lower my expectations about what I will achieve." That experience was very telling to me in many ways. I learned there is a severe stigma for women with autism, and I also learned that people often don't understand what it is.

ADHD and ASD often co-exist with mental health problems and because we have had such a large increase in diagnosis in these developmental disabilities within Gen Z, it is important to discuss how we can better support individuals with these developmental disabilities and also highlight the ways in which they exemplify systemic failings within mental health care. The following chapter will explain what is currently known about autism and ADHD and explain why these developmental disabilities need more. These disabilities need more of…what exactly? More resources, more funding, and more attention to reducing stigma, especially for women, non-binary members, and people of color. My reasoning behind including this chapter is that as we begin to recognize the nuances of these conditions, we can provide resources to the many people who do not present psychiatric symptoms in the stereotypical way. Typically, those who fall in that category are left misdiagnosed and without necessary resources and educational/work accommodations. In turn, this leaves many struggling with their mental health due to society's failure to acknowledge their lived experiences with this often-invisible disability. Likewise, this rise in developmental disabilities is an example of how our system is failing us.

What is Autism?

Autism spectrum disorder (ASD) is a developmental disorder characterized by a wide range of symptoms, skills, and levels of impairment. [2] The term "spectrum" reflects the wide variation in challenges and strengths possessed by each person with autism. While there isn't a universally agreed-upon classification of "levels" of autism, clinicians often refer to different degrees of support needed based on the individual's level of functioning.[3] These levels are sometimes used to guide treatment planning and support services. Although these classifications have changed over time, here's a general overview of the current levels:

Level 1: Requiring Support

> At this level one may exhibit mild challenges in social communication and interaction. They might find it challenging to initiate and sustain conversations, understand nonverbal cues like facial expressions or body language, and grasp social nuances. Repetitive behaviors and routines are common, and they may have intense interests in specific topics. Sensory sensitivities, like being sensitive to certain sounds or textures, can also be present.[4]

Level 2: Requiring Substantial Support

> People at this level often demonstrate more pronounced difficulties in social communication and interaction compared to Level 1. They may struggle more significantly with understanding and responding to social cues, maintaining relationships, and adapting to changes in routines or environments. Repetitive behaviors and restricted interests may be more noticeable and impactful on daily functioning. Sensory sensitivities can be heightened and may interfere with daily activities.[5]

Level 3: High Support Need

> Individuals at this level exhibit challenges across multiple domains, including social communication, interaction, and behavior. They may have minimal verbal communication skills or be nonverbal altogether. Social difficulties are profound, with limited understanding of social cues and minimal interest in social interaction. Repetitive behaviors and sensory sensitivities can be severe and may considerably impact daily functioning. At this level, many people often require assistance with all aspects of daily living.[6]

Tailored interventions, cultural competence, and a holistic understanding of each person's unique strengths and challenges are essential for providing effective support and promoting inclusion for people with autism across all levels and identities, yet often these services are lacking from providers. [7] Despite progress, challenges persist in diagnosing autism in girls, women, and those with less obvious symptoms. Autistic people often face difficulties accessing appropriate support and services, leading to higher rates of homelessness, unemployment, and mental health issues. Furthermore, existing support systems are often inaccessible or insufficient, leaving many autistic adults and their families struggling to navigate complex bureaucracies and inadequate resources. [8]

What is ADHD?

Like autism spectrum disorder, Attention-Deficit/Hyperactivity Disorder (ADHD), according to *SimplyPsychology*, "is a neurodevelopmental disorder characterized by persistent patterns of inattention, hyperactivity, and impulsivity that interfere with functioning or development." [9,10] ADHD can manifest differently, depending on the person, with variation in severity and impact on daily life. [11] ADHD is often categorized into different levels of support, although this classification can be fluid. Here's an overview of the current levels:

Mild: Requiring Support

Persons at this level may exhibit mild symptoms of inattention or hyperactivity-impulsivity. They might find it challenging to stay focused on tasks, follow through on instructions, or organize activities. One may often appear to be daydreaming, lose things frequently, or forget daily routines. Hyperactivity might manifest as fidgeting, difficulty staying seated, or excessive talking. Impulsivity can result in hasty actions, difficulty waiting for turns, and interrupting others. While these behaviors are noticeable, they generally do not cause significant impairment in social or academic functioning. [12]

Moderate: Requiring Substantial Support

Individuals at this level often demonstrate more pronounced symptoms of inattention and hyperactivity-impulsivity compared to mild. Inattention might include consistent difficulties in sustaining attention, following multi-step instructions, and managing time effectively. [13] Hyperactivity can be more disruptive, such as an inability to remain seated for extended periods or excessive movement in inappropriate situations.[14] Impulsivity might lead to frequent interruptions, impulsive decision-making, and difficulty waiting for their turn in conversations or activities. [15] These behaviors can interfere with academic performance, social interactions, and daily routines.[16]

Severe: High Support Need

At this level one is more likely to exhibit severe symptoms of inattention, hyperactivity, and impulsivity that profoundly impact their daily functioning.[17] Inattention might include a pervasive inability to focus on tasks, extreme forgetfulness, and disorganization that affects all areas of life. [18] Hyperactivity can be so intense that the individual is almost constantly in motion, making it difficult to engage in sedentary activities or remain quiet in settings that require calmness.[19] Impulsivity at this level can lead to dangerous behaviors, severe social difficulties, and frequent disruptions in academic and occupational settings. [20] These individuals often require a lot of support to manage their symptoms and perform daily activities effectively.[21]

Like autism, ADHD manifests differently in each person, with significant diversity within the ADHD community, and gender, race, cultural background, and other intersectional factors can influence the presentation and management of ADHD symptoms.[22,23]

Why Are the Rates Higher?

Since the 1990s, there has been a continuous increase in the number of children diagnosed with autism spectrum disorder and ADHD. [24, 25] Scientists have been actively investigating the reasons behind this surge and trying to pinpoint when and why autism began to rise.

Regarding ASD, as of 2020, the CDC reported that about 1 in 36 children aged 8 in the United States were diagnosed with autism.[26] This is over a 300 percent increase in the last 20 years.[27] Some experts believe the higher rates could be due to the release of the DSM-5 in 2013[28] that removed Asperger's syndrome (the name Asperger is rooted in Nazism so it is no longer recommended to be used), which was merged and broadly categorized into ASD. This change could have potentially led to a higher number of people meeting the criteria for an autism diagnosis, consequently contributing to an increase in reported cases. Whether the DSM change alone is enough to explain this increase is up for debate.

Like ASD, ADHD has also seen a record rise. The prevalence of ADHD has steadily increased. In the past two decades, ADHD diagnoses rose from 6.1 percent to 10.2 percent,[29] sparking a debate about over-diagnosis and the overprescription of stimulant medications. Still others point to diagnostic disparities, especially in marginalized communities. The DSM-III (1980) introduced "attention deficit disorder" (ADD), and the term ADHD first appeared in the DSM-III-R in 1987, combining inattention and hyperactivity, with the DSM-IV later dividing it into three subtypes.[30] The DSM-5 in 2013 broadened the definition further, allowing ADHD and autism to coexist, contributing to increased prevalence due to more inclusive criteria and the high comorbidity with other psychiatric conditions.[31] So essentially, this rise in ADHD could be due to the changes in the DSM. However, this does not paint the full picture.

So, what has contributed to the increased rates in both these conditions in Gen Z? In addition to improved/different criteria for diagnostics, increased screening efforts are also at play. Ramped-up screening initiatives have been observed in the US, with a greater number of children undergoing autism screenings. In 2006, the American Academy of Pediatrics (AAP) advised screening for autism at 18 and 24 months of age during regular pediatric checkups.[32] Presently, the AAP suggests screenings for developmental delays at 9, 18, and 30 months of age for all children.[33] While the extent of adherence to these guidelines remains uncertain, this shift may have contributed to increased diagnoses among young children, particularly those exhibiting subtler symptoms. Beyond screening and the changes to the DSM, some researchers have argued these changes are not enough to explain this recent phenomenon. The increase in autism cases is puzzling because autism is believed to be heavily influenced by genetics, suggesting that its prevalence should remain stable or even decrease over time; yet the increase has been significant.

Various environmental factors during pregnancy, known as epigenetic influences, can override or mimic genetic factors, potentially contributing to the recent rise in autism diagnoses.[34] These prenatal influences, particularly those affecting dopamine activity, have been extensively studied and include factors like maternal stress, fever, genetic and hormonal factors, certain medications, urban living, and fetal oxygen deprivation.[35] While genetic factors have long been acknowledged in the development of autism, particularly evident in family, twin, and genetic studies, the interpretation of data from twin studies suggests that the role of genetics may have been overestimated.[36] This is because both gene-only effects and genetic-environment interactions are often categorized as genetic influences. However, it's important to recognize that environmental influences can work in conjunction with genetic predispositions or directly impact the intrauterine environment. For example, a meta-analysis found that a specific variant of the MTHFR gene, which impairs folate conversion to its active form, is associated with higher autism rates, particularly in countries without folate fortification in food.[37] Additionally, research has found that thousands of chemicals can interact with genes linked to autism, highlighting the complex relationship between genetics, environmental toxins, and the development of autism.[38]

Exposure to air pollution during pregnancy and early life, common in urban areas, has also been linked to a higher risk of autism and ADHD.[39,40] Similarly, exposure to pesticides and chemicals, like phthalates, during pregnancy may also increase the likelihood of autism and ADHD in children.[41,42] Investigations about the impact of chemical toxicity exposure have revealed evidence of harm extending to offspring with no direct exposure to these contaminants—meaning people may pass on harmful chemicals many generations later.[43] With a deeper understanding of epigenetics, there is a growing recognition of the need for a more comprehensive approach to assessing chemical risks, one that considers effects beyond the generation directly exposed to the chemicals.

Some researchers believe the rise in neurological and developmental disorders such as autism and ADHD among children today may be linked to exposure to pollutants both during pregnancy and even before conception. These chemicals might affect dopamine receptors and other neurotransmitters, potentially impacting mental health. Studies of people with autism have shown differences in dopamine receptor activity, particularly in dopamine transporter binding.[44,45] Thus, solely blaming the DSM or new screening techniques would be missing the whole picture. Hopefully, in time, science will uncover the truth in this matter. The data that does exist create startling questions about what environmental factors may be contributing to our mental health.

<u>The Harm in Under-diagnosis</u>

Both ADHD and ASD are conditions that can cause serious harm to mental health when not properly diagnosed. The prevalence of ASD diagnosis is significantly higher among boys, with over four boys diagnosed for every autistic girl, as per recent data from the CDC.[46] While genetic differences are often cited as contributing factors, there is increasing acknowledgement of the existence of many "higher functioning" autistic girls who go undiagnosed. These girls, often referred to as the "lost girls" or "hiding in plain sight," evade detection due to either not fitting into stereotypes or having their symptoms misinterpreted as something else. Additionally, they may exhibit better abilities to conceal their symptoms, particularly during childhood. Thus, even when symptoms in girls are evident, they can still be overlooked.

In a podcast episode from Boston University, researchers Gael Orsmond and Sharada Krishnan discuss the varying experiences of young women and men with autism.[47] They address the growing anecdotal evidence of late autism diagnosis among women, particularly highlighted on social media platforms like TikTok.[48] Some possible reasons for this phenomenon include biological differences, bias in testing, and the tendency for autistic women to present their disability differently.[49] They also discuss the concept of "masking," where one may hide their neurodiverse traits by adopting behaviors that appear more neurotypical, and also suggest that females may be more adept at masking their neurodivergent signs than males.[50]

Delay in diagnosis is not uncommon, as clinicians may be less inclined to consider autism in girls, leading to excuses for their behavior and overlooking key indicators.[51] Autistic girls often do not conform to the typical male-oriented diagnostic model of autism, which primarily focuses on deficits in communication and social skills, along with restricted or repetitive behaviors.[52] Instead, girls may exhibit a quieter presentation of autism, with less overt repetitive behavior.[53]

Like ASD, boys are a lot (three times) more likely to receive an ADHD diagnosis than girls, and girls are 16 times more likely to not get a diagnosis than boys.[54,55] Males are also more likely to receive medication than females.[56] ADHD also has similar issues with varied symptom presentation in different genders.[57] Due to a lack of research in this area, there also remain questions about how symptoms and diagnosis are maintained for individuals who are outside of the cisgender binary.

The issue with under-diagnosis is that, if untreated, people with these conditions suffer the consequences. Untreated ADHD can result in reduced productivity, strained interpersonal relationships, additional mental health issues, and may also lead to anxiety, depression, and substance abuse problems. Also, according to the Attention Deficit Disorder Association, masking ADHD symptoms can lead to burnout, anxiety, and lower self-esteem.[58] Additionally, girls who are able to "pass" as neurotypical may avoid diagnosis until later in life, despite experiencing significant challenges related to their condition. The consequences of a missed ASD diagnosis include an increased risk of depression, anxiety, poor self-esteem, and difficulties in social interactions.[59] Safety risks for autistic girls are heightened due to their vulnerability to bullying and exploitation[60] (caused by their difficulty with understanding social cues and desire to be accepted), making them easy targets for sexual predators.[61] They may struggle to recognize and respond to dangerous situations, further exposing them to harm. Early identification and acceptance of autistic girls is crucial for providing timely support and intervention. This requires greater awareness and sensitivity among parents, teachers, and clinicians to recognize the diverse presentations of autism in girls and ensure they receive the support they need. Thus, in both ADHD and ASD, under-diagnosis, especially in women and girls is both detrimental to life outcomes and mental health.

Conclusion

It's clear that understanding ASD and ADHD requires nuance—with personal experiences like mine highlighting the complexity of diagnosis and the impact of societal perceptions. There is need for greater awareness and sensitivity in the clinical realm, particularly regarding the unique presentations of autism in women and girls. The surge in ASD and ADHD diagnoses, especially among children, prompts critical questions about the evolving nature of diagnostic criteria, the influence of environmental factors, and the accessibility of support services. While advancements in screening methods have contributed to increased detection rates, disparities in diagnosis persist, particularly for people who do not fit within traditional diagnostic criteria or who mask their symptoms.

Part 2

Root Causes

Chapter 10: Disparities

We should measure the prosperity of a nation not by the number of millionaires but by the absence of poverty, the prevalence of health, the efficiency of public schools, and the number of people who can and do read worthwhile books.
–W.E.B. DU BOIS

Throughout my life, I have found myself upset at how it is commonplace to pass unhoused people with no empathy—or even disgust. And that it is routine for people to avert their eyes when a disabled person passes. Early on in life, I started to recognize that our systems have been designed to reward certain people over others. And now, it is apparent to me that by advantaging some, we've created a system of oppression for others. It would be remiss to expect anyone who is disadvantaged to have satisfactory mental health without proper accommodations.

I grew up in a time where a song by Katy Perry called "Ur So Gay" was popularized—ignoring the millions of people the song marginalized. My generation has been handed down a long history of disparities. It is clear we as a generation are enduring many forms of systemically rooted inequities.

According to the Agency for Healthcare Research and Quality (AHRQ),

> "Healthcare disparities are differences in access to or availability of medical facilities and services and variation in rates of disease occurrence and disabilities between population groups defined by socioeconomic characteristics such as age, ethnicity, economic resources, or gender and populations identified geographically."[1]

To put in simpler words, disparities are the variances in treatment between us that create inequality.

I think it's important to acknowledge my personal limitations on these topics; I am writing on a range of subjects that are heavy, controversial, and often difficult to discuss. Because I give a brief summary on these areas, I recommend that you learn about each issue from authors that are experts with lived experience in these subjects if you would like to dive deeper. I am not an expert with lived experience of being BIPOC, or a member of the LGBTQIA+ community. I am referring you to researchers/authors who I believe are more qualified to help you further explore these topics (you will find in footnotes). The only way we can grow is to start the process of learning.

In order for us to address the structural root causes of the Gen Z mental health crisis, we need to understand how the system needs equity in every part of life to actualize mental wellbeing for all. The basic things that keep us healthy, like having nutritious food, a clean environment, a stable job, and safety from violence, are all connected to bigger systemic problems like racism, ableism, and sexism. The documented disparities in access to mental health services accentuate systemic inequities that perpetuate unequal treatment and outcomes. Despite efforts to address these disparities, individuals from marginalized communities continue to face barriers to accessing and receiving quality mental healthcare. The intersectionality of race, ethnicity, and mental health adds another layer of complexity to an already multifaceted issue, highlighting the need for comprehensive and culturally competent approaches to mental healthcare delivery. Generation Z has been profoundly affected by racial disparities because we inherited a legacy of systemic discrimination and inequality that continues to shape our experiences and opportunities.

Racial Injustice in Mental Healthcare

As outlined in *Mental Health: A Report of the Surgeon General*[2] and its supplementary document *Mental Health, Culture, Race and Ethnicity*,[3] there is a disparity in access to mental health services among marginalized communities.[a] This inequity extends to a lower likelihood of receiving necessary care and an increased probability of encountering substandard care.[4] To demonstrate my point, only 22.4 percent of Latinx Americans and 25.0 percent of African Americans receive treatment, compared to 37.6 percent of White Americans.[5] A study by McGuire et al. indicates that overall spending on outpatient mental healthcare by

---

[a] To learn more about racial disparities, please refer to experts in the field such as: Angela Davis, David Cortez, Neal Lester, Celina Sue, Alejandro Portes, Rachel Rickets, Ta-Nehisi Coates or Ibram X. Kendi

Blacks and Latinx is approximately 60 percent, while Whites are at 75 percent. [6] Additionally, data suggest that members of the BIPOC community are more likely to delay or forgo mental health treatment, and once engaged in care, they are less likely than their White counterparts to receive optimal treatments for conditions like depression and anxiety.[7] There is also a higher likelihood that Black Americans will prematurely terminate their treatment.[8]

Beyond disparities in access there are also disparities in quality of care. If you look at the data of the American Psychological Association (APA), 86 percent of members are White, while only 10 percent are of color.[9] Provider bias and stereotyping contribute to health disparities,[10] and over the past four decades, there has been a call within the mental health field to enhance cultural competency through training, focusing on examining provider attitudes, increasing cultural awareness, and improving knowledge and skills. Despite these efforts, racial disparities persist, even when controlling for factors such as income, insurance status, age, and symptom presentation. Barriers faced by BIPOC individuals include:

- Lack of diverse cultural perceptions of mental illness[11]
- Experiences of racism and discrimination[12]
- Higher susceptibility to being uninsured and encountering access barriers[13]
- Communication obstacles[14]
- Fear and mistrust of treatment[15]

The barriers listed above paint a clear picture of another reason our system is currently failing, leaving the millions of BIPOC Gen Z members without essential care.

It is also worth pointing out that there is a strong link between experiencing racism and poor mental health outcomes. [16] Scholarly findings suggest that experiencing racism may result in alterations to cognitive-affective brain regions, including the prefrontal cortex, anterior cingulate cortex, amygdala, and thalamus. [17] These changes bear similarities to pathways associated with conditions such as anxiety, depression, and psychosis. Therefore, not only does the system fail by not providing quality, accessible, affordable, antiracist treatment, but the system can compound harm by allowing for these practices to continue.

Disability

Mental illness, as defined by the ADA,[18] is considered a disability because it can substantially limit one or more major life activities.[19,b] The effects of mental illness can vary widely from person to person, and the severity and duration of symptoms plays a crucial role in determining disability, but conditions such as depression, anxiety disorders, bipolar disorder, and schizophrenia may impair concentration, memory, decision-making, and emotional regulation; this can hinder a person's ability to carry out everyday tasks. Recognizing mental illness as a disability is essential for advocating for the rights and accommodations that one may need in various settings, including the workplace, educational institutions, and public spaces. Legal frameworks, like the ADA, aim to protect those of us with mental health conditions from discrimination and ensure equal opportunities for participation in society. Yet, people with disabilities are discriminated against every day, and the consequences are far reaching.

At least one in three people with a disability have experienced discrimination in the workplace.[20] People with disabilities not only face discrimination but are at greater risk of violence. And among people with disabilities, those with a mental disability are reported to be at the highest risk of violence and discrimination.[21] Moreover, experiences of disability-based discrimination are compounded by factors such as race, gender, and socioeconomic status.[22]

As mentioned, this type of discrimination comes with consequences, such as worsening existing mental health conditions and contributing to the development of a new illness or disability. The stigma and prejudice associated with mental illness may lead to increased stress, anxiety, depression, and other mental health challenges. People who face discrimination are often denied equal opportunities in education, employment, and other areas of life, resulting in restricted career options, educational attainment, and overall quality of life.[23] Discrimination in the workplace may result in job loss, reduced income, or limited career advancement—leading to economic hardships. The fear of discrimination

---

[b] To learn more about disparities in disability communities, please learn from experts in the field such as: Leah Lakshmi Piepzna-Samarasinha, Emily Ladau, Talila "TL" Lewis, Liat Ben-Moshe or Orison Swett Marden

can be a deterrent from seeking workplace accommodations. I have seen this play out recently. A friend of mine was being overworked to the point of a mental health crisis, but she will not ask for accommodations out of fear of discrimination or retaliation from her boss. Stigma can perpetuate a cycle of societal biases, leading to negative experiences, further reinforcing stereotypes, and sustaining a cycle of discrimination within our society.

The ADA aims to be protective for all people with disabilities, yet many of our current practices provide discretion for businesses and our government agencies to make decisions at will, meaning many of our institutions have "loose" regulations regarding what qualifies as discrimination. For example, as of now, our police are given the discretion to use the ADA laws on a "case by case" basis in many situations—such as in the field. That is concerning, given that the police often have our life or death in their hands. Likewise, employers are given the fine-print ability to exclude workers. As the law states, employers must provide reasonable accommodation for individuals with disabilities to perform the essential functions of their jobs unless it would cause "an undue hardship." Therefore, when a job description lists "must lift 40 pounds" as an essential requirement, many candidates, such as those with muscular skeletal or neurological conditions, are automatically discriminated against. This creative wording provides leeway for discriminatory practices and must be addressed. According to the US Equal Employment Opportunity Commission, approximately 30 percent of ADA charges in 2021 involved allegations of mental health discrimination. This represents a 20 percent increase since 2010. Increased mental health discrimination happens to coincide with many of us Gen Zers entering the workforce. This raises concern about the employment landscape we are inheriting and the impact it will have on us.

How Sexuality Has Been Disparaged

Studies have consistently shown higher rates of depression, anxiety, suicidality, and substance abuse among LGBTQIA+, with factors such as discrimination, stigma, and stress playing significant roles in these disparities.[24, c] One of the key factors contributing to these disparities is the pervasive discrimination in various facets of life, including employment, healthcare, education, and housing. [25] Discrimination and stigma can lead to internalized shame, low self-esteem, and a sense of isolation, all of which can worsen mental health issues.[26]

What's more, LGBTQIA+ members often encounter barriers to accessing culturally competent and affirming mental healthcare.[27] Many mental health professionals lack training in LGBTQIA+ issues and may hold biased attitudes or misconceptions about sexual orientation and gender identity. As a result, LGBTQIA+ individuals may hesitate to seek help or may receive inadequate or inappropriate care when they do. It is critical to point out that the intersectionality of race, ethnicity, and gender identity further complicate the experiences of LGBTQIA+ people of color, who may face compounded discrimination and marginalization. For example, transgender women of color experience alarmingly high rates of violence, homelessness, and unemployment, all of which contribute to poor mental health outcomes.[28] Contrary to what some believe, according to the Trevor project:

> "LGBTQ youth are not inherently prone to suicide risk because of their sexual orientation or gender identity but rather placed at higher risk because of how they are mistreated and stigmatized in society."[29]

Moreover, it is important that we recognize and change the ways in which we treat certain groups while also addressing the systemic barriers that continue to compound the mental health crisis.

Conclusion

Reflecting on the widespread injustices embedded within our system, it's impossible to ignore the deep-rooted history of racism, prejudice, and discrimination that continues to shape our present-day realities. Our system continues to discriminate against our most vulnerable. Why do we continue to allow people with disabilities to be treated without dignity? How is it okay for lawmakers to enforce a

---

[c] To learn more about Queer disparities, please refer to an expert on this topic such as: Ryan Thoreson, James Baldwin, Angela Davis, Leslie Feinberg or Alison Bechdel

system that oppresses people of color and our LGBTQIA+ members? The systemic inequities ingrained within our mental health system perpetuate unequal treatment and outcomes. Despite efforts to address these disparities, barriers to accessing quality care persist. The consequences of this have led to poor outcomes through perpetuating cycles of trauma and marginalization. Until we fix this, our mental health crisis will persist.

Chapter 11: Capitalism's Fuel to the Fire

We have deluded ourselves into believing the myth that capitalism grew and prospered out of the Protestant ethic of hard work and sacrifices. Capitalism was built on the exploitation of Black slaves and continues to thrive on the exploitation of the poor, both Black and White, both here and abroad.
-MLK

Although the next chapter will bring points of contention, I argue that capitalism produces inequality and, in turn, many people's needs are unmet. It is impossible to have good mental health when you are missing crucial elements of basic living. Though capitalism has the potential to be an effective form of economic system, it continues to fail in ways that directly impact us. Though some argue differently, for the purpose of this book, I argue that the U.S. economy operates a system of advanced capitalism.[1] In the simplest terms, our system is based on a few fundamental concepts: private property, production, profit/assets, and rule of law. It also serves as a social system, significantly shaping social relationships by creating a culture of self-interest, competition, materialism, and individualism. This contributes to shifts in greater exploitation and employment precariousness.

The formation of capitalism in the US unfolded through distinct historical stages and did not happen all at once. In his book, *Ages of American Capitalism*, Jonathan Levy explains that capitalism has existed since the inception of our country, but formed in a few different stages: the Age of Commerce, the Age of Capital, and the Age of Chaos.[2] According to Levy, capitalism found its real beginning with the Age of Commerce in 1660, where land and enslaved labor were intertwined, and progressed through the Age of Capital characterized by industrialization, where the nation experienced economic transformations and power shifts.[3] The exploitation of enslaved peoples as capital assets contributed to economic growth during the early stages of capitalism.[4] However, this exploitative foundation in the Age of Capital set the stage for enduring challenges. The Age of Chaos in the 1980s, a period of financialization and neoliberal ideologies, further heightened inequalities.[5]

The consequences of these historical developments are evident in issues that concern modern poverty. Capitalism's legacy of exploitation, wealth concentration, and insufficient regulation has contributed to systemic disparities, hindering equitable access to resources for a significant portion of the population. Many argue that poverty is a true consequence of capitalism because the means of production are constantly altered to reduce cost and, therefore, also reduces wages.

In his book, *Confronting Capitalism*, Philip Kotler argues capitalism is failing in fourteen ways, yet has promising solutions. I argue that a few of these failures, argued by Kotler, have detrimental effects on mental health in capitalist countries. If we, as a society, address these failings, many positive outcomes, including increased mental wellness, would result. For this chapter I want to focus on a few specific failings that I believe directly impact Gen Z mental health.

<u>Little to No Solution to Poverty</u>

Poverty is inextricably one of the worst issues our world faces. Over five billion people on this earth are poor or extremely poor.[6] Historically, poverty was not an issue many addressed, and the industrial revolution intensified poverty, when peasants became attracted to cities for work, leading to "shantytowns" and severely poverty-stricken areas within cities.[7] The concept of addressing poverty only seems to have revealed itself in the nineteenth century. President Lydon Johnson declared a "war on poverty" in the 1960s and passed new social programs like Medicare, unemployment insurance, Head Start, and more.[8] Also, at the turn of the century, the United Nations created a multilateral plan called Millenium Development Goals (MDG), through which they outlined an agenda to reduce poverty by 2015.[9] They have since renamed this plan into Sustainable Development Goals (SDG).[10]

The MDG goals were not reached, but instead superseded by a new plan. This new plan outlines 17 goals, eliminating poverty as the first goal. According to the SDG's 2023 report, there had been a positive trend towards lesser poverty, yet the COVID pandemic halted progress and instead has raised concern about the possibility of hundreds of millions of people being stuck in severe poverty by 2030. The report states:

> "The average annual reduction rate was 0.54 percentage points between 2015 and 2019, less than half the 1.28 percentage point rate observed between 2000 and 2014. In 2020, the number of people living in extreme poverty rose to 724 million, surpassing the pre-pandemic projection by 90 million 11 and reversing approximately three years of progress on poverty reduction."[11]

Therefore, their goal of "halving poverty" seems to be ambitious, if not a bit delusional. However, the impact of poverty is axiomatic.

Many people tend to blame poverty on the individual, [12] however, the cause of poverty (according to many experts) is a result of interrelated factors that I believe should be addressed with a systems approach. In the book, *The Bottom Billion*, Paul Collier identifies four reasons for poverty in our modern world: civil war, natural resource exportation (and corruption of leaders who steal the wealth of these resources), landlocked countries due to surrounding neighbors that block resources and opportunities, and bad governance (about three out of four countries are governed by a corrupt leader).[13] Though the 2022 census reports that poverty levels are at about 12 percent nationally,[14] when you ask most Gen Z members whether they can afford to buy groceries or healthy meals, pay rent, or eventually afford a house, the answer is usually no.

It seems convenient that the government lists the poverty threshold at about $16,000 a year for an individual, yet the average rent for a studio apartment ranges from $577-$2,000 depending on what state you live in.[15,16] Even in the lowest cost state (Arkansas) with an average of $577 for a studio apartment, making even $20,000 a year means that having the money for groceries and basic necessities is practically impossible.[17] It is now calculated that for someone to be making the bare minimum to survive, the number would look more like $57,000. [18] Therefore, if the government looked at individuals making less than

$57,000 annually, the actual poverty rate would be undeniably higher, and in my opinion a lot more accurate.

So, what does poverty have to do with capitalism and mental health? Living in poverty significantly increases the challenges faced by adults with mental illness, creating a complex interplay between economic hardship and mental wellbeing.[19] The intersection of poverty and mental illness introduces additional hurdles, including heightened healthcare costs, reduced productivity, and overall poorer health. According to the National Survey of Drug Use and Health (NSDUH), approximately 9.8 million US adults (aged 18 or older) grapple with serious mental illness (SMI)—with 2.5 million of them residing below the poverty line.[20] The intricate relationship between mental illness and poverty is bidirectional: poverty may amplify the impact of mental illness and increase the likelihood of its onset, and, conversely, experiencing mental illness may elevate the risk of living below the poverty line. Recognizing and addressing these dynamics is crucial for comprehensively understanding and mitigating the profound impact of poverty on mental health.

Failure to Pay Living Wages

Worker exploitation is not a new concept. As someone who is at the age when I have watched myself and my friends enter the workforce, I have noticed that most people who leave school cannot get jobs easily, and available starting jobs do not pay a living wage. In his book, *The Jungle*, Upton Sinclair depicts the harsh realities of industrialization in the nineteenth century and the conditions in Chicago for immigrants who worked in the meatpacking industry, highlighting health violations and unsanitary practices.[21] Sinclair warns about how working-class individuals were impoverished without social programs, which caused severe hopelessness and depression for many workers.[22] Even with a steady wage, workers could not afford the cost of living and were thus led to mental despair.[23] "The jungle" that Sinclair discusses mirrors today's living conditions, and the mental despair many of us are grappling with.

According to a 2021 report from the Pew Research Center, concerns about our health and financial stability are connected to increased levels of psychological distress.[24] This pattern is noteworthy because psychological distress is linked to various health consequences, including emotional exhaustion, compromised immune function, heart disease, and heightened mortality.[25] Studies found that a 10 percent increase in the minimum wage could lead to a 2.7 percent reduction in suicides among adults with limited education.[26] One study at the University of North Carolina found that a $1 per hour increase could have resulted in approximately 8,000 fewer suicides from 2006 to 2016.[27] These findings collectively magnify the potential positive impact of raising the minimum wage on mental health, particularly for those with limited education and lower income levels.

Despite the mounting evidence that payment for work needs to increase, the federal minimum wage still remains a mere $7.25 per hour.[28] Some states have raised their minimum wages, like California, which, on January 1, 2024, passed a minimum wage of $16 per hour.[29] This is a step in the right direction, yet the struggle for a living wage is evident as many recent graduates from university and high school find it challenging to secure well-paying jobs or afford the cost of living.[30]

Capitalism Exploits the Environment—and Us

The United States remains the world's second largest consumer of energy and materials after China.[31] Our beef industry alone is contributing to a high percentage of global emissions.[32] Though our sea levels have risen a concerning amount, our planet has warmed two degrees, many animals are now extinct, and over 38 percent of land has been degraded by modern farming, there are still people denying climate change.[33,34,35] It seems this trend is highest for Americans, who lag behind other countries—54 percent of US citizens believed climate change was a serious issue compared to 85 percent of Brazilians.[36] If we do not address what large corporations are doing to the environment, we risk serious consequences. For example, the earth is losing arable land due to soil degradation and if this continues, there will not be enough food produced to feed our world's population.[37] Though the topic of climate change is a complex and supremely important issue, what I want to express is how capitalist agendas are creating an environment that is not only unsafe, but also how capitalism has a detrimental impact on mental health.

As I write this, one of the most obvious mental health impacts of this crisis is growing up feeling this burden on my shoulders, like many others in my generation. Many experts agree that climate change will impact not only physical health but also mental wellbeing. The rise in ambient temperatures is expected to correlate with higher rates of aggression and suicides.[38] A survey of farmers found that prolonged droughts resulting from climate change may contribute to an increased number of farmer suicides and generally lead to impaired mental health and heightened stress.[39] The elevated frequency of climate-related disasters can trigger mental health conditions such as post-traumatic stress disorder (PTSD), adjustment disorder, and depression.[40] Also, the necessity for populations to migrate due to climate changes and global warming can give rise to acculturation stress. We need comprehensive strategies to address these challenges.

Capitalism has also contributed to an often-overlooked problem: light pollution. While people might generally know that artificial light can disrupt birds and insects, the consequences are more extensive and severe than commonly realized. Light pollution refers to the excessive use of artificial light, including bright electronic screens and the illuminated night sky caused by city lights.[41] Annually, outdoor lighting in the US consumes approximately 120 terawatt-hours of energy, primarily used for illuminating streets and parking lots.[42] This amount is estimated to power New York City for two years alone.[43] DarkSky, an organization working to eliminate light pollution, found that at least 30 percent of all outdoor lighting in the US is wasted, largely due to inadequately shielded lights. This results in a staggering cost of $3.3 billion and the emission of 21 million tons of carbon dioxide each year. If we wanted to counterbalance this carbon footprint, we would have to plant 875 million trees. Research has revealed that this has come at a huge expense to the environment, such as by impacting biodiversity and crop supply as a result of diminished pollinators, since these pollinators are confused by these unwarranted light sources.

Furthermore, light pollution, particularly in areas with high outdoor light pollution, is associated with a decrease in the average night's sleep length for adolescents.[44] This aligns with concerns about the negative impact of bright light from technology's screens. Sleep deprivation, linked to depression and other mental illnesses, is becoming more prevalent, especially among adolescents.[45] Inadequate sleep increases the risk of poor performance at work and school, heightened mood swings and irritability, and a greater susceptibility to depression and anxiety.[46] Thus, the capitalist-driven patterns of excessive artificial lighting have become a silent yet potent factor shaping both our environment and mental health.

<u>Conclusion</u>

It has become increasingly apparent that the current economic system perpetuates inequalities and fails to adequately meet the needs of Gen Z. While capitalism holds the promise of prosperity and progress, its shortcomings need to be addressed. The persistence of poverty continues to afflict millions nationwide. Poverty is inextricably linked to mental health, which is only amplifying the challenges faced by Gen Z. As so many of us struggle to make ends meet on meager wages, psychological distress mounts, contributing to a host of negative health outcomes. Further, capitalism's exploitation of the environment poses a dire threat to both planetary health and human wellbeing. The unchecked consumption of resources and heavy pollution contribute to climate change, biodiversity loss, and environmental degradation. These environmental changes, in turn, have profound implications for mental health: evoking stress, anxiety, and depression. Given that research has found that raising the minimum wage can reduce suicides and improving mental wellbeing, it is critical to rethink how we view money, work, and health.

Chapter 12: The Parenting of Gen Z

The best way to make children good is to make them happy.
-Oscar Wilde

One topic I have come across from my own lived experience is the catastrophic impact parenting can have. Freud gets a lot of hate, but many of his arguments about the impacts of childhood have remained relevant. The ways in which we are raised have a real influence on who we become as adults. Gen Z kids grew up in a unique period where a few key shifts in parenting norms had a lasting negative impact on our mental health. As a kid, I witnessed the moms of my friends being heavily involved—too involved. One girl I knew was not allowed to have doors. None. Not even to her bedroom or bathroom. Her parents over-controlled every detail of her life. That girl has now grown up to face severe mental illness and struggles to hold jobs or maintain friendships. Down the street from my childhood home, another boy was forced by his own mother to sell their homegrown weed to kids on campus, and she would call him "gay" every time he expressed emotions—completely invalidating and neglecting him. That boy grew up to be chronically homeless and dependent on substances. These instances are not rare but instead illustrate patterns within shifting parenting norms that are now proving to have had significant consequences for their children.

<u>The Failure of Our Parents</u>

Gen Z was born into a complex emotional landscape. Technological advancements introduced new challenges, such as increased exposure to social media and cyberbullying. I can remember back when I was 12 the detriment that MySpace had on my feelings of isolation. People had their "best friends list" posted publicly—an easy way to make many feel lonely and isolated. But, when I would bring something like this up to my parents, they would respond with either "I am sure it is not that bad," or "you are imagining it." I believe this is not because my parents were malicious, rather it is because they simply did not understand. How could they? Technology was growing exponentially quicker than any of us were ready for.

We Were Emotionally Neglected/Invalidated
These tech advancements influenced one of the most important failures I want to get across: emotional neglect and how it has affected my generation. Emotional neglect can be defined as parents exhibiting a persistent failure to meet the emotional needs of their children, often resulting in long-term psychological consequences.[1] It involves a chronic lack of emotional responsiveness, support, and validation, which undermines a child's emotional wellbeing and development.[2] This form of neglect is characterized by:

- parental inattention to the child's feelings
- dismissing or minimizing emotional experiences
- an overall lack of empathetic engagement

According to *GoodTherapy*, examples of emotional neglect may include a consistent failure to provide comfort or reassurance when a child is distressed, ignoring, invalidating or downplaying the child's emotional expressions, and being emotionally unavailable during times of need.[3] A neglectful caregiver might also fail to foster a secure attachment by not engaging in nurturing interactions or by being consistently indifferent to the child's emotional cues. This can look like a child coming home from school visibly upset after being bullied, only to have their parent dismiss their feelings with a "you'll get over it," without offering any comfort or support. Or even an example that I witnessed happen to a friend of mine in middle school. After getting an A on a very difficult test, and feeling proud, my friend Bianca went home for affirmation but was instead scolded by her parents for not getting an A+. In my own experience as a kid I would be invalidated by my own parents who would say things like, "when I was your age I had it worse because..." or "why don't you focus on something more productive?" This type of invalidation and neglect over time can teach a child to suppress their emotions, feeling that their feelings are unimportant and unworthy of attention.

It is important to note that the concept of emotional neglect can be observed on a societal level. Gen Z parents are generally the youngest Baby Boomers (born between 1946-1964) and Gen X (born between 1964-1980). Boomers experienced an up-bringing that included rapid economic growth, cultural upheaval, and changes in family dynamics largely due to the aftermath of the Great Depression.[4] While not all experienced emotional neglect, societal trends during this era often favored economic prosperity often overshadowing the importance of emotional expression and mental wellbeing.[5,6] Traditional gender roles, which position men primarily as breadwinners and women as homemakers, sometimes led to emotional disconnection within families. This historical context set the stage for certain trends that have persisted into subsequent generations, including Generation Z. The stigma surrounding mental health concerns, prevalent during the Baby Boomer and Gen X era, contributed to a lack of open dialogue about emotional needs and struggles. For example, the Boomers grew up hearing phrases like, "suck it up," or, "big boys don't cry."[7] My mom once shared with me that it was not uncommon for kids to shove each other into trash cans and laugh at them during her upbringing in the 70s and 80s. This is in stark contrast to receiving hate comments or messages online as a new more common form of bullying. In to 70s, parents could see visible pain on a child's face and tell them to "rub dirt in it," whereas the more invisible forms of bullying that take place today are easier to ignore for parents who did not grow up with it themselves.

Individuals who have experienced emotional neglect during their formative years may struggle with various aspects of their lives, impacting their mental, emotional, and even physical wellbeing well into adulthood.[8] One prevalent consequence is the challenge of forming and maintaining healthy relationships. The lack of emotional attunement and responsiveness during childhood may contribute to difficulties in expressing and understanding emotions, leading to issues with intimacy and connection later in life.[9] Also, it can significantly impact one's self-esteem and self-worth. Children who do not receive adequate emotional support may internalize a sense of unworthiness, which can persist into adulthood.[10] This, in turn, may manifest in self-sabotaging behaviors, a persistent fear of rejection, and challenges in setting and maintaining personal boundaries.[11]

According to Healthline,[12] the most common symptoms of emotional neglect in children include:

- depression
- anxiety
- apathy
- failure to thrive
- hyperactivity
- aggression
- developmental delays
- low self-esteem
- substance misuse
- withdrawing from friends and activities
- perfectionism
- appearing uncaring or indifferent
- shunning emotional closeness or intimacy

In adulthood, the repercussions of childhood neglect manifest beyond behavioral issues or struggles with relationships. This early neglect can contribute to issues later in life with mental health. These include enduring conditions such as PTSD, depression, and emotional unavailability.[13] Furthermore, people who experienced neglect can exhibit an increased propensity for developing eating disorders, as well as an avoidance of intimacy, alongside feelings of personal inadequacy and emptiness.[14] This neglect in childhood may lead to deficits in self-discipline, accompanied by overwhelming sensations of guilt, shame, anger, and aggressive tendencies.[15] Additionally, survivors of childhood emotional neglect frequently struggle with trusting others or depending on them for support.[16] This cycle could potentially perpetuate as some neglected children may turn into emotionally neglectful parents themselves,[17] lacking the understanding of their own emotions and consequently failing to nurture those of their offspring. Cognitively, the long-term effects of emotional neglect can create difficulties with self-regulation, problem-solving, and decision-making.[18]

It is crucial to recognize that the impact of emotional neglect is not uniform, so one may respond differently based on resilience, support systems, and life experiences. Therapy and counseling can play a vital role in addressing the long-term effects of emotional neglect, providing Gen Z with the tools to understand, express, and manage emotions in healthier ways. According to Laurissa Hampton, a licensed counselor, breaking the cycle of emotional neglect involves acknowledging its pervasive effects and actively working towards fostering emotional wellbeing at both the individual and societal levels.[19] Despite a growing awareness of mental health issues and increased advocacy for emotional wellbeing, the intergenerational impact of emotional neglect is real.

We Were Overprotected

The second failure of Gen Z's parents has been their overprotective, over-intrusive, controlling parenting style that shifted from their own generation. Gen Z has been called "the most sensitive generation," and there is a reason why. Dr. Jonathan Haidt, an NYU professor, asserts that the origins of the issue can be traced back to earlier times, specifically on the playground, where children lacked unsupervised time,[20] but now kids spend more time inside and online.[21] Generation Z parents are accused of overprotecting, or as Haidt puts it, "coddling," their kids by raising them in an environment perceived as a safety bubble.[22] Despite mothers having fewer children and spending more time working outside the home compared to 1965, they are dedicating more total time to caring for their children.

This excessive protection has reached a point where a child outdoors without adult supervision might prompt people to call the police. An extreme case involved parents facing 'neglect' charges for leaving their eleven-year-old unattended in their own backyard.[23] Concerns about children's safety were heightened by sporadic but tragic incidents of kidnapping during Generation Z's formative years.[24] These incidents—every parent's nightmare—fueled understandable paranoia. Missing children's images began appearing on milk cartons and pizza boxes, and cable TV sensationalized those cases for ratings. Mass media played a role in amplifying parental fears, portraying threats as more significant than they statistically were. As a case and point, the likelihood of a child being kidnapped is one in a million,[25] yet one in seven children suffer abuse or neglect.[26] Despite such statistics, the fear of harm to children, once witnessed, becomes etched in memory, distorting the perception about kidnapping and safety risks. In other words, parents misjudge the actual risk that strangers pose to their children.[27]

On the same topic of being overprotected, my generation lacks experience in handling challenges independently, having grown accustomed to constant intervention and arbitration by authority figures. [28] As a consequence, when we Gen Z are confronted with opposing viewpoints, we perceive a threat, feel unsafe, and are inclined to ostracize the dissenting party, because there is no parent or teacher to mediate as there was for us growing up.[29] Our reaction can resemble a form of PTSD,[30] seeking a protective shield to navigate surroundings, genuinely alarmed by divergent ideas. In contrast, when our parents were kids, they were advised as children to shrug off insults. Their childhoods looked lightyears different than ours. Interestingly, their generation had higher levels of reported trust for one another,[31] and historically as a society we have had declining levels of trust, especially after the most recent elections.[32] As trust levels decline, parents statistically place more restraints on their children.[33] All of this has led to cultural shifts as a whole, leaning towards expecting parents to be more protective and controlling.

Studies indicate that overprotective parenting correlates with risk aversion, dependency on parents, elevated risks of psychological disorders, a deficiency in robust coping mechanisms, and chronic anxiety.[34,35] Remarkably, the effects of overprotectiveness bear striking similarities to those resulting from neglect, albeit to a lesser extent. Ultimately, children raised in an overly protective environment are inadequately equipped to navigate the stresses of adulthood, as reflected in the data.[36] Current college students exhibit higher rates of severe mental illness and increased reliance on psychiatric medication compared to their counterparts a decade ago. [37] Campus counseling center professionals attribute this trend to a notable lack of coping skills among today's students.[38] Younger generations consistently report higher stress levels than older ones,[39] with part of this disparity attributed, arguably, to a deficient grasp of stress management skills acquired through independent thought and risk-taking earlier in life.

Conclusion

Parents have such a strong influence and impact on their children, and I believe this is often forgotten in adulthood. Given that emotional neglect, invalidation, and overparenting, which were common during my upbringing, correlate to depression, anxiety and other mental health issues in adulthood, there is a necessity to take a deeper look into the way Gen Z was raised as this may have been a large contributor to the mental health crisis. Because of the neglect and invalidation we endured, we need to find ways to equip Gen Z with the tools to understand, express, and manage emotions in healthier ways than many of our parents did.

Chapter 13: The Loneliness Epidemic

Ah look at all the lonely people
Ah look at all the lonely people
Eleanor Rigby, picks up the rice
In the church where a wedding has been
Lives in a dream
Waits at the window, wearing the face
That she keeps in a jar by the door
Who is it for
All the lonely people
Where do they all come from?
All the lonely people
Where do they all belong?
-The Beatles

Growing up, I documented my struggles with loneliness in my diary. It is heartbreaking rereading some of my entries where I said things like, "no one understands me. I am so alone. I have no real friends." I remember feeling very lonely throughout my life. In elementary school, I used to sit under a tree alone holding the class pet, wondering to myself why I was so disconnected. As an adult, I look back on these memories of feeling isolated from a more pragmatic perspective because it turns out I was not alone in feeling alone. At least 1 in 2 people feel this way,[1] or have felt it. More apparently, young adults are experiencing loneliness more than any other age group.[2]

The US surgeon general, Vivek Murthy, wrote a book highlighting how detrimental loneliness is in society and argues it is a major public health concern.[3] In 2023, he published an advisory that goes into detail about how the absence of social connections poses a significant threat to individual health and lifespan. In the advisory, it is noted that loneliness and social isolation contribute to a higher risk of premature death—comparable to smoking up to 15 cigarettes daily.[4] Additionally, inadequate social connection is linked to an increased risk of diseases, including a higher risk of heart disease or stroke, and may heighten susceptibility to viruses and respiratory illnesses.[5] What's more, insufficient social connection is associated with an elevated risk of anxiety, depression, and dementia.[6] Although we are the most connected we have ever been through digital devices, we are simultaneously the most disconnected, too. The rise of loneliness needs to be taken seriously. My generation is at the center of this crisis, and we need help.

Understanding Loneliness & Social Disconnection

When I think about loneliness, I immediately hear "Eleanor Rigby" by the Beatles ringing in my mind.[7] This phenomenon has been around long before we have, and I remember having conversations with my dad about times he has felt lonely throughout his life, too. Loneliness is a deeply rooted human experience that has evolved over time, influenced by a complex interplay of architectural, historical, and societal factors.[8] While contemporary discourse often blames social media for exacerbating feelings of isolation, the roots of loneliness stretch back much further. Urbanization and modernization during the mid-twentieth century, for instance, disrupted established social networks by dispersing individuals into new urban landscapes devoid of familiar surroundings. Also, architectural designs emphasizing individualism and privatism, such as high-rise apartments, have raised concerns about their impact on fostering loneliness.

Historical narratives also reveal the profound role of place and landscape in shaping feelings of belongingness.[9] The question is, what can historical narratives teach us about fostering genuine belonging in today's rapidly changing world? I think what they would teach us is that loneliness is a lot more complex than "you use your phone too much."

Loneliness is an internal, emotional experience driven by one's perception of social isolation,[10] while social disconnectedness is an external state characterized by an objective lack of meaningful social connections.[11] Over time, we are becoming increasingly disconnected socially, and rates of perceived loneliness raise concern. Social connection has declined, and the most pronounced decline is observed among Gen Z. For this age group, in-person time spent with friends has diminished by almost 70 percent over almost two decades.[12] The COVID-19 pandemic accelerated the trends of declining social participation, but the number of close friendships has also declined over several decades—and yes, that means before the age of social media. The people who say they are not lonely report having three or more friends.[13] Yet, almost half of Americans report having three or fewer close friends, compared to about a quarter reporting the same in 1990.[14] Social connection continued to decline during the COVID-19 pandemic, with one study finding a 16 percent decrease in network size from June 2019 to June 2020 among participants.[15] This decline in connection is cause for worry. The question is, why is this happening?

Changing Social Structures

The influence of social media has become one factor in shaping the loneliness epidemic, and it is important to address. However, I want to emphasize it is not the sole contributor, as many others may argue. With the advent of digital platforms, we are more connected than ever, yet the very technologies designed to bring us closer have been implicated in rising feelings of loneliness and social isolation. The curated nature of online platforms often showcases idealized versions of oneself. This "highlight reel" can engender a distorted sense of reality, leading us to compare ourselves unfavorably and unrealistically to others. It can also foster feelings of exclusion, for example, when you see your friends post that they are hanging out, but you were not invited—called FOMO (fear of missing out). I know that when I see it, I feel upset. Moreover, the quantity and frequency of online social interactions may not necessarily translate into genuine, meaningful connections. The nature of digital communication may contribute to a sense of emotional detachment, hindering the development of deep and authentic relationships.[16] As we grapple with the multifaceted impacts of social media, it is imperative to discern its role in both fostering and impeding the collective battle against the loneliness epidemic.

When the average American adult uses social media around 2 and a half hours a day,[17] and teens use it around 4 hours daily,[18] one needs to question the impact. In a US study, people who indicated using social media for over two hours daily were approximately twice as likely to report heightened perceptions of social isolation compared to those who used social media for less than 30 minutes a day.[19] Numerous detrimental effects arise from technologies that displace face-to-face interactions: they monopolize our attention, compromise the quality of our engagements, and erode our self-esteem.[20] These consequences can manifest as heightened loneliness, FOMO, interpersonal conflicts, and diminished social connections. For instance, extensive phone use during in-person interactions within families and social circles can result in heightened distraction, diminished conversational quality, and decreased self-reported enjoyment of shared time. [21]

Furthermore, victims of online harassment reported increased feelings of loneliness, isolation, relationship challenges, as well as lower self-esteem and trust in others. [22] Surprisingly, evidence suggests that even perpetrators of cyberbullying experience weakened emotional bonds with their social contacts and perceive deficits in their sense of belongingness. Therefore, I would emphasize that while loneliness has been a social issue for centuries, the rise in rates today could be in part attributed to social media, but there are many more causes than social media alone. I argue that social media only makes an existing issue worse but that it is not the root cause.

In addition to social media and the rise of individualized tech, our community engagement has eroded over the last few decades.[23] This can largely be attributed to decreasing participation in religious activities, but also a decline in overall community organizations. In 2018, a mere 16 percent of Americans reported a strong sense of attachment to their local community. [24] Research from Gallup, Pew Research Center, and the National Opinion Research Center's General Social Survey[25] noted a consistent decrease in religious preference, affiliation, and participation among US adults since the 1970s. [26] In 2020, only 47 percent of Americans claimed membership in a church, synagogue, or mosque—a decline from 70 percent in 1999 and marking the first instance of the response falling below 50 percent in the survey's history.[27] Religious or faith-based groups have the potential to foster regular social interaction, provide communal support, imbue life with meaning and purpose, cultivate a sense of belonging, and potentially reduce risk-taking behaviors. [28] The diminishing involvement in community entities may adversely impact health in diverse ways. This is not arguing, however, that the cure is going to church (though for some it might be). But there seems to be a connection between the increase in loneliness and the decrease in community engagement.

Lack of community engagement may explain why many people, in my generation especially, have had a declining sense of belonging.

Belongingness is the human need to feel a sense of connectedness, shaped by experiences of social interactions. According to a study conducted on the effects of COVID, "[increased] loneliness and reduced feelings of belonging were significantly associated with increased levels of psychological distress."[29] In other words, the more psychological distress we have, the less we feel we belong, and the lonelier we feel. A recent study called "The Belonging Barometer," conducted by the American Immigration Council and Over Zero, reveals troubling findings about Americans' sense of belonging in civic life.[30] The study introduces a new tool, the Belonging Barometer, to quantify levels of belonging across various aspects of society.[31] Researchers Nichole Argo and Hammad Sheikh found that a majority of Americans feel disconnected from their family, friends, workplace, and local and national communities. Specifically, the study reports alarming statistics: 64 percent of Americans don't feel like they belong in the workplace, 68 percent feel disconnected from the nation, and a staggering 74 percent feel a lack of belonging in their local communities.

Belonging is closely tied with loneliness. In their research, Dr. Franklin and Dr. Tranter found that one of the defining aspects of loneliness is feeling an absence of belonging.[32] An article published in the LA Times last year emphasizes this, "More than anything, the key to feeling okay is belonging."[33] But, given so many people struggle to feel belonging, it also tracks that we are struggling with loneliness. Social scientists attribute this concerning trend to a variety of factors. People are increasingly dedicating more time to their jobs, whether by choice or due to widening income inequality, which leaves less time available for nurturing relationships and building community.[34] Also, the way we use our leisure time has undergone significant transformation. Laurie Santos, a cognitive scientist at Yale University, highlighted this shift by pointing out that in the 1970s, options like Netflix and video games weren't available for solitary entertainment.[35] By 2018, the average American spent around 11 hours daily engaging in solitary activities such as watching TV and using smartphone apps.[36] Others contend that the prominent focus on the nuclear family since the 1950s has led to a reduction in our social networks, shifting us from larger, extended kin groups residing together to smaller, more isolated family units.[37] Whatever the reason, we are struggling to find belonging, and it is a key gen Z mental health issue. And by not belonging, loneliness is rising.

Changes in Urban Environments

Accessible neighborhoods, green spaces, and avenues for social engagement play pivotal roles in alleviating loneliness and fostering community connection. Unfortunately, most cities are not built with this in mind—at least, not anymore. In pre-industrial America, cities were designed with pedestrians in mind, as we once relied on walking or carriages. Boston illustrates this focus on walkability with dense housing and extensive sidewalk networks (Boston also scores higher on the Happiness Index).[38] Yet, after WWII, an economic boom in the 1950s surged car ownership, leading to urban sprawl and a rise in car-centric urban planning—marking a departure from the pedestrian-oriented cities of the past.[39] The oil crisis of the 1970s highlighted the economic strain of car ownership, leading to a resurgence of interest in walkable communities. [40] Since then, the benefits of walkability, including economic, environmental, social, and health advantages, have become apparent. With projections indicating that 68 percent of the global population will live in cities by 2050,[41] there's a growing need for cities to support healthy, sustainable lifestyles. Efforts to improve pedestrian environments have been bolstered by government initiatives like the 1998 Transportation Equity Act and the 2015 US[42] Surgeon General's Call to Action promoting walkable communities.[43]

Nonetheless, walkability now comes at a premium. In fact, homebuyers in America's largest metro areas will pay 35 percent more for walkable real estate, while renters will pay 41 percent more.[44] A 2003 study conducted in Galway, Ireland, disclosed that residents of walkable cities enjoy numerous social benefits. These individuals exhibit elevated levels of social capital, defined as the "value derived from positive connections between people," compared to those in other communities.[45,46] They are more likely to demonstrate trust in others, engage socially, participate in politics, and foster relationships with neighbors.[47] Walkable neighborhoods foster increased social interaction, contributing to a heightened sense of community. This finding is further corroborated by a 2013 study from Texas A&M University, underscoring the significant role of walkability in enhancing social wellbeing.[48] So, it is clear walkability is important, desired, and essential for our social and physical wellbeing, yet our city leaders have continued to allow this important feature of our built environment to disappear, with the result that suburb living potentially jeopardizes our health.

The same decline in walkability has happened with third spaces, which are public places that are neither work nor home but serve as a space in which the community gathers.[49] Examples of third spaces include cafes, parks, libraries, community centers, and recreational facilities. The rise in popularity of technology has fueled a surge in remote work and social media, facilitating online connections over in-person interactions. In addition, escalating rent costs have rendered prime locations unaffordable for many businesses, contributing to the dwindling availability of public gathering venues.[50] Absence of these communal areas heightens the risk of individuals experiencing social isolation, potentially resulting in mental health challenges like depression and anxiety.[51] Hence, the scarcity of public gathering spots can diminish community involvement and reduce social capital.[52] Accordingly, the absence of third spaces undermines the formation of interpersonal connections within communities, ultimately eroding social unity,[53] which in turn plays into the loneliness epidemic.

Mental Health and Loneliness

Depression and anxiety often manifest as social withdrawal, heightening the risk of both social isolation and loneliness. Social isolation and loneliness contribute to an increased likelihood of developing depression and anxiety, worsening these conditions over time.[54] A comprehensive review of multiple longitudinal studies revealed that adults reporting frequent feelings of loneliness are more than twice as likely to develop depression compared to those who rarely or never experience loneliness.[55] These patterns persist among Gen Z, with a synthesis of 63 studies concluding that loneliness and social isolation in children and adolescents amplify the risk of depression and anxiety, sustaining this heightened risk up to nine years later.[56] Notably, social connection appears to serve as a protective factor against depression. Even for people with a higher predisposition due to a history of adverse life experiences, with frequent confiding in others, up to a 15 percent reduction in the odds of developing depression exists when more connected.[57]

Regarding suicidality and self-harm, social isolation stands out as a robust predictor. Social isolation is considered one of the strongest and most consistent indicators of suicidal ideation, attempts, and lethal suicidal behavior, according to a 2010 study on the Interpersonal Theory of Suicide.[58] Despite the multifaceted nature of suicide risk factors, more than a century of research draws attention to the significant correlation between a lack of social connection and death by suicide, particularly among men.[59] All of the above suggests that loneliness and social isolation are detrimental to mental health.

Conclusion

As a child, I struggled with feelings of isolation, documented in my diary as a poignant reminder of those lonely moments under a tree, clutching onto a class pet, wondering why I felt so disconnected. Little did I know then that I was far from alone in my loneliness. Given that at least 1 in 2 people have experienced similar feelings, with young adults being particularly affected, and the health impacts of loneliness being dire, we cannot continue to ignore the detrimental effects of the loneliness crisis. Because of the decline in community engagement, including religious participation, we have seen profound implications for mental health, with loneliness and social isolation being strongly linked to depression, anxiety, and suicidality across all age groups. It's clear that our societal structures and urban environments (such as the availability of third spaces, and walkable neighborhoods), play a crucial role in fostering social connection and combating loneliness, yet these features are often overlooked in urban planning when they should be central.

Chapter 14: Nutrition & Exercise Crisis

Let food be your medicine and medicine be your food.
-Hippocrates

Research on public health has revealed something amazing: mental illness recovery is potentially high when good nutrition and exercise intervention are involved. The issue is that many countries, including the United States, are in a nutrition and inactivity crisis. I remember growing up and sharing my favorite snacks with my friends—like Cheetos, Dino Buddies, Fruit Snacks, and Go-Gurt. My generation was raised on cereal and granola bars, followed by microwavable meals and white bread. These foods, though deliciously addictive, are some examples of the highly processed, nutritionally depleted foods that are now commonplace. In fact, according to Prof Carlos Monteiro of the University of São Paulo, "in the UK and US, more than half the average diet now consists of ultra-processed food... [which] were directly linked to 32 harmful effects to health, including a higher risk of heart disease, cancer, type 2 diabetes, adverse mental health and early death."[1] I remember my daily activities also mirrored the deficiencies I had in my diet. Playing Barbies inside, or video games on the couch was normal. And when I had to run a mile once a month for physical education (P.E.) class, I walked most of it in pain as if the small amount of exercise would be the death of me. The World Health Organization estimates that "81% of kids between the ages of 11 and 17 are now inactive."[2]

If you talk to your grandparents about what they ate or how much time they spent being active outside, I guarantee it looked a lot different. The impact of this nutrition/inactivity crisis on mental health is profound. As we consume more processed foods (high in sugars, unhealthy fats, and artificial ingredients), our mental wellbeing suffers. There is a strong correlation between poor diet/exercise and increased risk of depression, anxiety, and other mental health disorders,[3] but there's hope. Just as nutrition can play a crucial role in mental health, so can physical activity. In this chapter, we'll explore the powerful relationship between physical activity, nutrition, and mental health.

The Gut-Brain Connection

In the last decade, a lot of new research has come out about how there is "beneficial" bacteria in our guts. Now, grocery aisles are flooded with "probiotics" and "prebiotics" as more people develop awareness. I remember the day when I first heard about this. I was in undergrad when my mom texted me an article about it. Like many others, I believed bacteria to be the enemy, avoiding fermented foods and raw vegetables. Growing up, antibiotics were top of the line treatment for conditions ranging from ear infections to acne. Now, as more research data is revealed, the harm of antibiotics includes overuse, which can create treatment-resistant bacteria and can disrupt our microbiome. [4] The microbiome can be defined in simple terms as all the tiny living organisms and their genetic material in the human body.[5]

Since initial discovery, scientists have found many pathways in which our microbiome and microbiota have impact on our health. The human gut hosts around 100 trillion microbes, comprising a diverse array of species, each influenced by factors like diet, genetics, medications, and stress.[6] The gut is often referred to as a "second brain" because it produces several neurotransmitters, such as serotonin, dopamine, and gamma-amino-butyric acid—which are also found in the brain.[7] These neurotransmitters play a crucial role in regulating our mood. Recent data have established connections between gut dysbiosis and various diseases, particularly those affecting mental health. The relationship is bidirectional (meaning the brain and gut influence one another) with specific microbes associated with different diseases.[8] Pathways like neuroimmune, neuroendocrine, and sensory-neural are implicated in this connection.[9] It turns out that these pathways have been found to be vital to mental health.

Microorganisms in our gut serve many important functions. They are involved in the production of vitamins and nutrients, gastrointestinal functions, food absorption, and maintaining intestinal integrity. Scientists have even discovered that 90 percent of the body's serotonin is produced in the gut.[10] These microbes also play roles in metabolism and contribute to the functioning of the immune system.[11] Additionally, they influence the expression of human genetics.[12] Bacteria regulate processes such as gut motility and the permeability of the intestinal barrier.[13] What occurs in the gut appears to have powerful effects on crucial processes in the brain. According to Dr. Aurora Clapp and colleagues, "when the human microbiome is challenged with changes in diet, stress, or antibiotics, the physiology of the normal microbiome undergoes change, leading to dysbiosis."[14] A dysbiotic state is when the balance of gut bacteria is disrupted, causing the gut lining to become "leaky" and allowing harmful substances to pass into the bloodstream—phenomenon aptly named "leaky gut syndrome."[15] A study in the *Journal of Molecular Psychiatry* looked into this concept and found that people with mental illness and chronic fatigue have elevated levels of gut dysbiosis markers, which positively correlated with severity of sickness behavior in these patients.[16] Their findings reveal that gut dysbiosis may underlie many of the symptoms presented in these conditions.

Another important concept beyond dysbiosis/leaky gut is the concept of inflammation and its impact on the microbiome. When the digestive system gets inflamed, it stresses our gut microbes by releasing certain substances called endotoxins.[17] These substances can travel through the body, affecting the brain—causing anxiety and depression. Studies have found a direct connection between increased levels of endotoxins and feelings of being down or anxious. One such substance is called cytokines TNF-a, which researchers found "increases the permeability of the blood-brain barrier," amplifying the effects of rogue molecules in the gut.[18] One study looked into this and found that when healthy subjects with no history of depressive disorders were given infusions of endotoxins, they triggered cytokine release and subsequent emergence of classical depressive symptoms.[19]

Though the research is relatively new, more and more studies are coming out to uncover the relationship between our microbiome and many mental health conditions. One study by Li and colleagues proposes a connection between autism spectrum disorders (ASD) and the colonization of Candida species.[20] Candida is thought to impede carbohydrate and mineral absorption and may promote toxin accumulation, and in turn is suggested to increase autistic behaviors in children with ASD.[21] Another study links heightened autistic behaviors to the interaction between propionic acid and ammonia released by Candida albicans, generating an excess of beta-alanine.[22] This interaction is considered a potential contributor to the development of ASD.[23] In a neuroscience study, Alzheimer's patients who consumed milk infused with four probiotic bacteria species for 12 weeks performed better on a cognitive impairment test compared to those who consumed regular milk.[24] It is important to note however, that there is still limited research. More studies with better controls for better understanding of how this relationship works are required. The important point to make is that it is now evident that our microbiome and the gut-brain axis are important to both our physical health and our mental health.

There are mixed opinions on whether probiotics are effective at treating mental health conditions, due to the research being so new. However, there are now quite a few studies within the last year confirming the positive effects of probiotic use for conditions like depression and anxiety.[25] A limited study published in the journal, *Gastroenterology*, concluded that women who consumed yogurt containing a blend of probiotics twice daily for four weeks exhibited greater calmness when exposed to images of angry and frightened faces compared to the control group.[26] Additionally, in the yogurt group, MRI scans showed reduced activity in the insula, a brain region responsible for processing internal body sensations.[27] Likewise, in a 30-day study, individuals without prior depressive symptoms were provided with either probiotics or antidepressants.[28] Those who received probiotics exhibited decreased cortisol levels and reported improved psychological wellbeing.[29] Similar investigations demonstrated that probiotic treatment lessened depressive symptoms and enhanced HPA-axis function, comparable to the effects of Citalopram and Diazepam.[30] Therefore, in the near future, it seems plausible that there will be probiotics specifically designed to be protective against conditions such as mental illness—the emerging data shows promising outcomes

Impact of Micronutrients

Micronutrients are vital for our brain processing. Just to produce melatonin, the sleep hormone for example, the body converts l-tryptophan, a protein found in beans and turkey, into serotonin using vitamin B6, niacin, and magnesium to convert to serotonin.[31] From there, the body uses micronutrients such as zinc and magnesium to convert serotonin into melatonin.[32] Without these micronutrients, the basic process of melatonin production for sleep becomes difficult.

Micronutrients are integral components of enzymes, coenzymes, and other molecules essential for cellular function. They participate in biochemical reactions that regulate metabolism, energy production, and the synthesis of important molecules. Micronutrients include vitamins and minerals, and each of them serves specific functions in the body. Even with a balanced healthy diet, experts are now saying many of these nutrients are lacking due to our modern farming practices.

The following are a few micronutrients and their potential impact:

- Omega-3 can optimize mood stability & cognitive function.[33]
- B-12 might prevent loss of neurons.[34]
- Vitamin B helps produce energy needed to make neurons.[35]
- Vitamin C helps mature neurons and form myelin sheath that protects neurons and transmissions.[36]
- Low levels of vitamin D correlate to poor memory and depression.[37]
- Vitamin E helps protect cells from oxidation.[38]
- Magnesium regulates receptors for brain development.[39]
- Zinc helps DNA maintain its integrity for cellular activity.[40]
- Potassium regulates central nervous system, and low levels correlate to anxiety.[41]

It is now known in the scientific field that micronutrients are critical for all health processes including mental health. For example, increasing essential fatty acids has an effect on the prevention and treatment of anxiety and depression.[42] Low vitamin D levels are associated with increased symptoms of depression and anxiety.[43] Likewise, the rise of nutritional psychiatry has given light to many diet choices that can reduce symptoms of many mental illnesses. There is now something called the "anti-anxiety diet" that has been shown to reduce anxiety and includes foods like dark chocolate, green tea, and leafy greens.[44]

Another study, which gave adolescents with ADHD broad spectrum micronutrients, found that about 80 percent of those who used and continued broad spectrum micronutrients were labeled as being in remission from their ADHD symptoms vs. 40 percent of those on medications and 20 percent of those who stopped all treatment.[45] By the same token, a study in China found that consuming a diet high in red and/or processed meat, refined grains, sweets, high-fat dairy products, butter, potatoes, and high-fat gravy, while having low intakes of fruits and vegetables, is linked to an elevated risk of depression.[46] Whereas, a dietary pattern, such as the Mediterranean diet, which has increased consumption of fruits, vegetables, whole grains, fish, olive oil, low-fat dairy, and antioxidants, along with reduced intake of animal products, is linked to a lower risk of depression.[47] This creates a clear picture: our diets, and the micronutrients we consume, are extremely important.

<u>Access to Nutrient-Rich Foods</u>

Food insecurity is deeply intertwined with poverty, with around 36 percent of households with incomes below the federal poverty line being food insecure.[48] "Food deserts" are areas characterized by a lack of access to affordable and healthy food options. These deserts can be found in various settings, including urban or suburban neighborhoods that lack grocery stores providing nutritious choices. Additionally, they are prevalent in rural areas where the nearest grocery stores are inconveniently distant. The occurrence of food deserts is often associated with neighborhoods predominantly composed of marginalized communities.[49]

Furthermore, these deserts are more likely to be present in areas with a higher percentage of residents experiencing poverty, irrespective of whether the area is designated as urban or rural.[50] Beyond food deserts, public health researchers have coined a new term called "food swamps," which are in areas, (urban, suburban or rural) where the local environment is saturated with stores that predominantly sell unhealthy, calorie-dense, and inexpensive junk foods.[51] These stores often offer a variety of high-sugar items, snacks, and soda, making it challenging for residents to access nutritional and healthier food options.[52] In essence, food swamps reduce the availability of nutritious foods while simultaneously making it easier for individuals to access unhealthy food choices. This matters because food swamps are predictive of obesity, especially in communities where residents face limited access to their own or public transportation and are confronted with income inequality.[53]

We know that healthy food is geographically inaccessible in many neighborhoods, but healthy food is also often expensive. In fact, one study in 2017 looked at six different cities across the US and found that healthier foods are on average two times more expensive than unhealthy alternatives.[54] Now, due to inflation, a healthy diet is four times more expensive,[55] thus accessing and affording this basic human need becomes a luxury. Even in the best circumstances where one can afford healthy food, many of us do not have the education or understanding of why our food choices matter.

In the late 1800s, a chemist named W.O. Atwater discovered that if you burn food to heat water, you can tell how much energy it has.[56] This led down a path towards the well-known idea that our existence is fueled by calories, and that we all need a specific number of calories to maintain life. The issue with this is that many have misunderstood what that really means, leading to a diet culture of "eat less, move more."[57] Though in theory this could make sense for people in specific circumstances trying to lose weight, it completely fails to recognize nuance and nutrition. When we view survival in terms of calories, it is easy to mistake eating processed foods at the right number of calories as sufficient. However, this type of diet misses key nutrients we need for our health and wellbeing. Maintaining a healthy diet extends beyond simply monitoring calorie intake. It involves incorporating a diverse array of nutrient-rich foods to ensure the intake of essential vitamins and minerals crucial for overall wellbeing.

Modern Farming & Lowered Nutrition

Many fruits and vegetables look quite different from the 1950s. This is because scientists developed new high-yield crop varieties and livestock breeds, along with the introduction of synthetic fertilizers, pesticides, and herbicides. Since there were a large number of food shortages during WWII, scientists aimed to enhance food production—and they did.[58] The new genetically modified crops, breeds and fertilizers, coupled with advancements in irrigation and the affordability of tractors, led to a prominent increase in crop productivity.[59] Between 1961 and 2014, the global cereal yield surged by 175 percent; and wheat's average yield soared from 1.1 tons per hectare to 3.4 tons per hectare within a comparable timeframe.[60] This is wonderful in terms of impacting world hunger, but raises new questions about how this impacts our health.

In the present day, we encounter a global food system that, in certain instances, prioritizes delivering calories and aesthetic appeal rather than nutritional value. This contributes to a phenomenon known as hidden hunger, where individuals may feel satisfied but lack essential nutrients for good health.[61] It may seem paradoxical, but obese folks can, in fact, suffer from nutrient deficiencies. And so can thin people. In fact, the National Health and Nutrition Examination Survey found that 95 percent of people are missing at least one micronutrient.[62]

Contemporary farming practices pose health risks not only because they expose us to cancer-causing inflammatory pesticides, but they also deplete essential nutrients from our soil. Research in the US and the UK reveals that commonly cultivated fruits and vegetables have witnessed significant declines—up to 40 percent—in vital nutrients like protein, calcium, phosphorus, riboflavin, and vitamin C over the past five decades.[63] Organic produce has been found to have less of an impact on nutrient deficiency (but only moderate).[64] Yet, organic options are considerably more expensive crop than conventional ones, and they still lack nutrients compared to older generations and add to the already expensive luxury of healthy eating.

The Crisis of Inactivity

Inactivity has become an international issue, and the global community is confronting an alarming rise in preventable diseases such as cancer, diabetes, high blood pressure, and dementia, unless urgent measures are implemented to encourage increased physical activity, as per recent analysis conducted by the World Health Organization (WHO).[65] A comprehensive study examining activity levels across 174 countries found that physical inactivity poses a major health risk worldwide. If no action is taken, governments can expect approximately 500 million new cases of preventable diseases by the year 2030.[66] Physical inactivity means not meeting the recommended levels of physical activity necessary for good health,[67] with the recommended minimum of at least 30 minutes of regular, moderate-intensity physical activity throughout our lives.[68]

What's more is that the economic burden of this crisis is costing governments around the world an estimated $300 billion.[69] The increasing trend of inactivity is especially prevalent among Gen Z, with far-reaching consequences for physical and mental wellbeing. The WHO identifies physical inactivity as the fourth leading risk factor for global mortality, necessitating urgent action to integrate more movement into daily routines of young people.[70] Additionally, a sedentary lifestyle during formative years is linked to poorer mental health outcomes. This inactivity crisis not only affects immediate health but also sets a precedent for adult lifestyle choices, making early intervention crucial.

Exercise and Mental Health

The role of exercise and mental health is quite important. Have you ever taken a walk on a bright sunny day and thought, "Oh wow, life feels good today?" Maybe that sounds niche, but every time I walk outside with the sun beaming on my face, I immediately feel better. The connection between exercise and mental health is increasingly recognized as a vital aspect of psychological wellbeing. Engaging in regular physical activity has been shown to significantly reduce symptoms of depression and anxiety, enhance mood, and improve self-esteem. According to the APA, exercise promotes the release of neurotransmitters such as endorphins and serotonin, and lowers cortisol, which can alleviate feelings of depression and increase feelings of happiness and satisfaction.[71,72]

What's more, physical activity can also improve cognitive function and reduce symptoms of anxiety, with regular engagement contributing to long-term mental health resilience.[73] The therapeutic benefits of exercise include not only immediate mood enhancement but also long-term preventive effects against mental health disorders. One study gave adolescents a 12-week fitness regimen and found notable improvements in their sleep quality and duration, demonstrating increased REM sleep and reduced very light sleep.[74] This was particularly evident in another meta-analysis of randomized controlled trials in adults with mental health conditions, where exercise improved sleep quality considerably.[75] The influence that better sleep has on adolescent mental health is well documented. All of this essentially makes the point that exercise is extremely important not just for sleep and cardiovascular health, but also for our mental health.

Conclusion

There is a profound connection between nutrition/exercise intervention and mental illness recovery. Growing up, our diets, laden with processed and nutritionally depleted foods, differed drastically from our grandparents 'era when mental illness rates were lower. Not only this, but our grandparents spent much more time outdoors being active—whereas we now spend more time inside with our eyes glued to our digital screens. Given that 95 percent of us is deficient in at least one of key micronutrient, it is critical we start taking nutrition more seriously. Yet, healthier foods are up to four times more expensive than unhealthy alternatives which has created food deserts and swamps that disproportionately affects those experiencing poverty. Because modern farming practices are driven by the pursuit of increased yields, they have contributed to the hidden hunger phenomenon. Beyond what we eat, it is also clear how important exercise is for our mental health. Therefore, both diet and exercise need more emphasis within public discourse surrounding mental health.

Chapter 15: The Media Dilemma

What is interesting is the power and the impact of social media... So, we must try to use social media in a good way.
-Malala Yousafzai

I remember the first time I heard the word MySpace. I was about 11 years old, in fifth grade, and amazed by the concept. My cousin, a year older, had asked me if I made an account already—and soon I did. But even before MySpace, I was introduced to the concept of interacting with others online from an early age. A website called "Club Penguin" that emerged in 2005 hosted a range of online games where strangers around the world could interact and chat. From there, I discovered a phenomenon called Webkinz, where the more stuffed animals you collected, the more pets you had in the international multi-player online world.[1] I learned pretty quickly, at a remarkably young age, that the online space can be unsafe, because even on these seemingly harmless platforms, I experienced harassment and bullying language from complete strangers.

When I was 13, my friend introduced me to an online video chat platform called Omegle (which has since been shut down). Both of us goofed around sending videos to strangers, only to find men exposing their genitals to underage young girls like us. We thought it was funny at that moment, but as an adult, that does not make me laugh in the slightest. The World Wide Web is the Wild west, even today—maybe even more so today. And, the more technology advances, the more we should question the safety and impact these programs have on us and our children. There's no denying the significant advantages social media brings to society, offering unprecedented access and connectivity to people, services, information, and opportunities. However, mounting evidence, especially concerning adolescent mental health, suggests a link between increased social media usage and elevated levels of depression, anxiety, sleep disturbances, diminished self-esteem, and body image issues.[2]

I think people forget how influential media is. A few years ago, I was spammed non-stop with *HelloFresh* ads on social media and on TV show commercials. The first time I saw an ad from them I thought, *oh that's an interesting new concept* and after the third ad I gave in and tried it. This is the power of media. I had no issue preparing meals myself but after a few celebrities made videos and ads on it I bought the product out of curiosity. Media, such as the shows and movies we consumed as kids, influences us in many ways and often negatively. And to be honest, I do not think it is surprising why we Gen Zers are currently influencer-obsessed and struggle with self-esteem given the media of our time.

Most of the shows and movies that were popular during our upbringing have centered on fame, talent, beauty, and chaotic relationships. For example, the top shows in the 2000s were *Gossip Girl, Dawson's Creek, Skins, Gilmore Girls, One Tree Hill, The Simple Life, Hannah Montana, Degrassi, The OC, Vampire Diaries*, and *The Secret Life of the American Teenager*.[3,4] Every show listed features traditionally thin, beautiful actors and actresses. Additionally, all twelve shows have problematic sex scenes, and all but one show has explicit drug use. More recently, newer shows have illustrated even more problematic subject matter. Shows that emerged after 2015 such as *Euphoria, White Lotus, 13 Reasons Why, Riverdale, Outerbanks, The Summer I Turned Pretty*, and *All American* continue to profit off of centering beautiful people (thin, symmetrical, youthful) and problematic storylines that undoubtably have influence on young minds. Gen Z was born into the influencer era, and this is, I believe, a consequence of the media we were exposed to growing up. There are many forms of media, but in simple terms, media are the tools to disseminate information and content—be it movies, TV shows, news outlets, blogs, influencers, etc. Taken together, it is important to unpack the ways in which media have affected us. Many books have come out about how social media caused our mental health crisis, and I argue it is more complicated than that. Books like *The Anxious Generation* by Jonathan Haidt claim that my generation is overcome by something he calls the "great rewiring."[5] But older researchers cannot understand the nuance and lived experience of our generation. It is only one small piece of the puzzle. And while social media, as I will explain, has many drawbacks, and does have negative influence on mental health, it also has positive features that cannot be ignored. The following chapter will underscore how the internet—and media—affects all of us, but more importantly, how it shaped my generation and beyond.

How Does Media Influence Us?

According to NYU professor Eric Arias, media influences people in two main ways:

1. **Direct Influence:** Media provides new information or trends that individuals adopt. For example, media promotes a new beauty trend, and people start following it.[6]

2. **Indirect Influence:** Media shares common information that helps people coordinate their actions. For example, media reports on a new diet product, and people start using it because they know others are doing the same.[7]

One example of such influence is through the new Ozempic craze. Media began promoting Ozempic, a new weight loss medication a couple years ago, after patients who used the medication to treat diabetes discovered strong weight loss properties.[8] This is an example of *direct influence*. During the 2023 Oscars, Jimmy Kimmel even made a joke about how all the celebrities around the room looked great and said, "When I look around this room, I can't help but wonder: Is Ozempic right for me?"[9] Normal people like me read articles and watch TV shows featuring celebrities who used Ozempic and wonder if we should try it too. Simultaneously, blogs and social media have been buzzing about how many people are using Ozempic and the results they are seeing. This has created a sense of shared experience, an example of *indirect influence*. There are over 91,000 people on TikTok talking about Ozempic.[10] With an increase of over 400 percent in Google searches for the weight loss drug, it is clear that media about Ozempic has created widespread influence.[11]

The ability of people to be persuaded is rooted in evolution and biology. Following the lead of high-status, high-prestige individuals in a group is seen in both humans and primates, where it is common to align one's gaze or copy the decisions of those with "high status."[12] Dr. Elizabeth (Zab) Johnson, with the Wharton Neuroscience Initiative states that "this behavior is seen in the wild when monkeys turn to look at whatever a higher-status monkey is looking at in the trees" and their behavior is remarkably similar to humans in the office when employees model their work after the top-rated employee.[13] Dr. Johnson further argues, "when [a] leader is successful, others require less evidence to make the same choice." We often blindly follow people that are perceived to be an expert or famous because of their influence. This becomes a concern when people we deem influential encourage us to believe prestige, consumption of overly expensive products, or eating disorder behavior is worth copying.

The Shows & Movies that Shaped Us

Many teens and young adults struggle today with body image, eating disorders, and low self-esteem. The National Organization for Women reports that by the time girls reach age 15, 53 percent say that they are "unhappy with their bodies."[14] This number grows to 78 percent by the time the girls reach 17.[15] These numbers have also been found in teen boys, where 75 percent of adolescent boys have reported dissatisfaction with their bodies, and up to a half them are using supplements such as protein powders during their teens in an attempt to boost muscularity.[16,17] The media has increasingly promoted a "thin/fit" ideal that is often unattainable in a healthy way for most. In a study of fifth graders, both boys and girls reported dissatisfaction with their bodies after watching a Britney Spears music video or a clip from the TV show *Friends*.[18] A 1996 study found that the time adolescents spent watching soaps, movies, and music videos correlated with body dissatisfaction and a desire to be thin.[19] This makes sense that young impressionable minds want to copy such ideals—seeing beautiful people on screen winning their love interest's hearts, finding fame and admiration. Who wouldn't want to be adored for being beautiful and cool? When we are subjected to media that tells us that being thin and fitting a certain ideal is "cool" or necessary to find love and happiness, many of us are going to copy it. When I watched *Hannah Montana* as a teen, did I also buy a blonde wig and try to write songs in my living room? Absolutely.

Reality TV is also a phenomenon that is undoubtedly influential. A study from the International Network Organization for Science

Research found that reality TV has significant impact on viewers, particularly children and teenagers. Reality TV often misrepresents reality through misleading editing and staged scenes, promoting vulgarity, materialism, and negative behaviors. The study found that shows like *Teen Mom* contribute to moral degradation and unrealistic life expectations.[20] Reality TV can increase tolerance for rudeness and negative behavior, influencing viewers to emulate these traits.[21]

The Psychological Impact of TV & Movies

A study in the UK in 2014 concluded that media is producing adverse effects on the psychological well-being of audiences.[22] Watching TV has been linked to more mood and anxiety problems. It was also connected to worse overall mental health, including lower self-esteem and life satisfaction, especially for girls.[23] Even back in 1997, the year I was born, researchers at the University of Sussex found that negative news is associated with anxiety, and depression.[24] To put simply, media does impact mental health.

One unfortunate example of the powers of media on mental health was the unusual show *13 Reasons Why* which tells the story of Hannah Baker, a 17-year-old who dies by suicide and leaves behind tapes explaining her reasons, sparking debate over its portrayal of teen suicide, self-harm, rape, and bullying. In the final episode, viewers, until it was later removed, were able to see Hannah's full suicide scene. All of it. As someone who watched it, I remember it vividly. Critics argue the show glamorizes and sensationalizes suicide, potentially increasing suicidal thoughts among viewers. But what studies after the show was released found is arguably worse than just suicidal "thoughts." Studies, including one by JAMA Internal Medicine, found that Google searches for suicide rose after the show's release,[25] meaning people who watched it did not just think about it, they investigated further. More consequently, teen suicides in ages ten to seventeen rose significantly and was associated with the release of the show.[26] Many influential organizations, such as the National Association of School Psychologists (NASP) expressed concerns about the show's impact on vulnerable youth, with some calling for its cancellation.[27] Medical experts and journals like the British Medical Journal have also called for better regulation of suicide portrayals in media since the show, emphasizing the potential harm to susceptible individuals.[28] Similarly, NASP advised that vulnerable youth, particularly those with suicidal thoughts, should avoid watching the series, as its compelling narrative might cause impressionable viewers to romanticize the character's decisions or develop revenge fantasies. That makes sense in hindsight. As someone who experienced bullying, younger me absolutely wished the perpetrators could understand the pain they caused. The way in which Hannah seeks revenge in the show might have influenced young minds to believe that suicide is a way in which one can seek justice (explaining the uptick in suicides after the show's release), when in reality it is far from it.

The Allure and Challenges of Social Media

On February 4th, 2004, Mark Zuckerberg launched Facebook at Harvard University, where 650 students made accounts within days.[29] Fast forward to the present day, and the platform boasts approximately two billion daily active users.[30] But do you know why Facebook was originally created? In 2003, Zuckerberg, then a sophomore at Harvard, developed the software for a website called Facemash. [31] He controversially used his computer science skills to hack into Harvard's security network, copying student ID images from the dormitories to populate his new site. [32] Facemash allowed visitors to compare two student photos side-by-side and vote on who was "hot" and who was "not."[33] In other words, the birth of one of the largest media platforms was founded on superficial principles. As Facebook experienced remarkable growth, there has been a simultaneous rise in concern regarding the mental health of teenagers and young adults.

Data from the CDC indicates that the suicide rate among individuals aged 10 to 24 remained steady from 2000 to 2007 but surged by 57 percent between 2007 and 2017.[34] The U.S. Surgeon General Vivek Murthy released an advisory about the youth mental health crisis because of concerns about social media. Social media use among youth is widespread, with up to 95 percent of youth aged 13 to 17 engaging with these platforms, and nearly 40 percent of children aged 8 to 12 also taking part, despite the recommended minimum age of 13. [35] A longitudinal study involving 6,595 US adolescents aged 12 to 15 revealed that adolescents spending over three hours per day on social media were twice as likely to encounter adverse mental health outcomes, such as symptoms associated with depression and anxiety.[36] All of this calls to question how much harm social media is having on my generation.

Why do we use social media? We are drawn to social media for multiple reasons. People like social media for social connectivity, self-expression, and for information sharing, where users engage in discussions, stay informed, and express their perspectives on various topics. However, this digital realm is not without its complexities. People have become increasingly aware of the "fake" personas that are created in a means to influence us into buying products.[37] The rise of influencer culture has given way to a toxic, unrealistic standard put upon my generation. Crafting online personas has become a common practice, influencing one's mental wellbeing by shaping their digital presence and identity. The pursuit of social validation and self-esteem through online interactions adds another layer to the psychological impact, as we seek affirmation and recognition online. To put it further, the Fear of Missing Out (FOMO) and the habitual comparison of one's life to curated content contributes to a landscape of negative self-image, struggles with anxiety/depression, and further exacerbates concerns like eating disorders, and loneliness.

I know for me personally, the more time I spend on Instagram or TikTok, the worse I feel. In fact, I made a new Instagram account as an experiment, and found that my "discover page"

was immediately saturated with pictures of "before and after photos" where women show their weight loss results. It is jarring that the algorithm put these as the first wave of "discoveries" for me on the app. Figure 2 depicts a screenshot of what I was shown. Pretty grating right?

Figure 2: My Instagram Experiment

I first downloaded Facebook when I was 12 years old. Within minutes of use, I was hooked. Not only could I see what my social network was doing daily, I was able to learn information about people easily making the concept of stalking commonplace. It also meant I could chat with boys (and predators) online. It seems ironic to me that I was hit on and solicited more as a 12-year-old than as a 27-year-old. Not only did I have easy access to a world of people, but I also learned all too young about the scary truth about some men. What did that do to my development? As a kid I did not understand that predators solicited me. As an adult, I am enraged. Dr. Ortega-Barón from University of Valencia and colleagues found that "around 23 percent of minors reported some sexual solicitation and 14 percent reported some sexual interaction."[38] This study also reports that those who are victims have lower quality of life scores in adulthood,[39] which undoubtedly has psychological repercussions for victims.

Addiction and Technology Dependency

Researchers have defined smartphone addiction as involving behaviors such as excessive smartphone use, tolerance (needing more engagement for the same benefits), and feelings of psychological dependence, withdrawal, and relapse.[40] This includes addictive behaviors like gaming, internet usage, and social media engagement. Various factors, such as instant gratification, reinforcement schedules, separation anxiety, and coping mechanisms, feed into the compelling cycle of this addiction. However, excessive smartphone use has been associated with both physical and psychological determinants like sleep disturbances, posture issues, repetitive strain injuries, obesity, hypertension, reduced confidence, loneliness, increased divorce rates, and lower productivity.[41] Smartphone addiction is also linked with mental health issues like depression, anxiety, stress, poor impulse control, and lower wellbeing.[42] Mental health concerns increase with society's reduced social interactions resulting from elevated technological use and dependence on social media for communication, further exacerbating loneliness.[43]

Despite extensive research, neither the APA nor the WHO recognizes smartphone addiction as a clinical disorder—and the literature lacks consensus on whether the addiction stems from the smartphone itself or the behaviors facilitated by it.[44] Some propose conceptualizing smartphone addiction as a spectrum capturing various disordered behaviors, while others advocate for creating a taxonomy to classify specific disordered behaviors and means of access. However, most research still focuses on the smartphone as the locus of addictive behavior, despite evidence suggesting a more nuanced understanding is needed. [45] The point is however, as a society, we are becoming increasingly dependent on our technology—sometimes to the point of detriment.

Body Image

It is no secret that social media can impact body image. Many studies have underscored the correlation between social media usage and body dissatisfaction. [46,47,48] Not only can it foster unrealistic beauty standards and unhealthy comparisons, but platforms often present idealized images, enhanced through filters and editing, fueling feelings of inadequacy and diminishing self-esteem. We also live in a world where now, the culture of comparison (defined below) on social media encourages us to strive for unattainable ideals, perpetuating dissatisfaction with one's body. Cyberbullying is increasingly becoming a public health concern, with more and more children and adolescents reporting cases; this form of bullying is prevalent on social media platforms.[49] Studies around the world have investigated this issue and have found that cyberbullying further intensifies negative body image, as people are targeted based on their appearance.[50]

Likewise, according to a researcher at Pennsylvania State University, victims of online abuse may experience "depressive affect, anxiety, loneliness, suicidal behavior, and somatic symptoms."[51] For those already grappling with body image disorders like body dysmorphic disorder, social media can intensify symptoms, triggering compulsive behaviors and worsening mental health concerns.[52] A study in China found that social media filters have given rise to a phenomenon termed "snapchat dysphoria," wherein people strive to emulate the altered appearance created by these filters.[53] Numerous plastic surgeons have reported instances of individuals seeking cosmetic procedures to resemble their filtered Snapchat images.[54]

According to the APA, adolescents and young adults who decreased their social media usage by half for a few weeks experienced notable enhancements in their body image and overall appearance satisfaction, as opposed to their counterparts who maintained consistent social media usage levels.[55] Recognizing the impact that social media has on our body image is extremely important, especially for our vulnerable youth. Growing up, I experienced and witnessed the impact of social media firsthand, especially on body image. My friends and I would do "photo shoots" and compare pictures of each other online. This behavior is apparently very common in youth since the emergence of social media. With such a strong emphasis on beauty and unrealistic standards, we are setting up youth to prioritize superficial values.

Comparison Culture

Social comparison theory proposes that we engage in self-evaluation to assess our worth relative to others.[56] In sociology, this phenomenon is a part of human social development. Psychologist Leon Festinger coined the theory less than a century ago in 1954.[57] Social comparison theory suggests that we evaluate ourselves based on comparisons with others, either in terms of abilities or opinions.[58] These comparisons can encompass various aspects of life, such as appearance, achievements, and wealth. There are different types of social comparison: upward, where individuals compare themselves to those better off; downward, where they compare themselves to those worse off; and lateral, where they compare themselves to peers.[59] Research indicates that people often engage in upward comparisons, which can lead to feelings of inferiority. However, recent studies suggest that upward comparison can also inspire positive changes.[60] social media, widely embraced by Gen Z, has amplified the impact of social comparison, with nearly 90 percent of youth using platforms like Instagram, Facebook, and TikTok.[61] While social comparison is common offline, social media intensifies its effects.[62]

Social media was developed to be addictive. In fact, if you saw the film *The Social Dilemma* (2022), you will remember how the makers of these apps did this on purpose.[63] According to Nancy Deangelis, CRNP, who serves as the Director of Behavioral Health at Jefferson

Health-Abington, social media platforms stimulate the release of dopamine in the brain, encouraging users to return frequently.[64] Shares, likes, and comments activate the brain's reward system, creating a sensation similar to that of gambling or drug use. It is the continuous utilization of social media that leads to social comparison and the negative consequences that come with it.

The Good Part of Social Media

While there is a lot of contention over its harm, social media use has been associated with positive mental health outcomes. From my observations, social media might positively affect mental health by offering continuous social connection, access to information and resources, and reducing stigma associated with seeking help. It provides a platform to build supportive relationships, access mental health resources, and engage in open conversations about mental health anonymously. Peer support groups and online communities on social media offer validation, empathy, and practical advice, contributing to overall wellbeing. For individuals with difficulties in face-to-face interactions, social media can serve as an alternative platform for communication and self-expression. Engaging in positive and uplifting content on social media can also act as a distraction from negative thoughts and promote self-expression and self-awareness. Social media can give people access to important information to help us get out of dangerous situations.

Research in 2019 showed that regular social media engagement correlated with improved mental health, self-rated health, social wellbeing, and resilience.[65] American teens also reported feeling more connected and supported through social media, emphasizing its role in combating loneliness and fostering support networks, particularly beneficial for those of us with underlying mental health concerns.[66] Moreover, social media offers new avenues for mental health information, connecting us to services and allowing us to build supportive relationships among users and caregivers.

Social media platforms provide constant opportunities for connectivity and interaction, regardless of time or location. This is invaluable for people who struggle with face-to-face interactions. For instance, those with impaired social functioning in schizophrenia spectrum disorders may benefit from social media, as it facilitates easier communication and socialization.[67] Research has shown that participants with schizophrenia found social media helpful in enhancing their ability to interact and socialize.[68] The capacity to connect anonymously online is crucial.[69] Researchers have found that people with serious mental health struggles[70,71] engage in online relationships and social connections on social media at rates similar to those in the general population. This finding is significant because people with serious mental disorders often have limited offline social interactions and experience heightened feelings of loneliness.[72]

Among those who receive publicly funded mental health services, nearly half report using media platforms weekly or more frequently as a means to combat loneliness.[73] In another study focusing on young adults with serious mental illness, most participants cited using social media to ease feelings of isolation.[74] Interestingly, frequent social media use was associated with increased community involvement, such as shopping, working, engaging in religious activities, visiting friends and family, and greater civic engagement, including participation in local elections.[75] Therefore, social media has been found to positively aid those with social difficulties.

On a similar note, social media platforms are increasingly being utilized by individuals with mental disorders for seeking information, connecting with mental health providers, and accessing evidence-based services to cope with symptoms and improve overall wellbeing.[76] Incorporating peer-to-peer social networking into digital mental health interventions has shown benefits in improving engagement, compliance, adherence, and perceived social support among individuals with psychosis.[77] For example, the Horyzons online intervention led to significant reductions in depression among patients with first-episode psychosis, with a high engagement in the peer-to-peer networking component.[78] Mobile apps like PRIME have been designed to resemble mainstream social media platforms to enhance engagement and quality of life for users with schizophrenia.[79] Ongoing research emphasizes the potential of leveraging online social networking to improve mental health outcomes and effectively support individuals and families managing mental health challenges.

Pornography Is Bad for Us

One of the scariest parts of growing up during the onset of the digital media age has been access to adult content as children. The first time I discovered porn was finding *The Joy of Sex* book in my grandparents living room library. I remember opening the book, with my eight-year-old eyes wide, mouth open, and shocked that people could be drawn doing such strange positions. It did not take long for me to Google what I had seen in the book, absolutely curious and dumbfounded by what I discovered. Within seconds I was brought into the world of pornography. Shocked, but also childishly foolish, the first thing I decided to do was bring my discovery to my friend at school. As we peered into the safari of my flip phone, I noticed he was not as curious as I. After he undoubtedly told his mom, I was no longer welcomed at playdates. The funny thing is, as an adult, it pains me that the young curious version of me was socially punished for something that was not my fault—it was the fault of the World Wide Web for making inappropriate material available for children to discover with complete ease.

So how did this access and prevalence of porn affect my generation? Pornhub's 2020 tech review reported a major viewership spike during the pandemic's onset, with daily hits reaching 130 million.[80] The review also reported that of the 130 million daily views, there was a 42 percent increase in US viewership at the pandemic's start, and 51 percent of viewers were aged 18-34. Meaning, Gen Z was a lot more involved than before. But what is the issue with this? Well, studies have linked high pornography consumption to greater feelings of loneliness among youth.[81] There has also been links between increased anxiety and depression and use of pornography,[82] as well as increased addictive behavior.[83] There is also great concern about the easy access of children using sites like YouTube and other video platforms because they are at thumb's reach. With content being uploaded every minute, these sites have difficulty vetting what is uploaded straightaway, and this undoubtedly has consequences for our children. According to Donna Volpitta, Ed.D., founder of The Center for Resilient Leadership,

> "Children who repeatedly experience stressful and/or fearful
> emotions may under develop parts of their brain's prefrontal
> cortex and frontal lobe, the parts of the brain responsible for

executive functions, like making conscious choices and
planning ahead."[84]

Thus, exposure to pornography at a young age has the potential to harm brain development. Additionally, the CDC noted sexual activity among high schoolers from 1991 to 2015 has dropped significantly.[85] But what is strange is that while Generation Z may prioritize relationships, our focus has apparently shifted more towards sexual rather than emotional connections.[86] So the limited relationships we are having might have less depth.

Despite pervasive media portrayals of young adults as sex-obsessed, millennials and Generation Z are having less sex than previous generations. [87] This decline is attributed to various factors including increased internet access and the influence of pornography. And what's more, is that the sex we do engage in is more often causal than other generations. In fact, Gen Z is increasingly embracing "situationships"— the middle ground between committed relationships and casual dating.[88] This trend reflects a shift in how youth approach love and sex, prioritizing personal freedom and career goals over traditional relationship milestones. While situationships offer flexibility and can suit modern, busy lifestyles, they also come with risks and potential misunderstandings if both parties aren't on the same page. So why is this related to porn? Well, research shows that use of pornography is correlated with a higher likelihood to engage in casual sex. This makes sense, given Gen Z is both engaging more with situationships and higher use of porn.

Yet, while some are engaging in hook-up culture, others are not—with some headlines even stating that we are in a sexual recession. Lisa Wade, a sociology professor and author, shares in her book, *American Hookup: The New Culture of Sex on Campus*, that about a third of students reject hookup culture, preferring to abstain rather than conform to its norms.[89] Wade noted in the *Scholars Strategy Report* that this culture could affect mental health. Susan Krauss Whitborne, a psychology professor and contributor to *Psychology Today*, observed that college students who had casual sex recently tend to report lower self-esteem, life satisfaction, and happiness than those who did not.[90] While casual sex itself doesn't cause depression, it often coincides with loneliness stemming from impersonal relationships.

Psychologist Nancy Sokarno adds that because casual sex is linked to loneliness, it can trigger anxiety, depression, suicidal thoughts, and unhealthy behaviors like disordered eating, substance abuse, and poor sleep.[91] Nonetheless, because recent studies have suggested Gen Z is having less sex than previous generations, there has been a splurge of headlines about "puriteens" and concerns over our sexual behavior. However, the actual story is more complex, as discussed on a recent *ICYMI* episode with Rachelle Hampton and Sarah Marshall from the *You're Wrong About* podcast. They explored why Gen Z might be less sexually active, pointing out that reduced alcohol consumption, increased online activities, porn use, and changing attitudes towards sex and relationships could all be factors.[92] The bottom line is that porn might have affected us, especially our views of what healthy sex looks like. It also raises concerns over body image and the sexualization of women and young girls. Therefore, it is important to assert that porn has significantly impacted us. The question is, *how bad was it really?* The answers are still being written, researched, and understood.

<u>Conclusion</u>

Media isn't just a tool for connection; it's a double-edged sword with profound implications for our mental health. It is important for us to recognize the incredible tools we have been given. By acknowledging the addictive nature of social media and fostering a culture of mindfulness and digital literacy, we can reclaim control over our online lives. Though there are drawbacks, there are many benefits to social media that balance the downsides. With the right education on media literacy, monitoring and evaluation, and more research on how these platforms affect those of us with mental illness, we can all benefit from social media—while leaving the negatives (like comparison culture) behind. In addition to social media, there is critical need for responsible media portrayals in general. Media's far-reaching influence on Generation Z—through TV, news, and movies—has harmed mental health, body image, and overall well-being, which evidences the importance of understanding and addressing these impacts. The power of media in shaping perceptions and behaviors cannot be underestimated. We need more research and understanding into the power of media on our generation. Media literacy was not a part of most of Gen Z's education, and it is reflected in the high rates of depression and anxiety. Now some states have adopted media literacy as part of public school curriculum[93]—too bad it is years too late for me and the many other young people who just graduated high school.

Chapter 16: Toxins are Everywhere

If you prick us do we not bleed? If you tickle us do we not laugh? If you poison us do we not die? And if you wrong us shall we not revenge?
William -Shakespeare

I'll probably get cancer from this, but oh, well, is a statement I have heard over and over since I was in elementary school. The lingering feeling that I was interacting with toxins everywhere I went was both anxiety-inducing yet numbing. At a certain point the amount of exposure is too much to wrap one's mind around. It is hard to know when exactly I first heard about these mysterious, invisible, and yet dangerous substances, but the awareness never left once it entered. At this point, it is common knowledge that our world is full of toxins, but older generations did not experience the same exposure nor anxiety about it like we face today. I believe including this factor as one of the intersections of the mental health crisis is important since the more science catches up, we learn how greatly these chemicals are affecting our health, from autoimmune disease to depression.

Sixty-two years ago, marine biologist Rachel Carson authored *Silent Spring*, a groundbreaking book renowned for raising awareness about the dangers of pesticides and other chemicals.[1] It is often credited with catalyzing a movement that led to the establishment of the US Environmental Protection Agency (EPA) and key environmental laws such as the Clean Water and Clean Air Acts. These laws have significantly reduced pollution over the past five decades.[2] However, experts argue that despite these advancements, health risks associated with commercial chemicals remain largely unchanged.[3] In fact, lead, a common neurotoxin has been found just about…everywhere. A Harvard study found that a quarter of public primary schools across our nation potentially may contain higher than safe levels of lead in school drinking fountain water.[4]

Sarah Vogel, senior vice president for Healthy Communities at the Environmental Defense Fund, acknowledges improvements in environmental standards since *Silent Spring*, particularly in areas like water pollution and pesticide use.[5] Yet, challenges persist, especially concerning chemicals found in consumer products. Vogel highlights the complexity of regulating chemicals in everyday items like paints, carpets, and plastics, which have seen the introduction of many new substances.[6] Despite efforts to address these concerns, progress has been slower in this area. Discussions with experts often turn to the Toxic Substances Control Act (TSCA) of 1976, a key federal law governing chemical regulation.[7] Despite being one of the last major environmental laws of the 1960s and 70s, it is widely criticized as one of the weakest.

My generation was exposed to many harmful chemicals, with the peak of production being around the time we were born. Research is finding that these chemicals not only affect mothers and their fetuses but also generations to follow.[8]

Because companies wanted to cut costs, they found a way to produce cheap goods by using these chemicals, but at the expense of both the environment and us. For example, exposure to certain "forever chemicals" and environmental pollutants known as endocrine-disrupting chemicals (EDCs) has been linked to neurological alterations, including ADHD and autism spectrum disorder.[9] These EDCs, found in everyday products, particularly phthalates and bisphenols, can disrupt the hypothalamic-pituitary-gonadal adrenal axis crucial for reproductive and neuronal processes.[10] These chemicals are widespread in food, air, and water, and as lipophilic compounds, they are easily absorbed through the skin and also can be ingested orally. Once in the body, they can bind to steroid receptors, and may start to create disturbing damage that we still know little about. Exposure during critical periods, including perinatal stages, is potentially associated with adverse health effects, possibly contributing to the predisposition to develop major depressive disorder (MDD). A study in Mexico found that phthalate exposure, particularly butyl-benzyl-phthalate, might increase MDD in female adults because of the way it interacts with female hormones.[11] "Forever chemicals," were initially identified in 1938 by Roy Plunkett, a chemist from DuPont.[12] The first application was used for the nonstick component in Teflon.[13] Although these chemicals have been out for only about eight decades, they can now be found in just about everything, such as shampoo bottles, stain-resistant couches, dental floss, and bicycle lubricants.[14] When these versatile compounds are used in food packaging, they migrate into the food itself.[15]

Mohan Manikkam and Michael Skinner at Washington State University conducted a study that explored the concept of transgenerational toxicity, showing how the effects of toxic chemicals can span multiple generations.[16] In their experiments, pregnant rats were exposed to common environmental chemicals, including insect repellents, plastics additives, and jet fuel. Subsequent generations of rats, despite no direct exposure to these chemicals, exhibited reproductive system damage, such as early puberty onset and reduced egg development in females, and higher levels of dead sperm in males.[17] In another study, researchers observed a 50 percent increased risk of obesity in the great-grandchildren of rats exposed to the pesticide DDT during pregnancy.[18] Epigenetic changes were also detected in these third-generation rats.[19] Besides epigenetic changes, new data have found that prolonged exposure to PFAS has been associated with heightened risks of certain cancers, weakened immune function, and complications in fetal growth.[20] Certain PFAS variants contain elements that may build in the respiratory system and have been correlated with more severe instances of COVID-19.[21]

During early industrialization heavy metal and toxin exposure began to be prevalent.[22] One well-documented example of this was the lead crisis. Though by the 1970s we discovered how bad it was, eliminating leaded gas and painting with lead paint, yet even today the harm is evident.[23] Lead exposure is estimated to contribute to 290,000 additional cases of ADHD in US children.[24] A study involving 270 mother-child pairs in Belgium revealed that doubling prenatal lead exposure, measured in cord blood, correlated with more than a threefold increase in the risk of hyperactivity in boys and girls at age 7-8. A more extensive study with nearly 5,000 US children aged 4-15 discovered that children with the highest blood lead levels were over four times more likely to have ADHD compared to those with the lowest blood lead levels.[25] MRI scans from participants in the Cincinnati Lead Study showed childhood lead exposure was linked to brain volume loss in adulthood. Individuals with higher blood lead levels during childhood exhibited reduced gray matter in certain brain areas, particularly impacting the prefrontal cortex responsible for executive function, behavioral regulation, and fine motor control.[26] In essence, the persistent repercussions of lead exposure (i.e., the alarming prevalence of ADHD and other neurological effects) underscore a concerning reality: the ongoing impact of industrialization continues to subject us to hazardous substances—contributing to widespread health issues that persist across generations.

Additionally, though the research is still being developed, there is now mounting evidence that a group of synthetic chemicals known as PFAS also interfere with immune function.[27] This is probably just the start of what we will discover about what these "forever chemicals" may harm. All of this to say that we are paying the price for industrialization and our society's push to cheapen products.

How do Toxins Play a Role in Mental Health?

The concept of hormones as chemicals has only been made known since the early twentieth century, so it is not surprising that the concept of toxins harming our bodies is also relatively recent in human history. By the time I was born, the array of toxins I was exposed to was reprehensible. From toys, to shampoo, to talc "baby" powder, to lead paint exposure, to everyday CO_2 exposure—it is almost impossible to avoid these harmful chemicals. And, the question is, what are they doing to our health? The Institute for Children's Environmental Health (ICEH) published a report detailing known ways in which the toxins we interact with daily can harm mental health.[28] In their report, many chemicals and agents are named. For example, some food additives like tartrazine (yellow dye number 5) and synthetic food colors combined with sodium benzoate can cause increased irritability, restlessness, sleep disturbances, and hyperactivity in children. Contact with metals such as lead, mercury, and aluminum can result in dementia, depression, anxiety, confusion, memory loss, poor concentration, and insomnia, with other metals like arsenic, manganese, thallium, and tin causing similar issues.

The National Institute of Environmental Health Sciences asserts that endocrine-disrupting compounds (EDCs) like bisphenol A (BPA) and phthalates, found in plastics and many household products, have been linked to schizophrenia.[29] This is possibly due to changes in brain development caused by hormone disruptions during prenatal development. Vinyl chloride, used in PVC plastic products, can lead to symptoms like nervousness, euphoria, irritability, depression, memory problems, hallucinations, insomnia, and fatigue when people are exposed to it through inhalation or skin contact. High levels of carbon dioxide can trigger panic attacks in some individuals. Boron, used in various industrial products, can cause euphoria, anxiety, depression, agitation, restlessness, sleep disturbances, memory problems, confusion, hallucinations, and recurring nightmares when people are exposed to it.

Pesticides, especially organophosphates like parathion and malathion, have been linked to a higher likelihood of depression among those with significant exposure, such as farmers.[30] These pesticides, which are chemically similar to nerve gas, can also cause various psychiatric symptoms. Even though chlorinated hydrocarbon insecticides like DDT are now banned due to their persistence and health risks, they still pose a threat. Carbamates, another type of pesticide, are less toxic but can still affect the nervous system. Essentially, there are a lot of everyday chemicals we are exposed to that have wide ranging effects on both our physical and mental health.

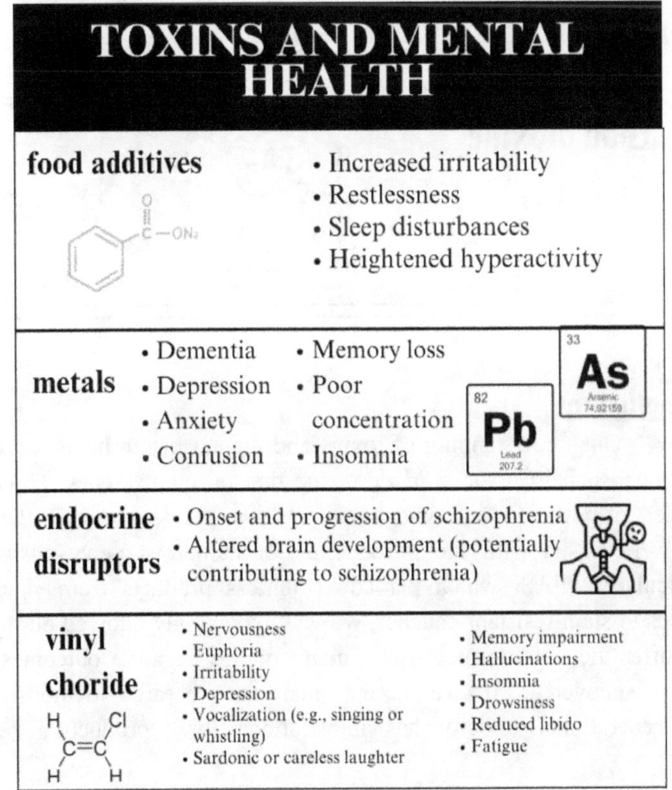

Figure 3. The Mental Health Symptoms Associated with Toxins created from ICEH Data

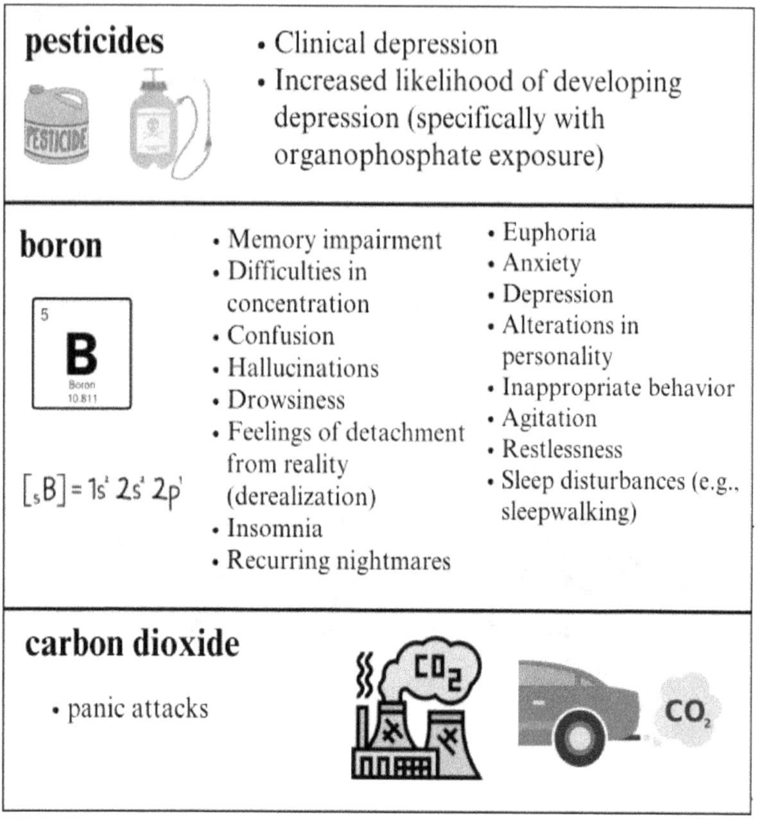

Figure 3 Continued.

Conclusion

Our understanding of toxins and mental health have evolved a lot since Rachel Carson's *Silent Spring* first raised awareness about the dangers of pesticides and other chemicals over six decades ago. Because we were raised with the introduction of numerous new substances, particularly PFAS, which pervade countless products from shampoo bottles to stain-resistant couches, we've unknowingly allowed our health to suffer the consequence—with many of the negative outcomes still being uncovered. If we accept that the research demonstrating transgenerational toxicity has implications for reproductive health, developmental disorders, and mental health issues across multiple generations, then it is obvious that our approach to toxicity needs remediation. Metals, pesticides, boron, carbon dioxide, vinyl chloride, endocrine disruptors, and food additives are just a few examples of the diverse array of toxins that can adversely affect mental wellbeing. From dementia and depression to panic attacks and schizophrenia, the range of psychiatric symptoms associated with exposure to these substances necessitates an imperative to take action against it.

Chapter 17: The College Dilemma

Education is the most powerful weapon which you can use to change the world.
—Nelson Mandela

Many people, including the 44th President Barack Obama (who unabashedly tweeted, "If you think education is expensive, wait until you see how much ignorance costs in the twenty-first century),"[1] have argued that education is one of the best ways to get people out of poverty. However, there's one big issue with that argument. For my generation, getting into college has become a crapshoot, and usually only wealthier kids get the best options. When my parents went to college, if you had good grades and applied, you usually got in and could afford it with little issue. Now, to stand out, you not only need perfect grades, but a high SAT score (although some colleges are now making this optional) and glowing service work/extracurriculars. Many wealthier kids have the option to hire college admissions advisors who can tailor applications to stand out (costing between $850 to $10,000 for a comprehensive package).[2] But for most people, hiring an expensive consultant is outrageously unaffordable.

Data suggest that going to college is worth the exorbitant amount,[3] yet the burden of student loans and stress to get there seems questionable. College education was once synonymous with the American Dream, representing upward mobility and opportunity. However, the rising costs of college and the uncertain job market, even with degrees, have shifted perceptions, with many families now clinging to the ladder of socioeconomic status rather than ascending it. College today, I argue, perpetuates inequalities by being inaccessible to many populations. Additionally, because of a weak job market, many of us Gen Z graduates are set up for stress, unemployment, and poor mental health.

What Went Wrong?

In painting the picture of where it all went wrong, some argue this phenomenon can be traced back to the GI Bill of 1944, the landmark bill that gave veterans access to free college. It was the first time in our history that we played with the notion of making education a public good.[4] The GI Bill marked a pivotal moment in expanding college access, offering free tuition and living expenses to returning veterans.[5] However, our government, with its long history of discrimination, ensured that this bill's access was not equitable, as Black veterans and women were often excluded or faced discriminatory practices in utilizing these benefits.[6]

Initially, college education, influenced by President Harry Truman's commission on higher education, was seen as essential for strengthening democracy and fostering global understanding.[7] Emphasis was placed on liberal arts education to produce well-rounded individuals capable of contributing to society and participating in democracy effectively. The surge in college enrollment following the GI Bill was driven not only by the need for a knowledgeable workforce but also by a desire to cultivate better citizens.[8] The curriculum expanded to include a broad array of subjects beyond career-specific skills, with a focus on literature, humanities, social sciences, and philosophy.[9] This approach aimed to promote global understanding and prevent future conflicts (particularly World War III). Yet, the 1960s saw a shift at college campuses as students became increasingly politicized and engaged in activism.[10] Civil rights movements, anti-war protests, and demands for educational reform became prominent, challenging the traditional ideals of a liberal arts education. This led to a backlash from the conservative establishment, who viewed these developments as excessive or disruptive.[11] Some people suggest that the initial aspirations of promoting democracy through education encountered "blowback" as students began questioning societal norms and advocating for change.[12]

Given those changes, the 1960s saw a backlash against the liberal culture on college campuses, with conservative figures like Ronald Reagan targeting universities as hotbeds of radicalism and questioning the value of public investment in higher education.[13] Today, that shift remains as there is a notable political divide regarding higher education, with Republicans often framing colleges and universities as bastions of liberal indoctrination.[14] Examples from states like Wisconsin and North Carolina illustrate efforts to exert political control over academic institutions and reshape their mission.[15] Unironically, I grew up hearing my conservative friends' parents casually mentioning how colleges indoctrinate people into being "liberals."

Believe it or not, in California in the 1960s, college tuition was free for residents.[16] According to a 1982 report by the NY Times, Reagan vigorously pushed for implementing tuition fees at four-year colleges through legislative efforts.[17] Despite his efforts, he was unsuccessful in achieving tuition fees. However, the California Legislature later approved an increase in student registration fees, which were previously minimal. Consequently, the official policy of not charging tuition fees in California's community colleges ended in 1982.[18] Due to political pushback against "liberal education," taxpayers grew upset about writing a check towards colleges. For example, in Pennsylvania in the late twentieth century, taxpayers paid 75 percent of the cost of public universities. Today, that number is only 25 percent.[19] By the 1970s, our economy shifted, and job growth slowed. This led to one of the first waves of unaffordable college moments. In 1978, Harvard became the archetype by raising their tuition by 17 percent and made the argument that their prestige was worth paying extra for, with some of the additional funds used towards helping some middle-class students in need.[20] This change became known as the high-tuition, high-aid model. Thanks, Harvard.

In their efforts to make more money, Harvard's scheme discovered their applications continued to increase every year, despite rising costs—leading to increases every year over the last 40 years. What does this mean for the cost of college for everyone? Harvard has always been touted as the trendsetter for many ideas in education.

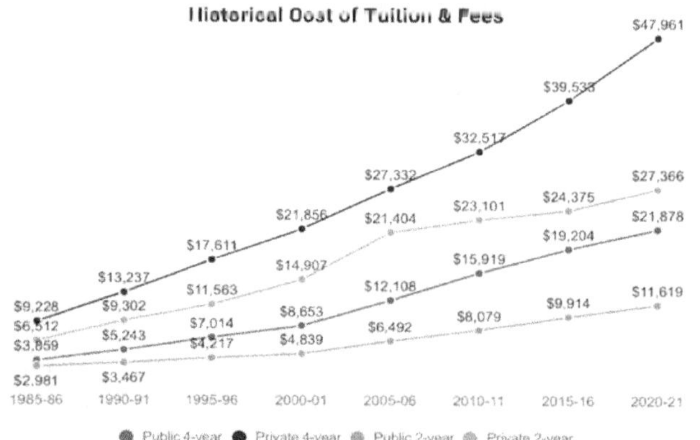

Figure 4: The Cost of Tuition from 1985 to 2021 from National Center for Education

<u>How Inequality Is Perpetuated in Our Schooling</u>

I remember the moment on June 29, 2023, when I opened my social media account to discover that the Supreme Court dealt a significant setback to the United States, ruling to invalidate the policy that allowed universities to consider affirmative action.[21] I wondered, "what will be the consequences of the end of affirmative action?" Affirmative action has historically aimed to address disparities in educational opportunities and outcomes for marginalized communities.[22] Ending these policies may exacerbate socioeconomic inequality by limiting access to higher education for students from low-income backgrounds and/or underprivileged communities, who already face barriers to academic success.

Inequity persists in accessing high-quality education through various means, notably evident in the disparity of resources among public schools. Typically, institutions situated in wealthy communities receive more substantial property tax funding for educational materials, resources, and faculty compared to those in impoverished areas.[23] Consequently, students from wealthier backgrounds enjoy superior facilities, lower dropout rates, expanded educational opportunities, increased earning potential, and advanced instructional support compared to students from low-income neighborhoods. Because of this, inequality continues to cycle within our education system. Our schooling and college system can perpetuate inequality in several ways. Schools in low-income areas often lack resources, experienced teachers, and extracurricular opportunities compared to schools in affluent neighborhoods.[24] This disparity in resources can contribute to differences in academic achievement and educational outcomes among students from different socioeconomic backgrounds.

Besides a lack of resources, by not having access to the right teaching tools, students can often be left behind in terms of studying for tests. Standardized tests, such as the SAT and ACT, are commonly used as part of college admissions criteria. However, many now realize that these tests may not accurately measure a student's potential or readiness for college and can disadvantage students from less privileged backgrounds who may not have access to expensive test preparation resources. Similarly, college admissions processes that prioritize factors like legacy status or extracurricular activities can further advantage students from affluent families.[25]

On top of testing expectations, the rising cost of college tuition and the reliance on student loans to finance higher education can further socioeconomic inequality. Students from low-income families may be deterred from attending college due to financial barriers, or may graduate with significant student loan debt, limiting their economic mobility and perpetuating cycles of poverty.[26] Wealthier students, on the other hand, have greater access to resources and financial support to afford higher education.

Systemic racism and discrimination can also contribute to inequality within the education system. Students from marginalized groups may face barriers such as discrimination, unequal treatment, and lack of representation in curriculum and teaching staff, which can negatively affect their academic performance and opportunities for advancement.[27] Tracking, or the practice of grouping students based on perceived academic ability, can perpetuate inequality by disproportionately placing students from disadvantaged communities into lower tracks with fewer opportunities for academic enrichment and advancement.[28] Similarly, racial and socioeconomic segregation within schools and school districts can limit access to resources and opportunities for students from disadvantaged communities.[29]

Also, something even more concerning, is that according to Georgetown University, "At the highest education level, Black/African American and Hispanic/Latino American individuals earn close to a million dollars less than their White and Asian/Asian American counterparts over a lifetime." [30] In other words, even if a student somehow makes it through all the systemic barriers, our systemic disparities still fail millions of people a year in the most disheartening ways. Addressing these systemic inequalities requires comprehensive reforms aimed at increasing access to quality education, reducing economic barriers to higher education, reforming admissions processes, addressing racial and ethnic disparities, and promoting inclusive and diverse learning environments. Yet, with the end of affirmative action, and the skyrocketing cost to attend college, is college still our best option?

Is College Still Worth it?

In the 1940s, more than half of Americans didn't graduate high school—and only about 5 percent had a bachelor's degree.[31] In 2021, approximately 37.7 percent of US residents aged 25 and older had completed college or attained a higher education qualification.[32] These stats matter, because more people are going to college than ever before, yet fewer people can afford basic living costs, which is a vast difference from our parents. In terms of annual wage growth rates, the top one percent experienced a significant increase of 465.1 percent since 1979, whereas wages for the bottom 90 percent grew by a modest 15 percent.[33] But the cost to go to college has increased by 135 percent.[34] Figure 5 is created using data from the Economic Policy Institute using Social Security Administration wage statistics, which emphasizes this shameful gap between the top one percent and the rest of us:

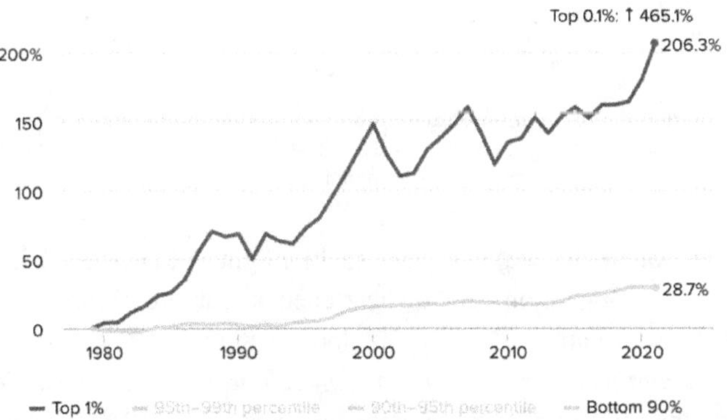

Figure 5. Comparison of bottom 90 percent with top 1 percent Wages 1980 to 2021
Source: EPI analysis of Kopczuk, Saez, and Song, "Uncovering the American Dream: Inequality and Mobility in Social Security Earnings Data Since 1937" (2007) and Social Security Administration wage statistics.

In other words, the rich can afford college, and continue to get richer, while the rest of us must struggle with the cost of college, the cost of living, and the burden of student loans—should we choose college. As you can see in Figure 6, the cost of living in the US, on average, has become an impossible target to meet, compared to our parents and grandparents. The federal minimum wage has not increased since 2010:

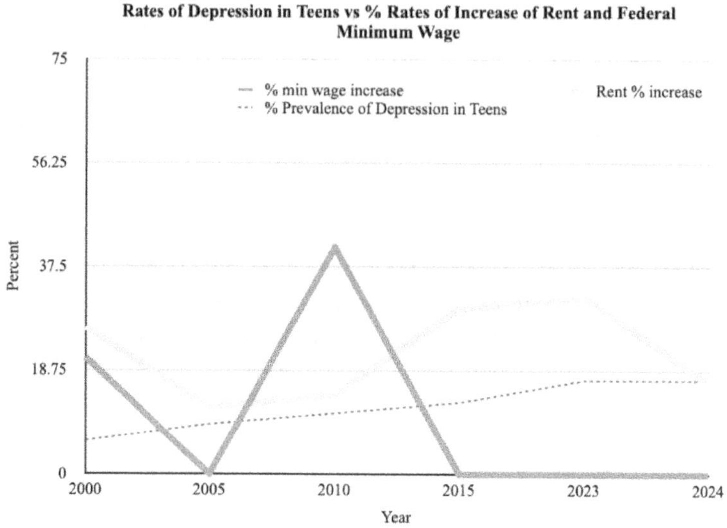

Rates of Depression in Teens vs % Rates of Increase of Rent and Federal Minimum Wage

Figure 6: Comparison of % increase in rent cost versus % increase in federal minimum wage from 2000 to 2024 using Statistica Data in comparison to prevalence of depression in teens using Gallup data

Through this data, I want to highlight a key idea that many people in my generation feel disheartened about our future potential, compared to our parents. Many of us look at the sticker price of college and think *I can just work in fast food for $20 an hour versus making the same amount, or less, working for the many entry-level jobs that require degrees.* Many 18-year-olds have no idea what they want their futures to look like, yet we expect them to make an enormous investment into their futures knowing around 30 percent of students drop out and end up losing even more as a consequence.[35]

With rising tuition costs, many students have had to rely more heavily on student loans to finance their education. As a result, student loan debt has ballooned, creating a significant financial burden for many graduates that can take years or even decades to repay. Given all the information above, it is clear that going to college is not what it used to be. But the question is, is it worth it? Well, despite the cost of attending college, many experts still argue it is worth it. The US Bureau of Labor Statistics reports that in 2022, bachelor's degree holders took home 68 percent more earnings than those who only hold a high school diploma.[36]

Based on findings from the Institute for Higher Education Policy, approximately 83 percent of institutions, catering to around 93 percent of undergraduate students, yield a return on investment within a decade.[37] This indicates that within the span of ten years, students regain the combined value of their high school diploma earnings alongside the expenses incurred in obtaining their college degree. Obtaining a Bachelor of Arts (BA) or Bachelor of Science (BS) degree translates to a 25 percent increase in wages within the first-year post-graduation.[38] Even in roles that do not explicitly demand a BA, individuals possessing a degree witness a 15 percent wage increase compared to their counterparts without one.[39]

I argue, too, that the benefits of college extend far beyond financial gain. College fosters an environment conducive to personal and professional development, nurturing critical thinking, problem-solving abilities, and intellectual curiosity. Additionally, the social and networking opportunities inherent in the college experience are invaluable assets for future career advancement. Through alumni networks, internships, and mentorship programs, students can forge connections that can prove instrumental in securing employment opportunities and fostering professional growth. The transformative potential of higher education extends beyond the individual, serving as a catalyst for social mobility and socioeconomic advancement. In essence, going to college can break the barriers of socioeconomic inequality, acting as a vehicle for upward mobility, but that does not excuse the cost, the perpetuation of disparities, and all the people strapped with loans.

What About Competition for Jobs?

There are way too many Starbucks baristas with college degrees, and yet, over and over, we are repetitively told college is the best option. Yet, there is a real risk of not finding a job (at least not related to the degree) post-grad. And most people who have not lived it, do not understand the stress, mental crisis, and the isolating feeling one has post-graduation. In fact, data from the Federal Reserve Bank found that 41 percent of recent college grads are underemployed, and 51 percent of grads regret the area of study they got their degree in.[40] Of course, over time things change, but the job market today is not just different, but light-years more complicated than what our parents experienced.[41]

While a college degree was once a ticket to a well-paying job, there is now increased competition for skilled positions, and the value of some degrees has diminished in certain fields. This means that the return on investment for a college education may not be as high as it once was. In the past, a college degree was often seen as the only path to a successful career. Yet, those of our parents who went to college did not struggle the way we do today, and it is time for this to be recognized. In the following section, I explain how Gen Z has been dealt a bad job market, with employers who are biased against us.

Apparently, according to the older generations who are conducting most job interviews, Gen Z lacks "professionalism."[42] A recent study reveals that many recent college graduates are struggling in job interviews, leading employers to favor older candidates. The study, conducted in December 2023 by *Intelligent*, surveyed 800 US managers, directors, and executives involved in hiring.[43] It found that Gen Z candidates often lack professional cues (such as eye contact) and exhibit behaviors like asking for unreasonable salaries or dressing inappropriately. Employers also reported issues with Gen Z candidates' ability to manage workloads, meet deadlines, and handle feedback. This seems interesting though, given they are only in the candidate stage. How are we supposed to prove we are capable if never given the chance?

Some Gen Zers have had virtual interview challenges, including candidates refusing to turn on their cameras,[44] but maybe it is because quite a few of us are exceedingly frustrated due to sending in hundreds of applications with little response. We have also been traumatized by the pandemic and are struggling with a mental health crisis. Despite these findings, experts like Joe Mull, author of *Employalty: How to Ignite Commitment and Keep Top Talent in the New Age of Work*, urge employers to consider the value and unique perspectives that Gen Z candidates bring to the workforce. Mull emphasizes the need for mentorship and tailored training programs to bridge the skills gap and support younger workers in their transition to adulthood and professional life. Indeed, the thousands of recent graduates who are struggling are not alone. We are apparently being discriminated against—on purpose.

Our governmental leaders love to talk about all the jobs they've created and how great the job market is. This is incredibly misleading. Despite the seemingly ideal market conditions for the class of 2022, one experiment revealed frustrating obstacles encountered by recent grads in their job searches. Companies ghost applicants, rescind offers, and post misleading job descriptions, leaving many disheartened. Business.com, the company that performed the experiment, joined departing interns to document their job-hunting processes, discovering that nearly 90 percent of 300+ online applications received no response, with only 5 percent generating interest and a mere 2 percent resulting in interviews, none leading to offers.[45]

While the experiment was small, and needs more research, this small investigation exposes the grueling and often futile nature of today's job pursuit for new graduates. They encounter overwhelming application volumes, AI screening pitfalls, limited professional networks, and misleading job listings. Despite the discouraging findings, experts recommend standing out, leveraging personal brands, and networking strategically to navigate this tough market with perseverance and patience.[46] It is a bit funny that we are told to persevere when we are struggling with the actual conundrum of unemployment, the brink of homelessness (or literal homelessness), or even worse: having to live with our parents again (if they let us…but not everyone has a safety net to lean on).

To push my argument further, in September 2022, the Bureau of Labor Statistics reported a record-high of 9.6 million available jobs, but in October of that year, non-farm payroll data showed a meager increase of only 150,000 jobs, leaving many puzzled by the disparity.[47,48] This disconnect reinforces the frustration felt by job seekers in 2024, evident on platforms like LinkedIn, where many young people have been flooded with rejection emails and recruiter silence. Clarify Capital's survey of 1,000 hiring managers revealed that 50 percent of them create job openings as placeholders, not intending to hire immediately, which contributes to the challenge of distinguishing genuine job postings from placeholders.[49] Reasons for posting "fake" jobs vary, from creating an illusion of company growth to appeasing overworked staff or waiting for an ideal candidate to emerge. Ultimately, these practices inflate job market numbers and prolong job searches, exacerbating job seekers' frustrations. This checks out though. It's no wonder it seems like we can send out thousands of applications to get one interview—because many of the jobs aren't real!

We also cannot talk about the changing job market without talking about AI. In May 2023, 3,900 US job losses were linked directly to AI.[50] And, 14 percent of workers claim to have lost a job to 'robots."[51] Advances in AI have led to the automation of many tasks that were previously performed by people.[52] This includes routine, repetitive tasks across various industries, such as data entry, basic customer service, and some aspects of manufacturing. As a result, jobs that once required specific degrees or qualifications may no longer exist or may require unique skill sets. And the truth is, as AI advances, there is no knowledge of what the future will bring.

College and Mental Health Outcomes

I remember the pressure I felt in high school to get into a good college. It was this pressure that made me push myself into doing a literal slew of extracurriculars that often left me feeling drained, beyond stressed, and hopeless. Sometimes, I thought, *What if I work this insanely hard and still do not get into a good college?* According to data from suicide.org, a distressing reality emerges: over 20 percent of high school girls have seriously contemplated suicide, with 11 percent of ninth grade girls attempting it and nearly 4 percent requiring medical intervention.[53] Teen suicide rates continue to be alarming, with one life taken every 100 minutes (making it the second leading cause of death among adolescents).[54]

The relentless pressure imposed on students to excel in the competitive college admissions arena is linked to mental health struggles. Many depressed and anxious students share a common narrative of feeling overwhelmed by unrealistically high expectations and fear of failure. Parents, viewing college admissions as a badge of successful parenting, often add to this pressure. Media portrayals further amplify the misconception that college prestige determines one's worth. Educational institutions inadvertently fuel this anxiety by demanding increasingly rigorous academic performances for admission consideration. The urgency to address this issue is clear.

A comprehensive review conducted in 2022 revealed a concerning array of mental health symptoms associated with academic pressure. These include anxiety, depression, and a decline in overall health and wellbeing.[55] Also, the study identified that it has detrimental effects on sleep quality, leading to the adoption of problematic coping mechanisms such as increased substance use. Notably, high levels of stress and burnout paradoxically result in diminished academic performance, alongside feelings of depersonalization and a reduced quality of life. The study also shed light on the prevalence of academic stressors among students, with a majority expressing concerns about poor grades and test-taking anxiety, even when adequately prepared. Below is a list of how academic pressure can affect adolescents and young adults:

- Feelings of nervousness or worry[56]
- Persistent feelings of sadness or hopelessness[57]
- Heightened reliance on substances[58]
- Social Isolation[59]
- Decline in physical and mental health[60]
- Difficulty sleeping[61]
- Intense stress and exhaustion, leading to diminished academic performance[62]
- Sense of detachment from oneself[63]
- Decreased overall wellbeing[64]
- Depression[65]
- Anxiety[66]

A Path Other Than College?

So, do we have other options? What do we do about this? With the rising costs and competitive nature of college admissions, it's crucial to explore viable alternatives. One significant option is the trades. Trades offer practical skills that are in high demand, often with shorter training periods and less financial burden compared to a four-year college degree. A recent study by Georgetown University's Center on Education and the Workforce revealed individuals without a bachelor's degree may surpass the earnings of those who hold one. The study examined data from 2017 to 2019 and discovered that, on average, 16 percent of high school graduates, 23 percent of workers with some college education, and 28 percent of associate degree holders earned more than half of all workers with a bachelor's degree.[67]

In fact, air traffic controllers, construction inspectors, respiratory therapists, and cardiovascular technicians all earn as much as or more than the median income of bachelor's degree holders.[68] Learning a trade can also be incredibly fulfilling, offering hands-on work that results in tangible outcomes instead of sitting at a desk all day. Basically, what I am saying is that trades are a great option, and if we continue to let Boomers and Gen X tell us otherwise, we might waste thousands upon thousands of dollars on a degree that might not even help us get a good job—or worse, paying off loans for a degree we did not finish or did not use. And as the demand for skilled tradespeople continues to grow, many current workers in these fields are nearing retirement—so even more of these jobs are opening up for us.

<u>Conclusion</u>

Even though the education system is failing in terms of increased cost and disparities, the potential opportunities plus financial mobility still make college a worthwhile decision (despite the cost) for many. However, the benefit is not nearly the same as what was granted to our parents. The issue with our system is how it has become a money-making enterprise, putting profit over the American Dream. My generation was dealt a stressful, expensive, nearly impossible living standard with less opportunity, yet going to college is still somehow the best option. People who make it to college still find better opportunities, higher pay, bigger networks, and overall better outcomes, but that discounts all the people who must drop out, or who could not or chose not to go. The issue is, as our system stands, inequality continues to be perpetuated and our wealthiest folks continue to reap the benefits. By making college absurdly expensive and putting undue pressure on our teens to get into good colleges, we are adding to an already difficult array of factors contributing to mental health. And, to add fuel to the fire, those of us who do go to college are entering an unexpectedly competitive, anti-Gen Z job market. So, essentially, we are living in a catch-22. Going to college is our best option…and yet the stress and our futures outside of college continue to be complicated, stressful, and impactful on our mental health. Nonetheless, we have other options such as associate degrees and trades, which can offer a fair alternative. Still, why should we continue to support a system that perpetuates mental illness in such a significant way?

Chapter 18: The Cult of Guns in America

(Gen Z has always known school shootings)

The right to bear arms ... does not and never will overpower the individual's right to life, liberty and the pursuit of happiness. We cannot protect our guns before we protect our children
—Delaney Tarr, Parkland school shooting survivor

When I reflect on the Second Amendment, I think of a time when people were quite literally engaged in warfare. At the time the Second Amendment was written, there was a citizen's militia.[1] Now we have a national military. It is frustrating that many Americans vehemently defend this right, often completely overlooking the consequences—namely, that thousands of innocent young lives are lost to gun violence. In fact, each day in America, 12 children die from gun-related incidents, and another 32 are injured.[2] Crazy idea but, maybe we should consider the relative rights of our children going to school without the fear of being shot?

My generation's experience has differed markedly from those before us. While our parents participated in earthquake drills by climbing under their desks, we practiced hiding under desks in dark classrooms to prepare for the possibility of a gunman entering the school. Essentially, we were taught that we were powerless against the Second Amendment, trained to respond to violence with silence and fear. In 1999, two years after the first Gen Zers were born, the Columbine shooting heralded a new era. Prior to that, school shootings were virtually unheard of. Since then, an eruption of violence has resulted in more than 370,000 students in the US experiencing gun violence at school.[3,4] You know what the craziest part about all of this is? <u>A majority of the shooters themselves are Gen Z.</u>[5,6]

Before you think it, I realize that the automatic weapons that many of these shooters use are not protected under the Second

Amendment specifically. But the loose regulations that are highly supported by the National Rifle Association (NRA) have led to many people having the ability to access these weapons with little difficulty. The connection to the mental health crisis affecting Generation Z is clear. In the next section, I will delve into how deeply gun violence has afflicted our country, explain the profound impact of exposing children to constant threats to their safety, and discuss why the perpetrators epitomize our system's failures.

<u>Guns and Mental Health—A Bad Combination</u>

The first thing to discuss is why gun violence is important to our mental health story. According to the CDC, more Americans died from gun-related injuries in 2021 than in any previous year on record, including unprecedented numbers of both homicides and suicides involving firearms.[7] Media reports on mass shootings often lead people to believe that mental illness usually results in violence. However, studies show that most people with serious mental health issues are not violent—and actually tend to be victims, rather than perpetrators.[8] What's more, even though they don't get as much media coverage as gun-related murders, most gun deaths in the US are actually suicides. In 2021, more than half of all gun deaths (54 percent) were suicides, according to the CDC.[9] Murders made up 43 percent, with a total of 20,958 cases.[10] The rest included accidental shootings, incidents involving police, and deaths where the details weren't clear. Essentially, many of the deaths related to guns are suicide and homicide.

The profound mental health impact of school shootings on students extends beyond the immediate threat to safety, influencing educational achievements, and future economic prospects—all of which are intersectional with mental health (remember. systems thinking). Data shows that by their mid-twenties, students who have experienced school shootings earn significantly less than their peers, with an average annual earnings reduction of 13.5 percent.[11] This translates into an estimated $115,550 decrease in lifetime earnings per affected student. [12] Considering the frequency of such events, with about 50,000 children exposed to school shootings annually, the aggregate economic cost is staggering—approximately $5.8 billion per year in lost earnings. [13] Furthermore, beyond the impact on our economy, students' educational outcomes suffer dramatically in the wake of school violence.[14] Data from

Texas public schools reveal that student absenteeism surged by 27.8 percent and the likelihood of needing to repeat a grade more than doubled following a school shooting.[15] These disruptions contribute to a decrease in high school graduation rates and lower college attendance and completion rates among students exposed to gun violence at their schools.[16]

But what is the relationship between guns and mental illness? One study compared antidepressant prescriptions in areas close to and farther from schools that experienced shootings, finding a 21.3 percent increase in prescriptions near affected schools in the years following these tragic events.[17] In Jefferson County, Colorado, the same place where the Columbine shooting happened, there was an increase in deaths, including suicides and accidents, among teens aged 14 to 18.[18] Additionally, the extensive media coverage that follows a school shooting can significantly heighten anxiety among American students. This heightened state can make any exposure to gunfire in a school—whether intentional or accidental—especially traumatic, potentially triggering overwhelming fear.[19] A study published in the *Journal of Social Science and Medicine* concluded that indirect exposure to gun violence is common, particularly among marginalized communities, and is linked to more mental health issues.[20] This suggests that healthcare providers should pay close attention to the mental health of individuals indirectly affected by gun violence. Additionally, efforts to reduce gun violence are imperative, because they could improve mental health across communities.[21] Knowing this, why do we continue to allow guns to be widely distributed?

Are Guns Still Popular or Do We Have Minority Rule?

Gun ownership in the US is based on the Second Amendment of the Constitution, which basically says that because a well-regulated militia is necessary to keep the country safe, people have the right to own and carry guns and not have the right taken away.[22] Even though the US has less than five percent of the world's population, it holds about 46 percent of all civilian-owned guns globally.[23] The US also leads in the number of guns owned per person and has the highest rate of gun-related homicides among the world's most developed countries.[24] However, many people who support gun rights argue that these numbers don't necessarily mean that more guns cause more crime, or more suicides[25]…but the data indicate that they do. In fact, more guns are tied with more crime, and unlike the popular statement "if everyone had guns, we would stop more crimes," data shows quite the opposite.[26] The question is, how did America become land of the "we demand our right to guns?"

The NRA, initially founded in 1871 as a recreational organization promoting rifle shooting, has evolved into one of the most formidable political forces in the US.[27] It actively opposes gun control legislation and champions the view that more guns enhance national safety, grounding its stance in its interpretation of the Second Amendment. Despite several legal troubles, the NRA claimed a membership spike to nearly five million following the 2012 Sandy Hook school shooting.[28] The NRA has been a controversial figure for its staunch opposition to gun control, even in the face of numerous high-profile mass shootings. It has famously resisted calls for tighter regulations, instead advocating for increased security measures like arming school staff, a stance backed by former President Donald Trump in 2018.[29] This approach was evident when, days after the tragic Uvalde school shooting in Texas in 2022, the NRA proceeded with its planned meeting in nearby Houston, despite public outcry.[30] So, why does the NRA have so much influence in America?

Do most citizens want gun control? Polls indicate that many Americans do want at least some form of gun control—even gun owners.[31] However, it seems we the people do not have much power in influencing such regulations. The NRA wields arguably the most influence regarding gun legislation and engages in several key activities to shape policy. It heavily lobbies lawmakers at both the federal and state levels to support gun-friendly legislation and to resist restrictive measures. Additionally, the NRA makes substantial political contributions, predominantly backing candidates who oppose gun control, thereby ensuring the continuation of their favored policies.[32] In 2022 alone, it received $97 million from membership dues, although this marked a 40 percent decrease from its 2018 peak.[33] The NRA spent $4.2 million on lobbying in 2021 and has directed over $140 million to pro-gun election candidates since 2010.[34] Its power is also demonstrated by its grading system for Congress members on their gun rights stance, influencing elections significantly. The NRA grading system evaluates Congress members based on their voting records, public statements, and responses to NRA questionnaires regarding gun rights.[35] These grades serve as a signal to NRA members and pro-gun voters which politicians align with their views on gun control.

Publicly, the NRA conducts extensive media campaigns and organizes events to mold public opinion in favor of gun rights and influence public discourse.[36] Legally, it often engages in litigation to oppose laws perceived as infringing on gun ownership rights. However, the NRA's methods and the extent of its influence have generated concern about corruption. Critics argue that the NRA's activities obstruct the passage of gun control laws that have broad public support—like better background checks and bans on assault weapons. [37] Financial controversies have fueled a broader debate about the impact of money and lobbying on American politics, leading to calls for reforms to curtail the power of influential groups like the NRA.[38] Despite this, the NRA maintains that it is safeguarding constitutional rights, highlighting the deep divisions in American views on gun control.

Okay, But Why Does Gun Control/Reform Matter?

If our leaders do not address and legislate guns, the human rights of parents to keep their children away from guns and gun violence remain unprotected. Gun violence jeopardizes our rights to health, education, and life. Only through effective gun regulation and violence prevention programs can we put an end to this epidemic. Half of our country wants stricter gun laws,[39] yet the ability for people to buy a firearm remains relatively easy across the nation. I believe that although the NRA has too much influence, our education system also fails to properly educate citizens about the dangers of firearms; many members of the public continue to believe that having a gun in the home is safer than without,[40] yet the data shows the opposite.[41] Gun ownership has increased by over 177 percent since 1997, the year I was born, and about 70 percent of gunowners cite "for protection" as their reasoning.[42] The gun lobby, by promoting a misleading narrative to the American public and crucial voter groups, has effectively obstructed common sense legislation. At the same time, it continues to produce a steady flow of propaganda aimed at boosting gun ownership in the US through fear.

Between 2012 and 2020, states with the least amount of gun laws saw a 46 percent increase in gun deaths, while states with the most robust gun laws experienced only a 7 percent rise during the same timeframe.[43] Furthermore, individuals residing in homes with guns are twice as likely to be victims of homicide and three times more likely to commit suicide compared to those in gun-free homes.[44] Handgun owners are seven times more likely to be shot by their spouse or intimate partner than those residing in a household without guns.[45] And, as I assert above, gun violence directly impacts mental health and wellness and is correlated with a host of poor outcomes. The key point: gun ownership (or "good guys with guns") does not increase our nation's safety. Instead, this false narrative has led to a country that is unduly influenced by the gun lobby and suffers the consequences.

In Summary

It's clear that our relationship with firearms is not just a matter of constitutional rights, but a deep-seated cultural crisis that threatens the mental health of students. Generation Z has never known life without the threat of being shot while at school. We continue to cling to a past that no longer exists, at the expense of thousands of innocent lives each year.[46] The distressing daily toll of gun violence on children and the alarming normalization of school lockdown drills starkly contrast with the ostensibly protective intentions of gun ownership. As we move forward, it's crucial to question narratives propagated by entities like the NRA, which obscure the real cost of gun ownership under the guise of security and freedom. These narratives not only exacerbate the public health crisis of gun violence but also impede meaningful reforms that could mitigate these harms. The cost of inaction is too great, measured in the lives and mental health of our youngest and most vulnerable.

Chapter 19: The Problem with Individualism

Alone, we can do so little; together, we can do so much.
– Helen Keller

I remember from a young age having conversations with my mom about how people my age seem lazy, selfish, flaky, and self-important. I'd say things like "I swear it's like we need classes now or something on how to make and keep friends." And over the last few years, I wondered if this was a trend, and if other people noticed that people in my generation are more selfish than other generations.

Our society loves to praise individualism—to the point that we idolize people like Elon Musk and Bill Gates. There is a meta-narrative that success is built on selfishness, hard work, and the power of the individual. Yet, Musk did not get here alone at all—he benefited from our system and the work of others.[1] And Gates did not make it on his own either—having the help of his family wealth and business savvy mother, among other boosts.[2] Still, we glorify the idea that people like Gates or Musk made it on their own, or that they're "novel thinkers." The notion of individualism is deeply ingrained in our culture. We're often told to pull ourselves up by our bootstraps and listen to claims that America is the best country because of individual freedom. This mindset, while present in other cultures, is particularly intense in the US.

There is a strong connection between where someone is born and their future income, leading researchers to create maps like the Opportunity Atlas.[3] The expected income for people born from wealthy families is significantly higher than for those from poor families.[4] Individualism overlooks these connections, focusing on hard work and personal qualities instead of birth circumstances as the largest predictor of success. In Florence, Italy, wealth has remained within the same families for over 600 years,[5] defying the notion that individual hard work determines success. Despite this, individualists blame individuals, not structures, for suffering. Individualism fragments communities, pits workers against each other, and weakens solidarity.

COVID-19 epitomized how dangerous our individualistic country is. Collectivistic countries, like Germany, managed to collectively address the pandemic as a community, eradicating the spread more quickly than individualist countries. [6] Meanwhile, Americans complained about social distancing, got into fights on planes about wearing masks, and even blatantly went against guidelines to "stick it" to the government.[7] In other words, as a nation, we acted selfishly. Unlike other collectivistic countries, like India or Japan, Americans, along with other individualist countries like Australia or the UK, have an affinity towards believing in individual value versus the greater good for the group. This difference has made me wonder for quite some time about what type of impact this has on our mental health. One question I googled was, "does Gen Z have more narcissists?" And sure enough, articles lined my screen answering my question: possibly yes. So, if people in my generation have been found to have more narcissistic traits, what does this mean? Why did we become like this? How does it affect our mental health? The following section outlines the impact of one of the key root causes of our mental health crisis: individualism.

What is Individualism in Terms of Our Culture?

Scholars have debated the concept of individualism for about 250 years, but the concept of individualism was popularized through Geert Hofstede's survey of American culture in 1980. [8] Hofstede conducted a global study of 116,000 employees and found that the most independent people came from the US, Australia, Great Britain, Canada, and the Netherlands.[9] Conversely, the most interdependent people came from Venezuela, Colombia, Pakistan, Peru, and Taiwan. Hofstede's work asserts that individualism emphasizes rights over duties, a focus on oneself and immediate family, personal autonomy, self-fulfillment, and identity based on personal accomplishments. Other sociologists have expanded on this, such as Schwartz, who described individualistic societies as contractual, with small social networks and specialized social relations centered on achievement.[10] In essence, individualism is the idea that people are valuable as individuals, and that worth is within personal gains—self-reliance over the collective.

Social scientists place individualism opposite to a concept called collectivism. Individualism values the self over the group, while collectivism emphasizes group cohesion and prioritizes the group over the self. Individualistic societies see social ties as transient and goal-oriented, while collectivist societies are structured around lasting in-groups and strong social bonds.[11] In individualistic cultures, the word "I" is encouraged, while in collectivist cultures, it is avoided.[12] Individualists have independent selves, while collectivists have interdependent selves. The two cultural orientations also differ in traits like extraversion, emotional expression, and occupational mobility.[13] Individualist cultures value personal success and self-esteem. Maintaining a positive sense of self is a basic endeavor, and relationships are often seen as means to attain goals but costly to maintain. And in this model, people often leave relationships when costs outweigh benefits. [14] In other words, individualistic societies are arguably more selfish.

Individualism and Mental Health

The reason I bring up individualism in a book about mental health is because they are related. There are both advantages and disadvantages of individualism. Some advantages include more acceptance of diversity, and creative thinking, which in turn influences change-making. However, the disadvantages are important to consider. For one thing, it decreases empathy. Sara Konrath, from the Research Center for Group Dynamics at the University of Michigan, asserts that,

> "Cultures that tend to be more collectivistic also tend to have higher empathy scores. Collectivism involves seeing oneself as being part of a larger, interconnected group of familial and other close relationships, with a priority on fitting in with others and maintaining harmony. So, it's not surprising that empathy would be higher in such cultures."[15]

This means individualistic countries might have less empathy. As you can imagine, this is alarming, as empathy is one of the most crucial elements in ending disparities. The rise of individualism in Western societies is believed to contribute to the challenging cultural environment faced by Gen Z.[16] When people are primarily focused on their own needs, they tend to have smaller and less satisfying social support networks, struggle to manage their emotions and those of others, are less inclined to seek help for personal issues, and experience higher levels of suicidal thoughts. [17] In fact, individualism is often linked with lower life satisfaction, increased depressive symptoms, and suicidal thoughts among young people.[18] On the other hand, collectivism, when coupled with strong social support, can be a protective factor.[19] Two studies on American undergraduates found that wellbeing was negatively associated with individualism, and positively correlated with collectivism, while also showing personal as well as collective self-esteem to be a mediator in these relationships.[20] So, good self-esteem and feeling valued within a group are important for overall happiness. Beyond individualism being suicidogenic, it is also tied to loneliness. In Chapter 13, I explained how harmful isolation is for mental health.

Our generation stands out due to the significant influence of technology and social media. While each generation is unique, Gen Z's trends and values can seem perplexing to older generations, who often criticize our perceived self-infatuation.[21] We grew up with many media platforms like Instagram, Snapchat, Vine, Tumblr, Twitter, and Facebook. These platforms encourage self-promotion, leading us to invest more in our online personas than in our real lives. This constant self-evaluation fosters narcissistic traits. Recognizing this impact can help us understand why older generations see us as egotistical. While individualism isn't inherently bad, our extreme self-focus is unhealthy. Research by Tasha Eurich shows only 12 to 15 percent of Americans have good self-awareness.[22] Instead of reflecting on relationships and experiences, we perfect our social media profiles, becoming infatuated with our online selves.[23] This is to say, social media is not the cause, yet the means to which toxic individualism is exploited and dispersed.

Self-Help, Self-Love, & Self-Care

On top of social media influencing traits within our generation we have another topic to consider: "self-love." Promoted by politicians and pop stars alike, self-love is a hot topic. New York Rep., Alexandria Ocasio-Cortez, in a Vogue makeup tutorial, calls it "the foundation of everything." Nicole LaPera, the psychologist behind Instagram's @theholisticpsychologist, tells her 6.4 million followers that "self-love is our natural state."[24] In her hit song "Flowers," Miley Cyrus sings, "I can love me better than you can." Self-love has become central to modern wellness culture, promising good health and freedom. Sharon Kaiser's book, *The Self-Love Experiment*, claims that self-love is key to achieving weight loss, career goals, finding a soulmate, and getting out of debt.[25] But is self-love really what it's cracked up to be?

In today's world of extreme individualism, self-love has become a survival tool. However, it often comes at a price, especially when shaped by corporate ads and social media. This version of self-love isn't genuine; it's more like self-sabotage, making us focus too much on ourselves and harming our connections with others. Dan Siegel, a psychiatry professor at UCLA, calls our intense isolation a result of our "culture of separation."[26] In his book, *Intraconnected*, Siegel explains that our society values separation over connection, independence over interdependence, and individuality over shared identity.[27] This focus on autonomy has led to widespread disconnection. Social media illustrates this, as women are bombarded with ads for Botox, Pilates machines, skincare wands, and hair growth serums under the guise of self-love and self-care.[28] These products promote self-obsession, negative social comparison, and insecurity rather than bringing people together.

Besides self-love, we have an epidemic of "self-help," which is another way in which individualism has crept up to negatively impact mental health. According to a therapist, Mark Travers, many people go to therapy frustrated that self-help content isn't helping them. They often ask: "I read so many self-help books, but I feel inferior because others don't seem to need them as much. What's wrong with me?"[29] The self-help industry is a multi-billion-dollar market.[30] While seeking self-improvement is fine, self-help isn't a cure-all and can sometimes do more harm than good.

How does self-love and self-obsession over social media affect our mental health? When self-love turns into self-absorption and materialism, it can harm our collective mental health. Studies show that excessive self-focus is linked to anxiety and depression.[31] Research also highlights a cycle of consumption and loneliness: buying material possessions in the name of self-love can make us feel lonely, leading us to buy more to feel better, but this only worsens our loneliness.[32] This loneliness cycle affects our health. As we discovered in Chapter 13, loneliness is connected to increased inflammation, heart disease, and even premature death.[33,34] Also, in terms of self-help, a study found that those who read self-help books had higher cortisol levels (the stress hormone) and were more likely to experience depressive symptoms compared to those who didn't.[35] Then again, seeking self-help programs and content is more of a symptom of a greater issue. In fact, it can be really harmful, especially for teens.

A study involving 2,150 adolescents from six schools explored the impact of extreme self-reliance regarding mental health and help-seeking behaviors.[36] The research found that adolescents who believed they should always solve their problems on their own were less likely to seek help, and this attitude was linked to depressive symptoms and suicidal ideation. For those identified as at-risk, extreme self-reliance at the initial screening predicted higher levels of suicidal ideation and depressive symptoms two years later, even after accounting for baseline symptoms. These findings suggest that promoting extreme self-reliance in adolescents can be harmful, as it reduces their likelihood of seeking appropriate help and exacerbates mental health issues. To improve mental health, we should not encourage people to believe that their health and happiness are solely based on being self-reliant.

Conclusion

Our intense focus on individualism fragments communities, pits people against each other, and weakens solidarity. COVID-19 starkly highlighted the dangers of this mindset, as collectivistic countries managed the pandemic more effectively through community cooperation, while individualistic nations like the US struggled with widespread resistance to public health measures. There is a broader cultural issue: Americans prioritize individual value over group mentality, leading to a society where narcissistic traits are more prevalent, particularly among Gen Z. The fact that research shows that individualism is directly linked to mental health challenges showcases how this societal trait is important to consider in the landscape of our mental health crisis. While it can foster acceptance of diversity and creative thinking, it also decreases empathy and increases feelings of isolation and loneliness. Empathy is essential for addressing disparities, yet individualistic societies exhibit lower empathy scores, which affects social support networks and increases depressive symptoms and suicidal thoughts. The rise of self-love and self-help movements, heavily promoted by social media and corporate interests, further complicates the issue. These trends often lead to self-absorption and materialism, fostering anxiety, depression, and a harmful cycle of consumption and loneliness. While self-improvement is valuable, extreme self-reliance can be detrimental, especially for adolescents who are less likely to seek help and more prone to severe mental health issues.

So, essentially, if we keep valuing ourselves over the collective, we are perpetuating behaviors that harm our mental health. Admittedly, I am not sure Americans can get behind a more collective community, given that public levels of trust have starkly declined since our parents ' generation,[37] and that there is a strong polarization of political parties. However, if we continue to isolate and value "self-love" over "group-love," we miss key factors towards better living. In other words, individualism will remain a root cause of the rise in mental illness because it fosters disconnection, undermines empathy, and perpetuates a cycle of loneliness and self-absorption. To improve our collective mental health, we must challenge this cultural norm and strive to rebuild a sense of community and mutual support.

Part 3

How Do We Change It?

Chapter 20: The Path Towards Systemic Change

Coming together is a beginning; keeping together is progress; working together is success.
—Edward Everett Hale

In considering how to solve our mental health crisis, many efforts have been proposed and enacted. These include concepts like coordinated care, adding more providers, and making services more accessible. But I will be honest: to me, these are <u>not</u> solutions. They are mechanisms of <u>allowing the problem to continue</u>—but with more help. The issue with current ideas and innovations is they fail to address *root causes*. To me, if we want to see genuine change in this crisis, prevention needs to be put at the center of the solution. As I've argued throughout this book, this systemic crisis is multifaceted.

One of my favorite theories is Maslow's hierarchy of needs. Within this theory, we need to reach all five levels to be self-actualized. At the bottom most basic level, "psychological needs," Maslow argues we need to have our fundamental survival objectives met, which includes, clean air, healthy food, shelter, clean water, and proper sleep. But to have mental health, we need to reach our biopsychosocial needs, which include community, safety, and purpose. And if we want to have self-esteem, we need respect, recognition, and freedom. To be fully self-actualized, we must have the desire to become the best version of ourselves. If we break this down into what our world looks like, most of us do not have all these basic needs met—maybe not even half. For example, half of all Americans cannot even afford a one-bedroom rental.[1] Therefore, it makes sense why so many of us in Gen Z are having mental illness, and a hard time affording treatment.

How are we supposed to be mentally well when basic needs like food, shelter, and utilities are incredibly stressful due to their lack of affordability for many of us? How can we feel good when we are surrounded by toxins and fear of the impending climate crisis? How do we feel happy when so many of us are lonely and disconnected? Why are Boomers blaming Gen Z for our struggles instead of helping us address the root causes? In the following I will make a case for how we can innovate the mental health crisis through a proposed Basic Income system, massive community initiatives to address our loneliness epidemic, making creativity accessible, changing societal expectations about college through a national service program, and lastly, holding our government accountable for its corruption and reducing political polarization.

Making Mental Health A Public Service

A while ago, while sitting in the waiting room to visit my therapist, I overheard the receptionist tell someone over the phone, "we have a sliding scale of $120 to $160, so we can save you about $40 which is great!" I shook my head silently thinking I don't know how anyone affords that (and felt grateful for my insurance). I commented about overhearing this to my therapist, and she said, "you know I am a therapist, and I can't even afford therapy."

To me, the cost of therapy is prohibitive and short sighted.[2] When conducting research for this book I consistently wondered if it would be possible to make therapy and psychiatry free for everyone in need—since lack of access and lack of affordability are two of the biggest failings of our system. I discovered there is a debate online: some people love the idea, and others argue it could be problematic. I've decided to "enter the chat," and make the argument that this objective is not only possible, but essential: we need to make mental health a public service. There is an obvious way this can be achieved: universal basic healthcare (UBHC).

If you ask most people what their experience is like finding mental healthcare, they may respond with "I had to wait weeks to get a doctor referral to see a psychiatrist, and then months to book with a psychiatrist that is covered under insurance, and then another few days or weeks for a therapist referral, and then waiting weeks or months to book with a therapist who takes insurance."

It might be easy to get mad at providers for not accepting insurance, but I urge you not to. The insurance system is inherently flawed. According to Dr. Manoj Kanagaraj, co-founder of GrowTherapy, providers find it hard to work within insurance systems because the process of getting credentialed and contracted with insurance companies is lengthy and complex, often taking months. Additionally, managing the administrative tasks of submitting claims and dealing with multiple, outdated insurance portals can be overwhelming, especially for solo practitioners. These challenges are compounded by insurance companies' use of third-party entities to manage behavioral health plans, adding further administrative complexity and reducing reimbursement rates. Therefore, given all of the barriers impacting insured services, it makes sense why many providers opt to forgo accepting insurance.

Obamacare was one of the biggest steps our country has taken towards addressing healthcare coverage—yet it still failed to insure millions of people, and still required a private insurance scheme. A census bureau analysis found that there is possibly over 220 billion dollars in American medical debt.[3] That same analysis found that almost 1 in 12 people have medical debt. KFF, an independent research company states:

> "Despite over 90% of the United States population having some form of health insurance, medical debt remains a persistent problem. For people and families with limited assets, even a relatively small unexpected medical expense can be unaffordable."

Given the high levels of debt despite insuring millions of people through Obamacare, it is clear that operating out of a private insurance system is costing Americans our health.

I have a friend I spoke to recently on this topic, where she disclosed to me that after freeing herself from a toxic relationship, she started attending therapy thinking it was covered under her insurance. After a few months she discovered her insurance would not cover the sessions and she accrued over 10 thousand dollars in debt to her therapist's office. She jokingly said, "I need therapy because I went to therapy."

It is critical now more than ever that mental healthcare is reassessed and redefined as an essential need, not a privilege granted to the elite. In order for us to lower the rising rates of anxiety and depression, we need to provide care to everyone in need in an accessible way. Are free mental health services possible, and if so, is universal basic healthcare the answer?

How We Can Make Universal Basic Healthcare the Future of Mental Health Care

Countries across the world have managed to create UBHC, so why haven't we? According to Katherine Baicker and colleagues, "Implementing a publicly financed basic policy with automatic enrollment could facilitate a move toward universal coverage in a financially sustainable way that ensures access to care with substantial health benefits."[4] Other experts such as Liran Einav and Amy Finkelstein also assert UBHC is possible, emphasizing the need for automatic enrollment, and affirming that basic coverage must be free with package options to allow individuals to make upgrades.[5] Einav and Finkelstein also contend that the government can create a "fixed" budget that "would cap the amount that taxpayers spend on health care." I would take this a step further, and assert that within this public insurance system, we also create a public pharmaceutical system that sets a price cap for essential medications. Within this basic care model, thus, mental health services including therapy and psychiatry would be offered for free and automatically applies coverage to everyone who needs it. As part of this plan, we will also need to make mental health provider education and licensing part of the national service program that I describe in detail below, given the worker shortage. We should be incentivizing mental health care professionals by making their education free, and giving them living stipends during their schooling to ensure success.

The cool thing about other countries beating us to the UBHC "finish line" is that we now have a wealth of examples of where we can use certain practices from other successful models (such as Sweden or Denmark)[6] while eliminating the negative (Like England's long waiting times/staff shortages)[7]. In addition, we do not need to "reinvent the wheel." The way in which we can be confident in providing a UBHC model in America is that it is successful in other countries. Moreover, the sooner we implement this as a solution within healthcare, the sooner we can provide free therapy and psychiatric services to the many who need it. In doing this we also change the discourse on the fundamental right for mental wellbeing.

<u>A Third Option to Finance College: A National Service Program</u>

Pete Buttigieg, who gained notoriety during his run for president in 2020, proposed a comprehensive National Service Program aimed at fostering a sense of civic duty and unity among young Americans.[8] And his idea is revolutionary and would provide opportunities for people aged 18 to 24 to engage in a variety of service activities, ranging from traditional forms like military service to community-based initiatives focused on areas such as infrastructure, education, healthcare, and environmental conservation.[9] Participants would receive compensation for their service in the form of educational benefits, including college tuition help and vocational training opportunities, as well as stipends to support their living expenses.[10] The program aimed not only to address critical societal needs but also to promote personal growth and development among participants, instilling values of leadership, teamwork, and empathy.[11] Buttigieg emphasized the importance of making national service accessible to all, regardless of socioeconomic background, and proposed expanding existing service programs like AmeriCorps and the Peace Corps to accommodate a broader range of participants and service opportunities.[12] His idea could dramatically change millions of lives.

Buttigieg's National Service Program idea comes with several potential advantages and drawbacks. We can take what works and challenge/shift the rest. Some of the best parts of the program encourage youth entering the workforce to contribute to their communities and country. Arguably the most important part, however, is that the program would offer educational incentives, such as tuition help and vocational training opportunities, making higher education more accessible and affordable for participants.[13] It might help address critical societal needs by mobilizing a diverse workforce to tackle challenges in areas like infrastructure, education, healthcare, and environmental conservation.

All of that is great, but here's where the problems arise, which I describe and address below. Some critics argue that there may be concerns about equity and access, as those from marginalized or disadvantaged backgrounds may face barriers to participation because of factors such as socioeconomic status or geographic location. To resolve this, a national service program can and should be designed to leverage partnerships and to enhance outreach efforts. Likewise, if implemented, it is important that the program provides stipends to help ensure participants of all backgrounds can access it. Conversely, some take issue with implementing a large-scale national service program because it would require significant financial and logistical resources—raising questions about funding sources and sustainability. While this may be true, the cost of *not* implementing it is vital. The services provided would be an asset to our nation and provide value themselves.

Another issue people find with the program idea is that the effectiveness of national service programs in achieving their stated goals may vary. This would be mitigated through program evaluation, monitoring, and continuous improvement such that the programs are backed by outcomes-based efficacy data. Finally, some argue that expanding national service initiatives like AmeriCorps and the Peace Corps could potentially divert resources and attention away from other important social programs and initiatives.[14] While this is a legitimate concern, ultimately, a thoughtful national service program should enhance and complement existing programs and help to address unmet needs. It should only add to aid, not subtract from it. In understanding the benefits—like a future college education financed, important character building for youth, and added workforce for crisis management—we learn that though there are obstacles to such an idea, we could create a data-backed program with measurable outcomes.

When considering that 40 percent of students drop out of college, and many because they don't "know what they want to do," or "cannot afford" it, it seems evident that a solution is needed.[15] A National Service Program idea offers potential benefits in terms of civic engagement, skill development, and addressing social needs like discovering what one wants to choose for their career—and having a way to pay for the education to get there.

Therefore, I propose a practical solution. Imagine a program in which high school graduates could secure a two-year position where they can perform service for areas such as infrastructure development, environmental conservation, education support, health initiatives, disaster relief, social services, and cultural programs—contributing to community needs while gaining valuable skills. And imagine that, at the end of those two years of service, these kids would be able to afford college and have a stronger sense of their goals. This would arguably both fill a societal need while also fundamentally creating a cascading effect on mental health and future outcomes of the many afforded this opportunity.

So how do we implement a national service plan in the US? Our government would first need to establish a dedicated agency for oversight (after passing bipartisan legislation), implement monitoring mechanisms, and launch national awareness campaigns. It is integral that this program creates a network of partnerships with local organizations across the country to offer meaningful service opportunities and continuously evaluate and improve the program based on feedback and data. This program would need to establish stipends based on location and cost of living, and also design a funding stream that can pay for college tuitions. By having an option like this, the financial burden that my generation has experienced (especially in the form of student loans) could be largely mitigated through national service. It also gives young people the time to learn more about themselves intrapersonally, while also building important skills and making humanitarian contributions.

<u>Transformation Through Community</u>

We are living in a crisis of disconnection/loneliness, and if nothing is done, this trend will continue. While efforts to combat loneliness traditionally emphasize individual and group interventions, there is more to unpack because this tendency to "blame the individual" has been called to question by studies across the globe. Our built environment has a massive impact on our mental health and perceived loneliness.[16] But our cities have evolved over time to become car-centric, and in turn we have lost important areas that connect us and protect our mental health. These spaces play a crucial role in promoting social cohesion, supporting mental wellbeing, and enhancing the overall quality of life within communities. Recognizing the consequences of losing these important spaces is necessary.

The aftermath of the pandemic has left us with increased isolation and reliance on remote transactions that prioritize convenience over human connection—working at home has its benefits, but not seeing co-workers every day also has genuine drawbacks. Urban planning offers a potential solution to isolation through the enhancement of "social infrastructure," through spaces such as libraries, parks, and commercial districts. Residents in urban areas with abundant green spaces report lower levels of loneliness and higher social cohesion. This suggests that green spaces can facilitate and enhance social interactions within urban communities. [17] Conversely, neighborhoods perceived as having low walkability, safety, and community attachment are linked to higher levels of loneliness.[18] Taken together, these findings indicate that neighborhood designs that promote social contact, even in brief and informal encounters, play a crucial role in fostering social connections and reducing loneliness.

The Revival of Third Spaces and Walking Streets

In pre-industrial America, cities were pedestrian-friendly, but after WWII, car ownership led to urban sprawl and less walkable urban planning. [19] Government initiatives have supported efforts to improve walkability, but it now comes at a premium. Walkable neighborhoods foster social interaction and community cohesion, benefiting residents' social wellbeing. Despite its importance, walkability has declined in many cities, posing a risk to public health. Similarly, the decline in third spaces has contributed to social isolation and mental health challenges as discussed in Chapter 13. It's crucial for cities to prioritize walkability and the creation of third spaces to enhance community involvement and social capital.

Absence of third spaces undermines the formation of interpersonal connections within communities, ultimately eroding social unity.[20] But, the question remains, how do we change this, and how do cities prioritize making these areas more accessible? Fortunately, several solutions exist to address the decline of third spaces in society. One approach involves encouraging businesses to establish more public gathering areas, possibly through incentives like tax breaks provided by local governments. Additionally, repurposing existing public spaces, such as parks or community centers, to enhance their communal appeal can foster social interaction. Individuals can also contribute by organizing social events or creating communal spaces like community gardens. By collectively taking action to cultivate third spaces, we can bolster social cohesion and community engagement, mitigating the negative effects of their decline on mental health and societal connections.

In short, transfiguring walkability in cities, and renewing third spaces serves as one part of the gigantic puzzle in addressing the root causes of our Gen Z mental health crisis. The loss of these environmental features can have a detrimental impact on mental and physical health. However, it is important to note that merely establishing these areas is insufficient. We need city leaders to implement purposeful design choices that are essential to foster meaningful interaction and engagement within these spaces. Although I have discussed the importance of walking and third spaces, I also want to stress the potential integration of built-in environment strategies into the anti-loneliness framework. Such strategies encompass enhancements to the planning and design of built environment attributes, alongside the cultivation of perceptions regarding: (1) local resources and amenities, (2) walkability, (3) general age-friendliness and environmental quality (4) green spaces, (5) housing diversity, (6) third spaces, and (7) accessible and cost-effective transportation services. By thoughtfully transforming our perceptions about our built environments, we can create a significant improvement in the lives of the millions of people who currently struggle because of social isolation.

Here's How Cities Can Become More Walkable/Add Third Spaces

There are a few ways cities can create tangible change to disrupt urban environments and improve mental health through physical spaces. First, cities can focus on redesigning streets and public spaces to prioritize pedestrians and promote social interaction. This can be achieved by widening sidewalks, installing benches and public seating, adding greenery and trees for shade, and implementing traffic calming measures to slow down vehicles. Neighborhoods can pilot pedestrian-friendly zones where streets are temporarily closed to cars on weekends to encourage foot traffic and community gatherings. These initiatives not only enhance walkability but also create inviting environments conducive to the development of third spaces like outdoor cafes, markets, and public plazas.

182

Second, cities can incentivize the development of mixed-use neighborhoods that foster a sense of community and connectivity. This can be accomplished through zoning policies that encourage a mix of residential, commercial, and recreational spaces within close proximity. Local governments can offer developers density bonuses or expedited permitting for projects that incorporate third spaces, such as community centers, co-working spaces, or small-scale retail establishments. By promoting mixed-use development, cities can reduce reliance on cars, encourage walking between destinations, and facilitate the emergence of diverse third spaces that cater to residents' social and recreational needs.

Third, community engagement plays a crucial role in the successful implementation of third spaces and walkability initiatives. Cities should actively involve residents in the planning and design process through public workshops, surveys, and participatory budgeting exercises. By soliciting input from diverse stakeholders, including residents, businesses, and community organizations, cities can better understand local needs and preferences. Fostering partnerships with local businesses and community groups can aid in cultivating underutilized spaces and support the creation of vibrant third places. Collaborative efforts such as organizing pop-up events, farmer's markets, and cultural festivals can further revitalize public spaces and strengthen social ties within neighborhoods. Through inclusive and participatory approaches, cities can build consensus, mobilize resources, and sustain momentum for creating welcoming third spaces and promoting walkable environments that enhance community wellbeing.

Using Creativity For Change

I grew up in a generation of defunded art/music programs, and as an adult, I wonder what my generation would have looked like if we all had access to creative outlets that didn't include selfies and Twitter posts. Repeated research reinforces the pivotal role of arts and music education in children's holistic development and academic success. Arts education enhances cognitive skills, fosters reasoning abilities, and facilitates language acquisition, correlating with higher academic performance in core subjects like reading and math, as well as improved school attendance.[21] However, in California for example, only 20 percent of public schools offer dedicated teachers for traditional arts disciplines such as music, dance, theater, and visual arts, alongside newer creative outlets like computer graphics, animation, coding, costume design, and filmmaking.[22]

While Proposition 28 (the Arts and Music in Schools (AMS) Funding Guarantee and Accountability Act), a California legislation passed in 2022 that allocates one percent of funding towards the arts, represents a step forward, it alone cannot suffice.[23] Educational psychologist KH Kim, author of the recent book *The Creativity Challenge* indicated a notable decline in the nation's creativity over the past few decades.[24] Kim's studies, which encompassed over 270,000 individuals ranging from kindergartners to adults, examined various aspects of creativity such as generating original ideas, engaging in detailed and elaborate thinking, synthesizing information, and displaying open-mindedness and curiosity.[25] Kim regards these qualities as essential components of creativity. Her findings uncover that while Americans' creativity exhibited an upward trend from 1966 to 1990, it has experienced a significant downturn since then.[26] Given the mounting evidence that my generation has taken a loss in the creative sphere, as a nation, we must advocate for more robust initiatives to nurture creativity across our institutions.

To clarify, creativity can be interpreted as the ability to generate novel ideas, concepts, or solutions that are original, valuable, and meaningful.[27] It involves breaking away from conventional thinking patterns to produce something new or innovative. Creativity encompasses a wide range of activities, including artistic expression, problem-solving, scientific discovery, and entrepreneurship. It often involves combining existing knowledge, skills, and experiences in novel ways to produce something unique.[28] Creativity is not limited to any domain or discipline but can manifest in various forms, such as visual arts, music, literature, design, technology, and business. It plays a crucial role in human advancement, driving innovation, progress, and cultural enrichment. So, while I highlight the importance of art and music, it should be noted that creativity is not merely within those spaces.

Art, music, and creativity coursework has been eliminated or reduced in youth primarily due to changes in educational priorities, budget cuts, and changes in societal values. With an increased emphasis on standardized testing and core academic subjects, schools have often prioritized subjects like math and languages over arts and creative programs.[29] As a result, the arts are frequently seen as optional or non-essential, leading to reduced funding and limited access for students. When faced with financial constraints, schools may choose to allocate resources towards subjects perceived as more directly related to academic achievement, further marginalizing arts education. In many cases, extracurricular activities related to the arts, such as school bands, theater productions, and art clubs, have also experienced cutbacks.[30] This limits opportunities for youth to engage in creative expression outside of the classroom.

The proliferation of digital devices and screen-based entertainment has contributed to a decline in hands-on creative activities among youth.[31] Instead of engaging in art, music, or other creative pursuits, many Gen Z spend their free time-consuming passive media content. Societal pressures to excel academically, pursue lucrative careers, and conform to narrow definitions of success can discourage Gen Z from pursuing creative interests. This pressure to achieve can lead to stress, anxiety, and mental health issues among youth who feel constrained by expectations—as explained in Chapter 17.

By overlooking the importance of art, music, and creativity in our development, society is missing out on valuable opportunities to support mental health and wellbeing. Engagement in creative activities can reduce stress, boost self-esteem, enhance emotional expression, and promote overall psychological resilience.[32] Therefore, investing in arts education, providing access to creative outlets, and fostering a culture that values creativity can help address the mental health needs of Gen Z and cultivate a healthier society. But how do we do this?

Ways to Combat the Creativity Crisis

To start, we must first recognize what creativity looks like. According to Kim, author of *How to Combat America's Creativity Crisis*, in order to nurture creativity, it's crucial for managers, educators, and parents to understand the behaviors and attitudes commonly exhibited by creative folks and to provide recognition and support accordingly.[33] Essentially, we need to discern what creativity looks like in various contexts—whether in our children, employees, students, or even within ourselves. Kim's book outlines over 20 behaviors frequently observed in creatives, drawn from extensive research she reviewed. Many of these behaviors, particularly the following, are sometimes mistaken for rebelliousness and impracticality. But, considered from a new perspective, these characteristics could be celebrated, nurtured, and utilized for innovation and mental wellness. Below are some of these characteristics as highlighted by K.H. Kim.[34]

Big-picture thinking: Creative people think abstractly, seeking innovative solutions beyond the immediate details of a situation.

Spontaneity: Creatives are flexible and quick to seize new opportunities, approaching them with an open mind and playful outlook.

Playfulness: Creative individuals exhibit a lighthearted demeanor and a curiosity-driven exploration of the world.

Resilience: Creatives bounce back from failures and challenges, refocusing on novel approaches to overcome obstacles.

Autonomy: Creatives strive for independence in their thoughts and actions, relying on intrinsic motivation to pursue their objectives.

Defiance: Creatives often challenge existing norms and authorities to pursue their own goals, enabling them to envision possibilities others may overlook, though this may appear rebellious.

Risk-taking: Driven by optimism, many creatives will forego security for uncertain rewards.

Daydreaming: Through daydreaming, creatives imagine new perspectives and solutions, even if some ideas may seem far-fetched along the way.

This list should bring to light how important it is for us as a society to rethink how we view these characteristics. What some may view as impulsivity or far-fetched idea-making could be reconsidered and recontextualized into a valuable creative spirit that can be utilized.

Beyond recognizing the characteristics of creativity, it's crucial to consider how we can cultivate and promote it on a broader scale across society. Foremost, fostering a flexible mindset is essential, encouraging us to embrace new ideas and adapt to changing circumstances. Also, promoting diversity in all its forms—be it cultural, ethnic, or experiential—can enrich creative perspectives and spark innovative thinking. [35] Cultivating a culture of experimentation and continuous learning is vital, providing opportunities to explore new concepts and push boundaries. Embracing an adhocracy approach, characterized by flexibility and decentralized decision-making, can empower us to take initiative and pursue creative endeavors. [36] Lastly, emphasizing collaboration and teamwork promotes synergy, enabling the ability to leverage each other's strengths and generate innovative solutions collectively, [37] which not only helps aid in creativity, but also with belonging. By embracing these principles and values, we can provide an environment conducive to nurturing creativity and innovation nationwide. In other words, to combat this crisis, we must collectively foster cultural shifts in the way we view creativity. Additionally, it is important for schools, workplaces, and families to encourage and reinforce creativity through a revitalized emphasis on the arts. This can be through more funding, more programs, and altering current curriculum or projects to innovate a renewed culture of creativity.

Confronting Our Country's Dangerous Polarization

During my time in grad school, I had the opportunity to study abroad in Rwanda. The entire time I toured the beautiful country, I had one question consistently bugging me at the back of my mind: what psychology could possibly lead to such a violent history, where normal people could take part in a genocide? If you aren't familiar, Rwanda experienced one of the most violent, catastrophic moments in history. Just shy of 30 years ago, the two political parties completely turned on one another, and it led to an absolutely devastating outcome where at least 200,000 people lost their lives (but more likely around a million died, according to the Genocide Museum).[38] Though my class at the time was centered on the innovation and technological revolution currently happening in their country, I somehow ended up writing my final essay about what interested me more: the sociology of a genocide. What I found through my research raised alarm bells because a many of those sentiments have been expressed by Americans, often hiding behind social media, and at times openly by politicians.

Psychologists believe there is not an individual factor nor single instigator that motivates a person to commit these acts, but researchers argue there are three main factors that contribute to an ordinary person taking part in a genocide: the mindset of an individual, the need for categorization by an individual, and the effect of a group on an individual.[39] In Rwanda, government propaganda fueled fear and hatred towards the Tutsi, fostering a mindset that justified violence.[40] Norms shifted over time, leading to social pressure and conformity towards brutality.[41] Militias recruited impoverished youth with promises of rewards like land, further reinforcing group dynamics that normalized excessive risk-taking behavior.[42] Categorization and dehumanization of the Tutsis played a pivotal role in the genocide.[43] Considering these factors—mindset, group dynamics, and categorization—one may question their potential influence in other contexts, such as in the US. When I take these three factors into account: mindset, groupthink, and categorization, I wonder, when combined, could these factors influence the US similarly?

Okay, so why am I talking about Rwanda's genocide, and how does this relate to mental health in Gen Z? A few things stick out to me (and hopefully you) in terms of our current political regime. Both the Left and Right have created a stark divide that was further intensified when former President Donald Trump was elected. This mindset has become arguably dangerous, harming us not only from a national security perspective but also from a social perspective. The increasing polarization and demonization of the "other side" fosters an environment where violence and extreme measures may seem justified, echoing the dangerous rhetoric that preceded the Rwandan genocide.

One example of this is the January 6, 2021 insurrection when many people breached the US Capitol Building during the Congress' ratification of the Electoral College's vote, disrupting the vote count and resulting in five fatalities.[44] QAnon, a conspiracy theory movement, has significantly strengthened polarization in the US, and is credited for the insurrection at the Capitol.[45] What started as a social media post has emerged into a large lucrative threat by promoting baseless and often absurd claims, such as the existence of a secret cabal of Satanic pedophiles within the government and other powerful "deep state" institutions.[46] This has further heightened tensions and contributed to an environment of fear and hostility. Social media platforms have facilitated the formation of echo chambers, wherein individuals are exposed only to information that reinforces their beliefs and are shielded from opposing viewpoints.[47] This has reinforced existing ideological divides and made it increasingly difficult for people with differing perspectives to engage in meaningful dialogue or find common ground. This polarization that has created collective rationalizing of violence should illuminate a clear issue in our country: how easily we have been thrust into dehumanizing behavior...and maybe even worse. These factors have contributed to genocide in other countries—so why aren't we taking this more seriously?

According to Robert Talisse, a political philosopher, political polarization can be defined as the ideological distance between opposed parties.[48] Talisse asserts that there can be benefits from polarization like offering voters clear choices and can be beneficial by fostering debate and discovery of truths. The issue is that polarization can also erode democracy when interactions with like-minded individuals leads to more extreme views and increased hostility toward the opposing side, transforming political identity into a lifestyle. The U.S. has been classified as a "backsliding democracy" due to persistent false allegations of voter fraud and extreme polarization.[49] Talisse explains that there are two types of polarization (called political and belief polarization) and together, both types of polarization create a destructive loop, with citizens becoming more divided and politicians exploiting this division for electoral gain. This leads to increased conformity and intolerance to ideological deviation within groups, and extreme animosity between groups. The irony is that by taking on this mindset people come to believe democracy is only possible when everyone agrees with them, which is fundamentally anti-democratic.

Elisa Brietzke, a professor at Queens University, argues that polarization and politics have caused a setback for mental health.[50] Increased political stress can significantly affect mental health, causing anxiety, depression, insomnia, and even suicidal thoughts.[51] A 2019 study found that almost 40% of Americans reported significant anxiety due to politics,[52] with the impact more prominent among the young, politically engaged, or those opposed to the government. Brietzke found that political stress has increasingly become a central topic in therapy since 2019. Patients often want to know the political views of their mental health providers. A study found that two-thirds of patients talked about politics with their therapists, and a better therapeutic alliance was reported when patients believed their therapists shared their political orientation.[53] Thus, the polarization of our nation isn't just a threat to our democracy, but also a significant concern for mental health.

Therefore, if we want to see real change, we need to focus on reducing hostility and encouraging respectful disagreement, even among allies, to counteract conformity and rediscover the ability to respectfully engage with opponents. So how do we do this?

Ending Citizens United, and Confronting Government Corruption

As voters, we should have a fundamental right to understand the influence of wealthy special interests on our political system. But the truth is we do not because of a landmark US Supreme Court decision over a decade ago. In Citizens United v. Federal Election Commission (FEC), decided on Jan. 21, 2010, the Court invalidated restrictions on corporate independent expenditures, allowing corporations and outside groups to spend unlimited amounts on political campaigns.[54]

By upholding disclosure provisions from the Bipartisan Campaign Reform Act, the Court believed that transparency alone would prevent undue influence, but this relies on the erroneous assumption that unlimited corporate spending would not lead to corruption because it would be deemed "independent." [55] One mechanism facilitating this corruption is the establishment of super political action committees (PACs), which can accept limitless contributions from nearly any domestic source and expend unlimited sums to sway the outcome of federal elections.[56] These "PACs" are famous for labeling corporations as "people."

While super PACs are ostensibly mandated to disclose their funding sources by reporting their fundraising and expenditures to the FEC, this transparency is compromised when they receive contributions from covertly funded "dark money" organizations that conceal their donors from public scrutiny. This issue transcends party lines, as major super PACs associated with the leadership of both political parties have garnered tens of millions of dollars, with some receiving the majority or entirety of their funding from groups that maintain anonymity regarding their donors. [57] The Citizens United decision has undermined the transparency and integrity of our political system, allowing undisclosed corporate spending to wield undue influence over our elections.

The reason this corruption is important to the story of the failure of our mental healthcare system is because of the self-interests that are manipulated by the "dark money" within our political system. When our leaders are enticed with sizable sums of anonymous money through super PACs, it is no surprise that many of the root causes of our crisis could also be eased with leadership that dismantled this corruption. This is because such pervasive corruption often results in policy decisions that prioritize the interests of wealthy donors over the wellbeing of the public. For instance, mental healthcare reforms may be stalled or diluted in favor of policies favored by these influential donors, perpetuating systemic issues within the mental healthcare system and hindering meaningful progress towards improvement. Or, another example is when J&J and its subsidiary, Janssen Pharmaceuticals, promoted the antipsychotic drug Risperdal for uses not approved by the FDA, particularly in children, despite knowing the risks.[58] In the legal case, it was uncovered that J&J paid kickbacks to physicians and long-term care pharmacies, such as Omnicare Inc., to encourage the prescription of Risperdal and other drugs. These payments were disguised as "market share rebates, data-purchase agreements, grants, and educational funding." [59] While government officials themselves were not implicated in this case, and J&J received substantial fines and a corporate integrity agreement, it was our government courts that allowed such a business to continue to operate with little more than a proverbial "slap on the wrist."

Just as big Pharma funds many psychiatrists, so too are our top leaders funded by large corporations. When big oil companies fund campaigns, it is no surprise that making our air cleaner is not a top priority. Addressing dark money in politics is essential for creating a political environment where the needs of the people, including mental healthcare reform, are prioritized over the interests of wealthy donors. By reducing the influence of dark money, we can ensure that policy decisions are made in the best interest of society rather than serving the narrow agendas of special interest groups. To restore faith in our democracy and ensure that the voices of ordinary citizens are heard, we must address the issue of dark money in politics and advocate for greater transparency and accountability in campaign finance regulations. And an obvious way we can start this is by overturning the Citizens United decision. Only then can we uphold the principles of democracy and safeguard the integrity of our electoral process for future generations.

Stopping "Us" vs. "Them"

In the past, Democrats and Republicans engaged in healthy disagreements over policy matters, which is essential for a functioning democracy. However, nowadays, there is a deep-seated fear within each party that the opposing side will cause irreparable harm to the nation if they come into power. Our country is struggling with a strong culture of "us" vs. "them." Essentially, if one does not fit into a certain group's mold, there is an out-casting culture. I have experienced this personally, over and over throughout my life, as someone who has seen issues with both sides. In conservative rooms, I am too liberal and shunned. In liberal spaces, I am not liberal enough, and have been singled out and told I was a "bad person" for not practicing the same rules as others in this ideology. In the moments I felt singled out, I recognized that many other well-meaning people who choose not to eat, breathe, and live politics probably have felt the same sentiment. There's often an unspoken pressure to align with one side or the other, leaving little room for nuance or independent thinking. This strict adherence to a "side" has arguably created a dangerous threat to democracy, and if we continue to allow this discourse, a civil war, or worse, is not out of the question.

One thing that is evident in this conversation about polarization is the issue of nationalism. A former evangelical minister, Brad Onishi, was interviewed and explained why this topic is of grave concern:

> "[Nationalists] understand themselves to be playing a character. They are drawn into a narrative that says, you are at the last battle. You have a chance to do something that is much bigger than you. Will you answer that call? Will you come to D.C. on January 6? Will you ride with us to the southern border? Because these are the moments, these are the battles that will shape our country. This is the cosmic war between good and evil. Are you really going to sit on the sidelines? Some of us can laugh that off. We can think that that's a fringe ideal, but January 6 was not something to laugh off. And some of the events we have seen since then, the swatting of judges 'houses, the evacuations of capitols due to bomb threats, so many more examples, little fires everywhere, are not things we can laugh off."[60]

What Onishi describes is one way that nationalists are stirring anxiety over the fate of our country. Those that follow this rhetoric have the firm belief that they are actors in carrying out this mission.

Within this role, nationalists naturally dehumanize those who are not "within" their group. According to Bart Bonikowski, an associate professor of sociology and politics at New York University, nationalism in the US is characterized by exclusionary and nostalgic sentiments.[61] It perceives the nation as in decline and seeks restoration by those who consider themselves its rightful owners, potentially resorting to authoritarian measures. While this phenomenon may manifest differently in other nations, Bonikowski noted that the underlying mechanisms driving these movements can be strikingly similar. He describes how nationalists exploit existing societal divisions to rally supporters.[62] Opportunists (like politicians and Q Anon) have recognized this and acted accordingly.

Extreme nationalism relies on strong, exclusive beliefs and the creation of an insular group identity. It often promotes a sense of exceptionalism and superiority, viewing adherents as the chosen or righteous group. This fosters the "us versus them" mentality because outsiders are demonized or portrayed as threats to the group's identity or wellbeing. Also, it often involves charismatic leaders or figures who exert significant influence over followers. Leaders may manipulate followers' fears and insecurities, using them to reinforce loyalty and obedience to the group's ideology. Additionally, nationalism can create a closed information environment, where dissenting views are rejected, and critical thinking is discouraged. This echo chamber effect isolates followers from alternative perspectives and reinforces the group's beliefs.

Furthermore, nationalism employs tactics of social control, such as shaming or ostracizing nonconformists, to maintain cohesion and conformity within the group.[63] This can create a culture of fear and conformity, by which individuals are pressured to adhere to the group's beliefs and behaviors to avoid social or psychological consequences. Others such as Rob Reiner, an actor and filmmaker, spoke out about fear over this behavior being a tremendous concern in his documentary *God and Country*. One of the most powerful parts of the film is how it depicts to viewers how many of those who follow the nationalism movement are normal people who are seeking meaning and community.[64]

So, what is the relationship between nationalism and mental health, and how do we combat this? Polarization has been increasing in our country, and it is directly affecting our marginalized communities. This polarizing language is not just words, but reflects the laws enacted or rejected into practice. For example, according to the Center for American Progress, policies protecting marginalized communities from being discriminated against tended to be opposed or weakened, as seen in resistance to the Violence Against Women Act.[65] This is also directly related to why important legislation to help mitigate issues such as racism, like affirmative action, have been erased from our law. Therefore, not only can polarization isolate those who are marginalized, but it can also affect the very laws that protect people.

Clearly, policies that restrict opportunities for certain populations can have wide-ranging effects. As mentioned in Chapter 10, research has shown that experiencing discrimination is associated with poorer physical health, shorter life expectancy, and a reduced quality of life.[66] Discrimination can adversely affect mental and physical health, as well as financial stability for marginalized populations.[67] The 2016 elections saw a normalization of polarized rhetoric, which studies suggest could lead to increased distress.[68] This heightened distress was linked to various mental health symptoms, including depression, anxiety, trauma-related symptoms, and diminished self-esteem and quality of life perceptions.[69]

Is it possible to depolarize our nation? Honestly, it is an uphill battle. Though, one of the first steps we can enact is to stop allowing the "us" vs. "them" mentality to exist within our discourse. There are three key steps anyone reading this can take: promoting empathy and understanding, encouraging constructive dialogue, and building inclusive communities. One of the most effective ways to combat polarization is by promoting empathy and understanding among those with differing perspectives. Empathy involves putting oneself in another person's shoes, understanding their experiences, and acknowledging their emotions and concerns. By fostering empathy, people can develop a deeper appreciation for the diverse backgrounds and viewpoints of others, leading to greater understanding and tolerance. This can be achieved through educational initiatives, community engagement programs, and interpersonal interactions that encourage listening and empathy.

Along with empathy we need to create safe spaces for stakeholders to talk about the things that they care about. Through constructive dialogue, engaging in respectful and open-minded conversations with people who hold different opinions or beliefs, we can create safe spaces for people to connect. Instead of resorting to hostility or dismissiveness, constructive dialogue encourages active listening, genuine curiosity, and a willingness to find common ground. By creating spaces for dialogue and debate where people can express their views without fear of judgment or reprisal, we can foster greater mutual understanding and bridge divides. This can be facilitated through community forums, town hall meetings, and online platforms that promote civil discourse and exchange of ideas. This will be a challenge, as many people today struggle with emotional reactivity based on opposing views. However, the more we open our minds and hearts to hearing other opinions, the more we can shift beliefs towards a more equitable nation.

To foster constructive dialogue, we also need to build inclusive communities that celebrate diversity and promote inclusivity. Inclusive communities are essential for reducing polarization and fostering a sense of belonging among all individuals. Inclusive communities value and respect the contributions of people from different backgrounds, cultures, and perspectives, creating environments where everyone feels welcome and valued. This can be achieved through initiatives such as diversity training, cultural awareness programs, and policies that promote belonging and inclusion in workplaces, schools, and other social settings. By building inclusive communities, we can create spaces where people can come together, collaborate, and work towards common goals, transcending divisions and fostering unity.

Basic Income as A Pathway Towards Mental Health

The first time I heard about Universal Basic Income (UBI) I thought, *oh wow, we could just give people money? That could solve a lot.* UBI, a social welfare program that provides all citizens or residents of a country with a regular, unconditional cash payment (regardless of their employment status or other sources of income), is a path towards many potential positive improvements in our current system.[70] The key feature of UBI is to ensure that every person has a minimum level of income to meet their basic needs, such as food, shelter, and healthcare—

thereby reducing poverty and inequality. By providing a stable income floor, UBI could address issues such as job insecurity, automation-related unemployment, economic instability, and for my argument: a sizable chunk of our mental health crisis.

Because so many people in my generation grew up barely scraping by, so many of us have missed out on what makes us healthy, like having the free time to meet with community and friends or the finances to afford healthy food. The 40-hour workweek, with little time for vacation or relaxation, has produced a generation of hopeless people, knowing the long hours will never afford us a house, good retirement, or true security. Mental wellbeing is inherently connected to financial wellness. In knowing this, we can dismantle this key root cause of so many people's distress.

The concept of "free money" has transcended mere whispers of *"is this a good idea?"* to a substantiated notion, supported by extensive empirical evidence. Many global experiments have been conducted to investigate the effects of UBI. [71] Through meticulous comparative analysis between recipient groups and control cohorts, researchers consistently unveil a myriad of positive societal outcomes associated with UBI. These outcomes include diminished levels of inequality and poverty, alongside tangible improvements in vital metrics like reduced infant mortality rates, lowered healthcare expenditures, decreased crime rates, enhanced educational attainment, decreased truancy rates, augmented economic growth, heightened rates of social emancipation—and the list goes on.[72] This research unequivocally suggests that UBI stands as an efficient, cost-effective, and humane strategy in the ongoing battle against poverty and could have preventative/protective effects on mental health.

To illustrate, an experiment was conducted in Canada that administered a one-time cash transfer of $7,500 to individuals experiencing homelessness and found that recipients exhibited higher positive affect and improved executive function in the short term, showing the potential for UBI to enhance mental wellbeing.[73]

Figure 6. Map from the Stanford Basic Income Lab that shows everywhere in the world that pilots and studies are taking place.[74]

UBI represents a pivotal step toward addressing the mental health crisis. By providing individuals with a financial safety net devoid of bureaucratic hurdles or conditionalities, UBI fosters an opportunity to prevent financial stress that can lead to better mental wellbeing. Because there is a strong correlation between economic insecurity and mental health issues such as anxiety, depression, and stress,[75] UBI could serve as a preventive measure by alleviating financial strain and existential anxieties, thereby reducing the prevalence of mental health disorders. UBI empowers individuals to prioritize self-care and seek appropriate support services without the burden of economic constraints. This shift from reactive interventions to proactive mental health management helps to curb the escalating rates of psychological distress observed across diverse demographic segments. Thus, UBI not only addresses material deprivation but also nurtures psychological resilience and mental health.

Opponents of UBI claim that free money may make people lazy and unmotivated to work.[76] While on the surface, this argument makes sense, it has not been supported by research. This concern is rooted in economic theory, particularly the principle of moral hazard, which suggests that people may act irresponsibly or reduce their efforts if they are insulated from the consequences of their actions—yet study after study fail to support this concept, as you will learn below. UBI can provide us with the financial stability needed to pursue education, training, or entrepreneurial ventures, thereby enhancing our overall economic productivity and innovation.[77]

UBI often raises questions about its affordability and fiscal sustainability.[78] UBI has the potential to generate economic stimulus and growth, which could lead to broader tax revenue increases and offset program costs.[79] By providing a basic income floor, UBI can stimulate consumer spending, demand for goods and services, and overall economic activity.[80] This increased economic dynamism can translate into higher tax revenues from sources such as sales taxes, value-added taxes, and income taxes, contributing to the fiscal sustainability of the program and proactively support mental health endeavors.

Another argument against UBI is that it causes inflation. And many groups blamed the stimulus checks during the pandemic on the rise in inflation. According to FactCheck.org, the issue of inflation because of the stimulus is based on many factors, therefore it is irresponsible to put blame on the stimulus checks.[81] Researchers in Mexico studied cash transfers compared to in-kind food aid found that cash transfers did not significantly impact prices, while in-kind transfers led to a decrease in prices for essential goods.[82] In other words, villages getting the food saw prices fall by 3.9 percent—reducing the inflation cost of food.[83] Some argue that poor people don't know how to spend their money, which leads to overconsumption.[84] When economists studied the CARES checks, and what people actually spent their money on, they found that they utilized their stimulus checks for various necessities.[85] This casts a spotlight on the role of the stimulus in meeting essential needs like housing and sustenance.[86] Almost 70 percent of people find it difficult to afford groceries and 83 percent depend on coupons or loyalty programs to purchase food.[87]

What UBI Could Look Like in the US

There is a lot of confusion around the discourse surrounding UBI. Many people do not understand what it is, what it can look like, and how it could be beneficial. There are many ideas circulating in terms of the feasibility and optics of these programs. For the purpose of my argument, I want to explain how this program could look in the US, and how it can be used as a preventative tool in the mental health space.

Here's what I propose: instead of giving everyone money, which many UBI proponents argue for, I believe this program could be means tested and targeted directly towards those that would benefit the most. Imagine a system in which everyone over the age of 18 making under $100k received $1,000 to $1,500 (depending on state average living costs) per month. This idea creates a safety net for everyone—and we need one. UBI of $1,000 to $1,500 per month could have profound effects. For example, it might mean that a single parent struggling to make ends meet can afford better childcare while still being able to cover basic expenses like rent and groceries. It could mean that a recent college graduate burdened with student loans can use the extra income to invest in further education or training without the fear of falling into additional debt.

For someone stuck in a low-paying job with no prospects for advancement, UBI could provide the financial cushion needed to take risks, such as starting a small business or pursuing a passion project. Additionally, for individuals facing unexpected emergencies like medical bills or car repairs, having a guaranteed monthly income could provide peace of mind and prevent them from spiraling into a financial crisis. Overall, UBI at this level could empower us to make choices that align with long-term goals and wellbeing, rather than simply struggling to survive paycheck to paycheck. Implementing a targeted basic income scheme has the potential to ease poverty, stimulate economic growth, improve mental health outcomes, and enhance overall quality of life for millions of individuals and families across the country.

There are a few things needed for basic income (BI) to work. Note, it's just BI, because my plan is not universal, as it is means tested. For example, it would have to override current rules about disability, supplemental Nutrition Assistance Program (SNAP), Medicaid, Temporary Assistance for Needy Families (TANF), Supplemental Security Income (SSI), Earned Income Tax Credit (EITC), Section 8 Housing Choice Voucher Program, Children's Health Insurance Program (CHIP), Free and Reduced-Price School Meal Programs, and all other welfare programs. These BI payments would be in addition to these current programs. The second thing it would need is to address inflation. There are things that can be done to avoid or mitigate this potential side effect according to experts.[88] BI should be adjusted based on economic conditions, such as increasing during periods of high unemployment and decreasing as the economy approaches full employment. Because the focus of this book is on mental health, I recommend reviewing work from experts such as Ioana Marinescu, Andrew Yang, Yanis Varoufakis, or Robert B. Reich for further reading on the economics of BI if you are curious about how it can be successfully implemented.

One argument I can make is that a form of UBI has already happened recently, through the COVID-19 stimulus program, The Coronavirus Aid, Relief, and Economic Security (CARES) Act, the Coronavirus Relief Act, and the American Rescue Plan Act. This example can answer a lot of questions that opponents of this idea may have. Millions of people received aid through three rounds of federal checks after the onset of COVID-19.[89] These stimulus checks exemplify the power a cash sum can do for individuals in crisis. A University of Michigan study found that following the implementation of the federal income transfers, material hardship experienced a significant decline across the nation.[90] From December 2020 to April 2021, they found that key indicators of hardship such as food insufficiency, financial instability, and adverse mental health symptoms saw notable reductions, with food insufficiency alone falling by over 40 percent.[91] Importantly, these improvements were observed not only among low-income households but also higher up the income distribution spectrum. And the data also showcases how cash payments can directly improve mental wellness by giving stakeholders the means to have their basic needs met and reducing mental health diagnoses associated with strain of financial burden.

Conclusion: Is Change Possible?

Over the last 20 chapters I have taken you on a journey through our mental health crisis and outlined many of the root causes, and proposed solutions/efforts. I wanted to make this about my generation because it is clear that people my age are experiencing something very different from our predecessors. It is no coincidence that while our genetics have not changed, our rates of mental illness (specifically, anxiety and depression) have skyrocketed. We, as a society, must recognize the burden of intersectional factors that are ever present. We live in an increasingly unaffordable country, with an impending climate crisis, superPAC funded leadership, a nutrition/exercise crisis, marginalization, a compulsion of social comparison, a loneliness epidemic, and more.

As the rates continue to rise, our local and federal leadership have scrambled to create reactive solutions like adding more mental healthcare workers and building more treatment centers. Though the lack of access and affordability of care are key components to the issue, it fails to truly address what is at the heart of the crisis—maybe because there are too many factors to address at once. But as I have highlighted above, a few things could objectively make an enormous impact. This includes offering a national service program that would fund college for those who choose after two years, and this also includes universal basic income for those making under $100,000 annually.

Beyond money, we need community. As our surgeon general has fought to emphasize this issue, it is time for us to act. We can revive community connection through community initiatives and the rebirth of third spaces and town walkability. Beyond this, we also need to hold our government accountable for their role in perpetuating polarization, dark money, and self-interests. We can start to fix this through overturning Citizens United, promoting empathy and understanding, encouraging constructive dialogue, and building inclusive communities. We can also benefit from reviving and normalizing creativity. Art, music, and other creative pursuits have many psychological benefits and offer an untapped resource for all of us.

Since the 2020 pandemic, and the election of a leader who normalized marginalization, many people started to recognize that the mental health crisis is real—as evidenced by the uptick in suicides during the pandemic. [92] It was during the pandemic that I lost my best friend who passed away from her battle with mental health struggles. Through my grief, I felt empowered to tell the story of my generation, because I realized our story needs to be told. I hope that the power of our stories, and the wealth of research supporting my argument, will create genuine change. The truth is, it makes no sense that millions of people are living in our beautiful country feeling miserable, lonely, depressed, anxious, and misunderstood. There is a monumental opportunity for our nation to fight for the change we deserve. In the famous words of someone unknown: *life is short*. Because of that, it is key that we make efficient use of our time. But beyond utilizing the fleeting time we have, it is my deepest hope we can find a way for *everyone* to have the opportunity to enjoy the journey.

You've learned about systemic changes; the next step is for you to learn how you as an individual can make a difference.

Chapter 21: What You Can Do

Every great dream begins with a dreamer. Always remember, you have within you the strength, the patience, and the passion to reach for the stars to change the world.
—Harriet Tubman

In David Stroh's book, *Systems Thinking for Social Change*, he argues that people must shift their hope so that others will change to "seeing how they can first change themselves."[1] This book focuses on how our systems have failed us, but also emphasizes that we have the power within ourselves to create change. If you've made it to this final chapter, and you've resonated with the research, arguments, and systems solutions, you are still probably wondering what you can do. The following chapter highlights the ways in which Gen Zers, parents, teachers, and employers can make changes in our own lives for better mental health within ourselves and our networks.

What Gen Z Can Do

As members of Gen Z, we've gotten a lot of hate in the media. People call us the "snowflake generation," accuse us of having no resilience, and point out our "emotional immaturity."[2] We are known for being lazy/quitting our jobs unexpectedly, and worse: employers admit to avoiding hiring us because of our bad reputation.[3] As young children, we were told we are as unique as snowflakes—all of us were so different and special, and we received trophies for almost everything. While each of us *is* special, we cannot ignore the fact that people are talking about how over-sensitive we are…it must mean something, right? The good thing about hearing this discourse is that we can learn from it, grow, and change these issues within ourselves—and thus, also impact our own mental health and happiness.

Stop Being Judgmental and Let Go of Cancel Culture

A few months ago, I hosted a party and invited the man I was seeing at the time. My friends (ages 23 to 27) mistakenly thought his electrician company shirt supported a political group they opposed. He had no idea about the organization and disagreed with its principles once informed, but confirmed the shirt had zero relationship with the political org they imagined it to be. Despite my friends urging me to break up with him for being "ignorant/uneducated," I continued dating him. Weeks later, I brought him to a picnic without informing the group, thinking it wasn't a big deal since we were dating. They accused me of being insensitive for bringing him and claimed he refused to apologize for the "impact" of wearing his company work shirt, which they had misinterpreted. They left us in the park, saying "I can't with you" and that they were "done with us." Despite my attempts to clarify his work shirt logo, my friends refused to reconcile. In other words: I was canceled—years of friendship thrown away.

So why am I writing about this? Because it drives an important question about cancel culture within Gen Z. Currently, we are in a loneliness epidemic within a country that is deeply divided. This division only deepens people's innate psychology to silo themselves within groups that only share the exact same beliefs as them, with *little* room for "mistakes" or deviation of thought outside of narrowly defined belief systems. The following explains why we shouldn't shun and exile people. Perpetuating cancel culture is not just harmful, but it is becoming an increasingly detrimental issue within Gen Z. And it is inadvertently harming our mental health.

Ok, but why shouldn't we cancel each other as peers? Cancel culture often *mirrors systemic inequalities*, harming mental health by denying equal opportunities for personal and societal growth. When folks are publicly shamed or "canceled" for perceived shortcomings or past "mistakes" (violation of group norms), it disregards the structural barriers that may have shaped their actions or limited their knowledge, thus *perpetuating cycles of inequality* and disregarding the root causes of the behavior. This approach not only fails to educate or reform but exacerbates feelings of isolation and anxiety among those targeted, reinforcing a society where people are judged harshly without understanding or empathy. Human decency and moral integrity demand empathy and understanding.

Cancelling our peers reflects a lack of compassion and a failure to recognize the fundamental dignity of every person. *Society has a moral responsibility to support and uplift those who have been denied opportunities.* Cancel culture *is counterproductive to progress* because it alienates and demoralizes those who might otherwise be motivated to improve their situation. Constructive support and encouragement are far more effective in fostering personal growth and societal progress. Cancel culture also embodies a form of victim blaming by placing the responsibility of systemic failures on individuals rather than addressing broader societal issues. By focusing anger on the perceived failures of Gen Z instead of on systemic solutions, it stigmatizes and demoralizes, hindering social mobility and reinforcing disenfranchisement. This lack of compassion and failure to recognize the dignity and potential for growth in every individual undermines mental health by creating an environment of fear and suppression, where personal development is sacrificed for retaliatory public judgment.

Overall, cancelling each other often perpetuates a culture of being angry at someone for either a misunderstanding, or even just perceived "ignorance," especially concerning social issues. This is not just unfair—it's an embodiment of deeper systemic failings and an obstacle to creating a just and equitable society. The practice of shaming and alienating our peers, often compelling them to apologize publicly for misunderstandings or something they did years before, is toxic because it fosters a culture of fear and resentment rather than genuine understanding and growth. This approach tends to polarize communities, creating an environment where people are more concerned with avoiding condemnation than engaging in meaningful dialogue and self-improvement. Instead of fostering inclusivity and change, it perpetuates division and defensiveness.

To improve this, the movement should focus on constructive criticism and education, encouraging us to learn from each other and grow without fear of public humiliation. Creating safe spaces for open dialogue, where people can express their views and learn from different perspectives, is essential. Emphasizing restorative justice and empathy over punishment can lead to more lasting and profound changes in attitudes and behaviors. If we collectively decide to stop cancelling people because we perceive someone made a mistake, or did something we didn't agree with, perhaps a lot of us would be a lot less lonely, isolated, and fearful of rejection.

As a group, Gen Z tends to be judgmental, and this is coming at a huge cost to our mental health. TikTok alone evidences this through the over 45.5 million people who posted videos about this topic.[4] Being judgmental can be detrimental to our mental health because it fosters a culture of exclusion and negativity, and this behavior not only isolates and harms those who are judged but also perpetuates a negative mindset that harms us. Somehow, we are the most diverse and accepting of all generations, yet simultaneously have low tolerance thresholds for outside opinions. A Pew Research study discovered that nearly half of both Gen Zers (48 percent) and millennials (47 percent) view same-sex marriage as beneficial for society, in stark contrast to just one-third of Gen Xers and about one-quarter of boomers (27 percent). This openness aligns with Gen Z's embrace of diverse identities.[5] However, Gen Z's tolerance does not extend to differing opinions, especially evident in cancel culture. According to Christopher Griese, a Gen X teacher, "Many Gen Zers act as both judge and jury on social issues, often shaming others into submission, which can be as detrimental as the actions of those they criticize."[6] This trend of mass withdrawal of support, often over minor errors, reflects a broader intolerance for differing viewpoints. In other words, we are judgy "AF."

Knowing that as a generation we struggle with judgment, the question remains, why is this bad? A study featured in *Mindfulness Magazine* revealed that participants who scored high on nonjudgmental thinking experienced lower levels of depression, anxiety, and stress-related symptoms.[7] The research assessed various aspects of mindfulness, such as observing thoughts, feelings, and sensations, describing them, acting with awareness, and maintaining a non-reactive and non-judgmental attitude towards these experiences. Among these, acting with awareness and nonjudgmental thinking were key predictors of psychological wellbeing, with the former being especially linked to reducing depression.[8] The findings suggest that regularly practicing acceptance and non-judgment can help alleviate anxiety and depression, and that staying mindful may aid in managing depressive symptoms more effectively. By embracing a more non-judgmental lifestyle, we, as Gen Z, can improve our mental health.

Chapter 21: What You Can Do

According to the Berkeley Wellbeing Institute (BWI), there are tangible ways we can learn how to practice non-judgment. Non-judgment is an emotional skill that can be developed and improved over time. Here are some ways to build your non-judgment skills as recommended by the BWI.

1. *Self-Awareness*: Often, we judge ourselves and others without realizing it. Improving self-awareness helps uncover these judgments.
2. *Mindfulness*: Mindfulness combines awareness and acceptance (non-judgment). Practicing mindfulness can enhance your non-judgment skills.
3. *Positive Thinking*: We tend to be judgmental when focusing on negatives. By training yourself to notice positive aspects, you can improve your ability to be non-judgmental.

Be Mindful of the Media You Consume

As I have concluded in chapter 15, the media has influence on us. That means that the shows, movies, videos, social media, and creators we follow all shape what we think, believe, and how we act. Knowing this, it is imperative we take control over what we allow us to be influenced by. If you're like me and love the *Kardashians*, or *Love Island*, you may also find yourself buying into certain beauty standards and comparing yourself to the celebrities on those shows. It is no coincidence that Brazilian Butt Lifts (BBLs) became popular after the 2010s when the Kardashian family came to fame.

What I am saying is that if you want to be someone who values depth, meaning, learning, or growth, instead of the superficial, then you can choose your media accordingly. Since learning about the power of media myself, I've committed myself to lessening my affinity towards reality shows, and spending more time watching science and nature shows like *Planet Earth* or *Explained*. I also struggle with body image, so I've decided to center my movie and show selection around bodies that are more inclusive, therefore I am watching more shows like *Shrill, the Great British Baking Show,* and *Insecure*. Beyond TV and movies, it is also important to think about the social media influencers we follow. Are you following fitness gurus and models, or creators who aim to inform you about enlightening topics? Because media is such an incredible tool, perhaps we should start using it as such.

Build Resilience

Because life doesn't come with a roadmap, we all face twists and turns that cannot be predicted. These changes affect people differently, bringing many emotions and uncertainty. However, older generations have tended to adapt well over time, thanks to resilience. Yet, when it comes to Generation Z, many argue that we lack resilience. Critics often say that Gen Z is overly sensitive, easily overwhelmed, and less equipped to handle life's adversities.

Take Alex, a 19-year-old girl I knew in college, as an example. After receiving a lower-than-expected grade on an important assignment, Alex told me she was devastated. This seemingly minor setback triggered a strong emotional reaction, leading to feelings of worthlessness and intense anxiety—which spiraled into suicidal thoughts. And I did my best to be there for her. Alex's case, the fear of academic failure, was exacerbated by comparisons to peers on social media, where everyone seemed to be thriving. A few days later when I checked in with her, Alex told me she was unable to find the necessary resources or support her in crisis. And, because our other friends dismissed her concern as trivial, and the campus counseling services were overbooked, Alex was left to navigate her emotional turmoil mostly alone. Critics might see Alex's struggle as evidence of a lack of resilience, arguing that previous generations faced similar academic challenges without falling apart. The fear of repaying exorbitant loans and not finding employment (or good pay, at that) are real.

According to the APA, resilience helps us navigate difficult circumstances and empowers us to grow and enhance our lives. For Gen Z, it's about adapting to a rapidly changing world, finding new ways to cope, and redefining what it means to be resilient in the face of unprecedented challenges. The APA outlines five ways we can build resilience:[9]

1. *Build Your Connections:* Connecting with empathetic and understanding people can remind you that you're not alone during difficult times. Concentrate on seeking out reliable and empathetic individuals who acknowledge your emotions to help build resilience. Accept support from those who care about you, and prioritize genuine connections, whether it's a date night with your partner or lunch with a friend. Additionally, joining

civic groups, faith-based communities, or local organizations can provide social support and help you reclaim hope.

2. *Foster Wellness*: Encourage healthy habits such as balanced nutrition, sufficient sleep, staying hydrated, and regular physical activity to strengthen your body and reduce stress. Practice mindfulness through journaling, yoga, prayer, or meditation to build connections and restore hope. Avoid masking pain with substances; instead, give your body the resources to manage stress effectively.

3. *Find Purpose:* Figure out what gets you up in the morning. Is it to make the world a better place? Is it to be a good friend? Whatever it is, there are many ways to find out where you belong. For example, helping others through volunteering or supporting friends can provide a sense of purpose and boost self-worth. Embrace opportunities for self-discovery—go out there and try new things. I think on some level all of us are trying to find purpose every day, and maybe your purpose can be as simple as reaching one goal you set.

4. *Embrace Healthy Thoughts:* Your thoughts shape your feelings and resilience. Identify irrational thinking and adopt a balanced mindset. Remember that challenges don't define your future or make you helpless. Understand that change is inevitable. Focus on what you can change/control rather than what you cannot. You can maintain an optimistic outlook by visualizing positive outcomes, and by reframing past experiences—sometimes finding the silver lining is key. Reflect on what helped you in the past, and use your past strengths and lessons learned to continue to grow and improve your daily life.

5. *Seek Help If You Need It:* Getting help when you need it is crucial for building resilience. While personal strategies may be enough for some, others might need other support. Mental health professionals are trained to help you develop a strategy for moving forward. Remember, you're not alone on this journey. Although you can't control every situation, you can make progress by concentrating on the aspects within your reach, with the support of loved ones and trusted professionals.

Meet Your Basic Needs (If You Can)

All of us have bare minimum basic needs to meet to even begin to have good mental health. This starts with nutrition, sleep, exercise, freedom from substances, a creative outlet, a safe environment, clean air, self-esteem, having a social life, support from loved ones, financial stability, and a secure roof over your head. If you are struggling with any of these, this is a good place to start on your journey towards better mental health.

<u>What Parents Can Do</u>

Listen to Your Child

I know this sounds obvious, but listening is so incredibly important. I get it, as parents you think you know what's right…you might even think you know everything about your kid's life. But you don't. This is why if your teenager comes home sad, worried, distressed, or clearly not themselves, it is your duty as a parent to give them what they need—a supportive ear, and if needed, more. One way to effectively do this is through active listening, which means focusing on understanding your child or teen's point of view instead of immediately trying to solve their problems.[10] To do this, you can listen to understand their feelings, restate their words to them, and acknowledge/validate their emotions. A great way to validate your kid is by asking one simple question, "how can I help you in this moment?"

Recognize If You Are Overparenting

Do you micromanage your children, get into power struggles, try to control all your kid's influences, have overly high expectations, or don't allow them to be independent? Well, if so, you might have fallen prey to overparenting. There are some ways you can stop, and here are some practical tips.

The prevention of overparenting involves finding a balance between being supportive and allowing your child to be independent. It is important you encourage your child to make their own decisions, learn from their mistakes by giving them age-appropriate responsibilities, and trust them to handle tasks on their own. You can set clear boundaries and establish rules without micromanaging, allowing your child the freedom to navigate within these limits. Instead of immediately stepping in to solve problems, you can instead guide your kids to find their own solutions by asking questions that help them think through the issue.

You also need to allow your child to experience the natural consequences of their actions, helping them understand the impact of their decisions. In other words, let them fail sometimes. This means you must practice self-restraint by resisting the urge to intervene in every situation, evaluating whether your involvement is necessary and whether the potential consequence of said situation would be too disastrous. Focus on offering support and guidance without controlling every aspect of their life and encourage open communication. You can also be the role model of healthy behaviors by demonstrating how you handle stress, make decisions, and solve problems. Also, please educate yourself on the developmental stages of children to set realistic expectations—this means understanding that your middle schooler does not in fact need to learn calculus right now (I promise). If you find it difficult to stop overparenting, seek advice from a parenting coach, therapist, or support group for guidance in developing healthier parenting habits.

Educate Yourself on Neglect and Invalidation

About a year ago I went on a family trip to Costa Rica with my parents to celebrate my graduation. At the time I was deep into my research on the impact of parenting and had learned how much my childhood wounds were affecting me presently. I started sending my parents article after article about invalidation, because they were both culprits of it. Growing up with an undiagnosed chronic disease, I was often in pain. Because the doctors told my parents it was all in my head, my parents would say "stop complaining"—often. They are not bad parents. I was literally on a vacation that they brought me on to celebrate my life accomplishment, but that didn't change that I could have been validated more. If you remember in Chapter 12, I outline the impact of emotional neglect. It can leave lifelong wounds for people, and it can impact mental health on many levels. I urge you as a parent to look inward and recognize if you may have made this mistake too. It is a quite common parenting mistake, and you are not alone. And the good news is that it is fixable. The following is a list of things you can say that will validate your child.

"I can see why that is upsetting."

"That would upset me too."
"What I am hearing is…and I understand that it is making you feel like…"
"I hear you, and I am sorry that happened."
"It is not wrong to feel that way."

Take Responsibility

Whether you know it or not, your actions, role modeling, and parenting style have had a huge impact on your kid. I invite you to take a deep exploration into ways you may have copied patterns from your own childhood that you let carry over into this generation. Maybe your parents put high pressure on you, and now you pressure your kid in the same way. Or perhaps your parent had a habit of shaming you for being emotional, and now you also tell your kid to "suck it up." Whatever it may be, take time to recognize your faults and apologize. From a kid's perspective, this is incredibly healing. For my own story, my mom came to me and apologized for the years I suffered with chronic pain, and for her part in only listening to the doctors and not me. She not only apologized but made amends by taking me, at my sickest, to appointments and helping me advocate for answers when I was too physically disabled by the diseases and couldn't. Her apology and acts to make amends helped me heal my inner child that once felt so alone. You can do the same and help your kid heal from their own traumas simply by apologizing.

Harvard has a description on how to give a *real* apology. To be effective, an apology must be sincere. A meaningful apology acknowledges the other person's feelings and takes responsibility for the harm caused. It should express genuine remorse, show care for the hurt individual, and include a commitment to prevent similar incidents in the future.[11] Psychiatrist Dr. Aaron Lazare, an apology expert, argues a good apology has four elements:

1. <u>Acknowledge the offense.</u> Dr. Lazare emphasizes one must "take responsibility for the offense, whether it was a physical or psychological harm, and confirm that your behavior was not acceptable."[12] Further, it is important to "avoid using vague or evasive language, or wording an apology in a way that

minimizes the offense or questions whether the victim was really hurt."[13]

2. <u>Explain the situation</u>. In order to make sure you and the person you hurt are on the same page, it is important to explain to them what happened in your own words without excusing or minimizing it. Lazare asserts that "sometimes the best strategy is to say there is no excuse."

3. <u>Show repentance.</u> In situations of conflict, showing the other person you feel sorry can go a long way, even if you state the words "I feel shame," you can help validate the other person. Be sincere.

4. <u>Offer to make amends.</u> If you hurt someone's feelings, acknowledge the pain and agree you will not repeat the same behavior.

<u>What Educators and Employers Can Do</u>

Be a Safe Space for Gen Z

There is something so powerful about feeling seen and heard by someone—and when it is a trusted adult, it can mean everything. As an educator or employer, you are a role model and can make a true difference in young people's lives. As an educator myself for the last seven years, as both a tutor and now running my own therapeutic art program, it became clear to me how much my words and actions mean.

Below are seven ways to help create a supportive and healing environment for Gen Z, one person at a time, by becoming a safe space for them.

1. <u>Connect with Us</u>
Engage in conversations with us. Keep the topics neutral and friendly, avoiding controversial subjects. A simple smile and a bit of humor can go a long way. Ensure your interactions are genuine and brief, so we feel comfortable and not pressured.

2. <u>Ask Us How We Are Doing</u>
When you ask how we are, show sincere interest in our wellbeing. Listen attentively to our responses and remember personal details to

follow up on later. This demonstrates that you care about our lives beyond the classroom/workplace.

3. <u>Show That You Care</u>
    Your facial expressions and body language should convey unconditional positive regard. Make sure we feel that our time with you is valued. Offer your undivided attention and let us know you are available to listen if we need to talk about anything.

4. <u>Maintain Confidentiality</u> (when it does not breach mandated reporting requirements)
    Be trustworthy by keeping conversations with us confidential. If we share something personal, ensure that you respect our privacy and do not gossip or disclose our information to others.

5. <u>Avoid Giving Unsolicited Personal Advice</u>
    Rather than telling us what to do, encourage us to talk through our issues and come to our own conclusions. If we seek your advice, ask us what we hope to hear from you. This approach helps us reflect on our own solutions.

6. <u>Practice Active Listening</u>
    Give us your full attention when we speak. Make eye contact, nod, and show that you are listening through your body language. Avoid interrupting and let us express ourselves fully before responding.

7. <u>Show Compassion, Not Judgment</u>
    Demonstrate compassion through your tone of voice and expressions. Ensure we know that we are in a judgment-free zone with you, where we can share our thoughts and feelings without fear of being judged. When you need to evaluate as part of your job, please show compassion instead of criticism. When criticism is part of your job, like grading papers or giving a performance review, ensure you give constructive feedback (meaning you don't just say what went wrong, but give examples of where to go right).

Be Inclusive/Learn Cultural Competency

You know what the golden rule is? Treat people how you want to be treated. But you know what's better than that? Treat people how *they* want to be treated—not what you think is right or wrong. Because the only right thing should be to be kind and not cause harm. Part of this is learning the ways in which your words could unintentionally be harmful. All of us have blind spots, and it is impossible to know every way to be inclusive. However, you can still try. And you can apologize when you do make a mistake (because all of us make mistakes). Below are steps and strategies to develop cultural competence, based on insights from the APA experts:[14]

1. Learn About Yourself

    Start with self-reflection to understand your own cultural background, beliefs, values, and biases. This self-awareness helps you recognize how culture shapes your worldview and interactions. This can help uncover blind spots you may be unaware of.

2. Learn About Different Cultures

    As a teacher/employer, you are probably working with diverse people who come from unfamiliar backgrounds. You should expand your knowledge through academic literature and cultural insights. Memoirs, novels, and documentaries can provide rich, nuanced perspectives that academic articles might not capture.

3. Interact with Diverse Groups

    Be the type of role model that we will value through engaging with diverse groups outside of the classroom/workplace. One way to do this is through volunteering. Volunteering at community centers, religious institutions, or soup kitchens can provide hands-on experience with people you may normally not interact with. These interactions help you understand diverse perspectives and improve your ability to work with people from different backgrounds. Participate in social events, religious services, or cultural festivals where you are in the minority. This helps you see beyond your normal settings and appreciate the everyday experiences of diverse groups.

4. Attend Diversity-Focused Conferences

    Conferences like APA's Annual Convention and the National Multicultural Conference and Summit offer formal training and networking opportunities focused on diversity-related issues. These events can enhance your knowledge, introduce you to the latest research, and connect you with potential collaborators. If cost is a barrier, consider volunteering at conferences for reduced fees or apply for travel grants. APA's database of scholarships, grants, and awards can be a valuable resource.

Also, your district/employer may also offer these trainings, and it is worth asking the higher ups.

5. <u>Lobby Your Department</u>

   If your school/workplace lacks adequate training in cultural competence, advocate for it. Gather support from peers and present your case to faculty and management. Highlight the importance of cultural competence in today's increasingly diverse society and push for comprehensive training.

6. <u>Ongoing Learning</u>

   Cultural competence is not a one-time achievement but a lifelong journey. Stay committed to continuous learning and expanding your understanding of different cultures. Remember, competence with one group doesn't imply competence with another. I highly recommend taking your reading further than this, and investigate diverse authors like Tressie McMillan Cottom, Rachel Rickets, Kiese Laymin, and Lily Zheng.

Tips for Supervisors

By now, it's clear: Gen Z is not like previous generations. While older generations might be okay with annual feedback, we thrive on regular check-ins and data-driven insights. Gen X loves their hierarchies, but Gen Z excels in flexible, collaborative environments that prioritize well-being.[15] Flexible work hours are also crucial for Gen Z.[16] While Gen X relies heavily on email, Gen Z prefers open, transparent, multi-channel communication [17]—think chat, video conferencing and social media communication.

Gen Z is hungry for learning and growth whilst maintaining work life balance; [18] therefore, creating a continuous learning environment with mentors, tuition assistance, paid time off, more vacation time, and online courses is key to attracting and keeping Gen Z talent.

You can also retain talent by being more aligned with social and environmental concerns. Meaningful work that aligns with values and contributes to a bigger cause is important to many of us. According to the *Harvard Business Review*, Gen Z gravitates towards companies with strong ethical practices and environmental initiatives.[19] So by not only improving your company's reputation through environmental and ethical standards and helping the planet, you'll also be able to retain more young talent that can inevitably help you grow your business. In essence, more meaningful perks you have for us, the more likely you will retain us.

Conclusion

In this final chapter, I really want to emphasize the power of individual action in addressing the Gen Z mental health crisis. Real change begins with each of us. By understanding and acknowledging the failures within our system, we recognize that we hold the power to create positive change in our own lives and the lives of those around us. Whether you're a member of Gen Z, a teacher, a parent, a politician, an employer, or a concerned citizen, the practical steps outlined in this chapter provide a roadmap for improving mental health within your community. For Gen Z, this involves letting go of cancel culture, practicing non-judgment, and building resilience. For parents, it's about active listening, avoiding overparenting, and taking responsibility for past mistakes. For educators and employers, creating a safe and inclusive space for students is paramount. Many members of Gen Z may require accommodation for their mental health disabilities in order to perform optimally. Instead of making assumptions about us, please ask us what we need.

By connecting genuinely with students and employees, maintaining confidentiality, practicing active listening, and showing compassion, teachers and employers can foster a supportive environment that significantly impacts Gen Z's mental health. Ultimately, the journey to better mental health is ongoing and requires a collective effort to build a more empathetic, inclusive, and supportive society. By taking these steps, we can help heal the divisions and traumas that hinder our wellbeing, fostering a healthier and more connected community for all.

Epilogue

The secret of change is to focus all of your energy not on fighting the old, but on building the new.
–Socrates

I used to think that my voice didn't matter. In fact, I was often that person who was too painfully shy to speak in class or talk to strangers. And then my best friend died during a global pandemic after her long battle with mental health struggles, and I realized I was *done being quiet*. I initially started fighting for equality within my city and even helped establish a non-profit. Yes, that shy little girl *found her voice*. Through our advocacy work, a few passionate people and I managed to organize a movement—one that had thousands of our local citizens marching through our streets for equality—and together we helped pass new policies that will directly impact our city's functioning with more equitable practices. After three years of fighting for equality, there remained one pressing issue that I still sought a way to impact: our mental healthcare system. After losing my friend, I spent those years brainstorming, while working toward improving other intersectional areas that hopefully will positively affect mental health. But I wondered for years: what can I do? And then I remembered the power of words.

If you are reading this, and you made it this far, you are now equipped with much of the information you need to understand the scope of the problem and the solutions landscape. I know it sounds crazy, but I believe in you. Yes, you! You can be an agent of change, and I am going to leave you with four actions you can take toward change.

Lead By Example

To lead by example, find a specific area you are passionate about, such as youth mental health, destigmatization, access to care, or support for specific conditions like depression or anxiety. Focusing on a niche can make your efforts more directed and effective. The cool thing about what you have learned through this book is that many areas indirectly impact mental health. If your cause is climate change, then fight for it! If you care about improving our prison system, be that changemaker! Even if it is indirect, it still matters. Once you find your niche, educate yourself in that focus area, and share your passion with others—being a beacon of knowledge and empathy for those you interact with. Leading by example isn't just about what you achieve, but also how you achieve it. By embodying the qualities you wish to see in others, you can influence behavior and drive change effectively.

Work With Others

One of the best ways you can create change is through community networking and organizing. You can join local or national mental health organizations. Volunteering with these groups can provide practical experience and networking opportunities. Organizations often need help with events, fundraising, and educational campaigns. Establish connections with healthcare providers, educators, and community leaders. Attend and speak up at local city council and school board meetings, seminars, and workshops. Networking can lead to partnerships and collaborations that amplify your impact. And, if for some reason your city does not have an organization within your niche, you can start your own group through social media. In other words, you do not need to do this alone! FYI, this is also a chance to meet cool like-minded people and make friends.

Use the Tools You Have

Think about what you can do. Can you make art? Are you good at hosting events? Are you a social media expert? There are many tools that you have within your own expertise and those that are easily accessible, like social media. You can leverage social media platforms to raise awareness, share information, and mobilize supporters. Platforms like Twitter/X, Facebook, TikTok, and Instagram can be powerful tools for reaching a large audience quickly. Also, because you are a human with the ability to read this, this means you also have the ability to engage with policymakers by writing letters, making phone calls, or scheduling meetings with local stakeholders to discuss mental health issues and the changes needed in healthcare policies. Prepare clear, research-backed arguments to support your points. Likewise, if you have access to a park, or a space of your own, you can host or take part in events such as workshops, seminars, health fairs, and discussion panels.

Events can be platforms for education, raising awareness, and advocating for policy changes. Think about the tools and connections you have and use them!

Stay Informed and Adapt

As I have highlighted in Chapter 2, the evolution of our system is constantly making fresh waves in innovations and solutions. This is why it is important for you, my new fellow activist, to keep up to date with the latest news, research, and policies. As you are aware, the only constant in our lives is change. Adapting ensures that your strategies and skills remain relevant and effective. The book, *The Practice of Adaptive Leadership*, underscores how leaders who are adaptable and knowledgeable inspire confidence and loyalty in their teams. [1] By demonstrating a commitment to staying current and flexible, leaders can encourage a similar approach among their team members, fostering a culture of continuous learning and resilience. And I mention leadership, because as a changemaker, I believe in you to lead with me. If every person who reads this book decides to help make change in their cities, together, we can literally change the mental healthcare system

Book Club Discussion Questions

<u>**Chapter 1.**</u>
1. What impact did James' father's addiction have on his own mental health and behavior?
2. How did Sam's experience with the troubled teen industry shape their understanding of mental health and community?
3. What were the significant turning points in Ethan's life that affected his mental health?
4. How do the personal stories in this chapter illustrate the broader systemic failures in addressing mental health?

<u>**Chapter 2.**</u>
1. What were some of the earliest recorded treatments for mental illness, and how were they perceived in society?
2. How did the treatment of mental illness evolve from the Middle Ages to the 20th century?
3. What were some of the controversial treatments mentioned in the chapter, and what were their consequences?
4. How has the Diagnostic and Statistical Manual of Mental Disorders (DSM) influenced the diagnosis and treatment of mental health issues?

<u>**Chapter 3.**</u>
1. How does the author describe their personal experiences with stigma related to mental health?
2. What impact does media representation of mental illness have on public perception and stigma?
3. What are the different types of stigma identified in the chapter, and how do they affect individuals with mental health issues?
4. How does stigma contribute to the challenges faced by people with mental illness in seeking and receiving treatment?

<u>**Chapter 4.**</u>
1. What barriers do people face in accessing effective mental healthcare, according to the author?
2. How have emergency rooms become a primary source of mental health treatment for children and adolescents?

3. What are some examples of unprofessional behavior or low standards of care in mental health services mentioned in the chapter?
4. How do the costs and shortage of mental healthcare providers impact access to treatment?

Chapter 5.
1. What is the significance of early intervention in mental health treatment, and what challenges prevent it?
2. How does misdiagnosis of mental health conditions affect individuals, especially in terms of over or under-diagnosis?
3. What role do overlooked physical health conditions play in mental health struggles?
4. How does medical gaslighting impact individuals seeking help for mental health issues?

Chapter 6.
1. What are the potential drawbacks of using medication as the first line of defense against mental illness?
2. How does the pharmaceutical industry's influence affect mental health treatment practices?
3. Why does medication matter to address mental healthcare's failings?

Chapter 7.
1. How does the criminal justice system intersect with mental health treatment

Chapter 8.
1. How does the drug epidemic contribute to the mental health crisis among Gen Z?
2. What are the systemic issues that exacerbate substance abuse problems?
3. How does the author link the drug epidemic to broader social and economic factors?

Chapter 9.
1. What factors does the author attribute to the rise in autism ADHD diagnoses?
2. What are some challenges faced by individuals with autism/ADHD in accessing mental health care?
3. How are these conditions related, and why do they illustrate systemic failings?

<u>Chapter 10.</u>
1. What are some examples of systemic bias and disparities in mental health care mentioned in the chapter?
2. How do these biases affect the quality of care received by different demographic groups?
3. What role do social determinants of health play in exacerbating mental health disparities?
4. Why do disparities represent a root cause of the mental health care crisis?

<u>Chapter 11.</u>
1. What is the link of capitalism to the mental health crisis?
2. What are some ways in which economic instability impacts mental health, according to the chapter?
3. How do workplace pressures and the gig economy contribute to mental health struggles?
4. In what ways does capitalism impact our mental health care system?

<u>Chapter 12.</u>
1. How have parenting styles and societal expectations changed for Gen Z compared to previous generations?
2. What are some unique challenges faced by parents of Gen Z children in supporting their mental health?
3. How do modern parenting practices impact the mental health of Gen Z?

<u>Chapter 13.</u>
1. What factors contribute to the loneliness epidemic among Gen Z, as discussed in the chapter?
2. How does loneliness impact mental health and well-being?
3. What role do social media and technology play in both exacerbating and alleviating loneliness?

<u>Chapter 14.</u>
1. How does the author link nutrition and exercise to mental health?
2. What are some specific dietary and exercise-related issues that contribute to mental health problems?
3. How do modern agricultural practices and food industries impact the mental health of Gen Z?

<u>Chapter 15.</u>
1. How does social media use impact mental health, according to the chapter?

2. What are some positive and negative aspects of social media on mental well-being?
3. How can individuals and society better manage social media usage to mitigate its negative effects?
4. What role do tech companies play in addressing the mental health impacts of social media?

Chapter 16.
1. What types of environmental toxins does the author discuss, and how do they affect mental health?
2. How does exposure to toxins affect certain populations and who do they affect?
3. Why is it important to address toxicity? Why does the author believe it is a root cause of the mental health crisis?

Chapter 17.
1. What challenges do youth face that affect their mental health in terms of education?
2. How has the higher education system changed, and what are its shortcomings in supporting students' mental health?
3. Why isn't college the same for gen z as it was for their parents?

Chapter 18.
1. How does the prevalence of guns in America impact mental health?
2. What are some specific ways in which gun violence affects individuals and communities?

Chapter 19.
1. How does the author link individualism to the mental health crisis?
2. What are some negative consequences of an individualistic culture on mental well-being

Chapter 20.
1. What current solutions are being implemented to address the mental health crisis, according to the author?
2. How effective are these solutions in addressing the systemic issues highlighted in the book?
3. What are some innovative approaches to mental health care mentioned in the chapter?

Chapter 21.
1. What comprehensive strategies does the author propose for addressing the mental health crisis?

2. How can policymakers, communities, and individuals contribute to these proposed changes?
3. What role does advocacy play in driving systemic change for mental health?
4. How would the future of mental health care look if the suggested changes are implemented?

End Notes

INTRODUCTION

[1] https://www.pewtrusts.org/en/research-and-analysis/articles/2023/03/03/youth-suicide-risk-increased-over-past-decade

[2] https://www.cnbc.com/2023/12/05/youth-suicide-rates-rose-62percent-from-2007-to-2021.html

[3] National Alliance on Mental Illness. (n.d.). Mental health by the numbers. Retrieved from https://www.nami.org/about-mental-illness/mental-health-by-the-numbers/#:~:text=22.8%25%20of%20U.S.%20adults%20experienced,represents%201%20in%2020%20adults

[4] Riley, W. J. (2012). Health disparities: gaps in access, quality and affordability of medical care. Transactions of the American Clinical and Climatological Association, 123, 167–174; Mental Health America. (n.d.). State of mental health in America. Retrieved from https://mhanational.org/issues/state-mental-health-america

[5] National Institute of Mental Health. (n.d.). Suicide statistics. Retrieved from https://www.nimh.nih.gov/health/statistics/suicide

[6] NYU Stern. (n.d.). An anxious generation: How the great rewiring of childhood is causing an epidemic of mental illness. Retrieved from https://www.stern.nyu.edu/experience-stern/faculty-research/anxious-generation-how-great-rewiring-childhood-causing-epidemic-mental-illness

[7] NPR. (n.d.). Body electric. Retrieved from https://www.npr.org/series/1199526213/body-electric

[8] State of Connecticut. (n.d.). Declaration of Independence & U.S. Constitution. Retrieved from https://portal.ct.gov/sots/register-manual/section-i/declaration-of-independence-us-constitution#:~:text=We%20hold%20these%20truths%20to,and%20the%20pursuit%20of%20happiness

[9] U.S. News & World Report. (2024, April 24). $282 billion: What mental illness costs America each year. Retrieved from https://www.usnews.com/news/health-news/articles/2024-04-24/282-billion-what-mental-illness-costs-america-each-year

CHAPTER 2: HISTORICAL PERSPECTIVE

[1] Spanos, N. P. (1978). Witchcraft in histories of psychiatry: A critical analysis and an alternative conceptualization. *Psychological Bulletin, 85*(2), 417–439. https://doi.org/10.1037/0033-2909.85.2.417

[2] Faria M. A., Jr (2013). Violence, mental illness, and the brain - A brief history of psychosurgery: Part 1 - From trephination to lobotomy. *Surgical neurology international, 4*, 49. https://doi.org/10.4103/2152-7806.110146

[3] Gerry Greenstone, M.D. The history of bloodletting. BCMJ, Vol. 52, No. 1, January, February 2010, Page(s) 12-14

[4] Virtual Mentor. 2013;15(10):886-891. doi: 10.1001/virtualmentor.2013.15.10.mhst1-1310.

[5] George, P., Jones, N., Goldman, H., & Rosenblatt, A. (2023). Cycles of reform in the history of psychosis treatment in the United States. SSM. Mental health, 3, 100205. https://doi.org/10.1016/j.ssmmh.2023.100205

[6] Chaturvedi, K., Vishwakarma, D.K., & Singh, N. COVID-19 and its impact on education, social life and mental health of students: A survey. Children and Youth Services Review 121 (2021) 105866

[7] Freudenthal, R., & Moncrieff, J. (2022). 'A landmark in psychiatric progress'? The role of evidence in the rise and fall of insulin coma therapy. History of psychiatry, 33(1), 65–78. https://doi.org/10.1177/0957154X211062538

[8] https://www.webmd.com/schizophrenia/features/insulin-coma-therapy

[9] Charlton GE, Brinegar WC, Holloway Or. Curare And Metrazol Therapy of Psychoses: Report Of A Fatal Case. *Arch NeurPsych.* 1942;48(2):267–270. doi:10.1001/archneurpsyc.1942.02290080113005

[10] https://www.health.harvard.edu/blog/transcranial-magnetic-stimulation-for-depression-2018022313335

[11] Tan, S. Y., & Yip, A. (2014). António Egas Moniz (1874-1955): Lobotomy pioneer and Nobel laureate. *Singapore medical journal*, 55(4), 175–176. https://doi.org/10.11622/smedj.2014048

[12] Caruso JP, Sheehan JP. Psychosurgery, ethics, and media: a history of Walter Freeman and the lobotomy. Neurosurg Focus. 2017 Sep;43(3):E6. doi: 10.3171/2017.6.FOCUS17257. PMID: 28859561.

[13] https://www.webmd.com/brain/what-is-lobotomy

[14] Washington University School of Medicine in St. Louis. (2024). Stereotactic neurosurgical procedures. Retrieved from https://neurosurgery.wustl.edu/items/stereotactic-neurosurgical-procedures/

[15] De Jesus O, Fogwe DT, Mesfin FB, et al. Neuromodulation Surgery for Psychiatric Disorders. Updated 2023 Aug 28]. In: StatPearls Internet]. Treasure Island (FL): StatPearls Publishing; 2024 Jan-. Available from: https://www.ncbi.nlm.nih.gov/books/NBK482366/

[16] WebMD. (2022). What is lobotomy? Retrieved from https://www.webmd.com/brain/what-is-lobotomy

[17] BetterHelp. (2024). A brief history of therapy: Where it all began. Retrieved from https://www.betterhelp.com/advice/therapy/a-brief-history-of-therapy-where-it-all-began/#

[18] Counselling Directory. (2024). History of counselling. Retrieved from https://www.counselling-directory.org.uk/history.html

[19] Kawa, S., & Giordano, J. (2012). A brief historicity of the Diagnostic and Statistical Manual of Mental Disorders: issues and implications for the future of psychiatric canon and practice. *Philosophy, ethics, and humanities in medicine: PEHM, 7, 2.* https://doi.org/10.1186/1747-5341-7-2

[20] Surís, A., Holliday, R., & North, C. S. (2016). The Evolution of the Classification of Psychiatric Disorders. *Behavioral sciences (Basel, Switzerland), 6(1), 5.* https://doi.org/10.3390/bs6010005

[21] Davis, L. C., Diianni, A. T., Drumheller, S. R., Elansary, N. N., D'Ambrozio, G. N., Herrawi, F., Piper, B. J., & Cosgrove, L. (2024). Undisclosed financial conflicts of interest in DSM-5-TR: cross sectional analysis. *BMJ (Clinical research ed.), 384,* e076902. https://doi.org/10.1136/bmj-2023-076902

[22] https://www.madinamerica.com/2022/02/new-dsm-coming/

[23] Majerus B. (2016). Making Sense of the 'Chemical Revolution'. Patients' Voices on the Introduction of Neuroleptics in the 1950s. *Medical history, 60(1), 54–66.* https://doi.org/10.1017/mdh.2015.68

[24] David, D., Cristea, I., & Hofmann, S. G. (2018). Why Cognitive Behavioral Therapy Is the Current Gold Standard of Psychotherapy. *Frontiers in psychiatry*, *9*, 4. https://doi.org/10.3389/fpsyt.2018.00004

[25] https://www.healthcentral.com/article/5-reasons-cognitive-behavioral-therapy-may-not-work-for-you

[26] National Alliance on Mental Illness. (2024). Psychotherapy. Retrieved from https://www.nami.org/about-mental-illness/treatments/psychotherapy/

[27] National Alliance on Mental Illness. (2024). Psychotherapy. Retrieved from https://www.nami.org/about-mental-illness/treatments/psychotherapy/

[28] Popova, V., Daly, E. J., Trivedi, M., Cooper, K., Lane, R., Lim, P., ... Singh, J. B. (2019). Efficacy and Safety of Flexibly Dosed Esketamine Nasal Spray Combined with a Newly Initiated Oral Antidepressant in Treatment-Resistant Depression: A Randomized Double-Blind Active-Controlled Study. *American Journal of Psychiatry*, *176*(6), 428–

[29] Subbiah, V. The next generation of evidence-based medicine. *Nat Med* 29, 49–58 (2023). https://doi.org/10.1038/s41591-022-02160-z

[30] Menta, A. K., Subbiah, I. M. & Subbiah, V. Bringing wearable devices into oncology practice: fitting smart technology in the clinic. Discov. Med.26, 261–270 (2018).

CHAPTER 3: THE HARM OF STIGMA

[1] https://www.psychiatry.org/patients-families/stigma-and-discrimination#:~:text=The%20study%20found%20that%20viewing,of%20mental%20illness%20is%20universal.

[2] Ahad, A.A., Sanchez-Gonzalez, M., & Junquera, P. (2023). Understanding and Addressing Mental Health Stigma Across Cultures for Improving Psychiatric Care: A Narrative Review. *Cureus*, *15*(5), e39549. https://doi.org/10.7759/cureus.39549

[3] Corrigan, P.W., & Watson, A.C. (2002). Understanding the impact of stigma on people with mental illness. World psychiatry: official journal of the World Psychiatric Association (WPA), 1(1), 16–20.

[4] See chap 21

[5] https://www.psychiatry.org/patients-families/stigma-and-discrimination#:~:text=Structural%20stigma%20is%20more%20systemic,relative%20to%20other%20health%20care.

[6] Corrigan, P. W., & Watson, A. C. (2002). Understanding the impact of stigma on people with mental illness. World psychiatry: official journal of the World Psychiatric Association (WPA), 1(1), 16–20.

[7] https://www.nami.org/mhstats

[8] Wong, E. C., Collins, R. L., Cerully, J., Seelam, R., & Roth, B. (2017). Racial and Ethnic Differences in Mental Illness Stigma and Discrimination Among Californians Experiencing Mental Health Challenges. *Rand health quarterly*, *6*(2), 6.

[9] Henderson, R. C., Williams, P., Gabbidon, J., Farrelly, S., Schauman, O., Hatch, S., Thornicroft, G., Bhugra, D., Clement, S., & MIRIAD study group (2015). Mistrust of mental health services: ethnicity, hospital admission and unfair treatment. *Epidemiology and psychiatric sciences*, *24*(3), 258–265. https://doi.org/10.1017/S2045796014000158

[10] Østerud K. L. (2023). Mental illness stigma and employer evaluation in hiring: Stereotypes, discrimination and the role of experience. *Sociology of health & illness*, *45*(1), 90–108. https://doi.org/10.1111/1467-9566.13544

[11] Jahn, D. R., Leith, J., Muralidharan, A., Brown, C. H., Drapalski, A. L., Hack, S., & Lucksted, A. (2020). The influence of experiences of stigma on recovery: Mediating roles of internalized stigma, self-esteem, and self-efficacy. *Psychiatric rehabilitation journal*, *43*(2), 97–105. https://doi.org/10.1037/prj0000377

[12] Oexle N, Müller M, Kawohl W, Xu Z, Viering S, Wyss C, Vetter S, Rüsch N. Self-stigma as a barrier to recovery: a longitudinal study. Eur Arch Psychiatry Clin Neurosci. 2018 Mar;268(2):209-212. doi: 10.1007/s00406-017-0773-2. Epub 2017 Feb 10. PMID: 28188369.

[13] Rössler W. (2016). The stigma of mental disorders: A millennia-long history of social exclusion and prejudices. EMBO reports, 17(9), 1250–1253. https://doi.org/10.15252/embr.201643041

[14] Mental Health: A Workforce Crisis," American Heart Association CEO Roundtable, 2018.

[15] https://psychnews.psychiatryonline.org/doi/10.1176/appi.pn.2019.6b21

[16] Sarkar, S., Menon, V., Padhy, S., & Kathiresan, P. (2024). Mental health and well-being at the workplace. *Indian journal of psychiatry, 66*(Suppl 2), S353–S364.

[17] https://nypost.com/2024/02/06/lifestyle/from-boomers-to-gen-z-women-of-all-generations-feel-this-subject-is-still-stigmatized/

<u>CHAPTER 4: INADEQUATE RESOURCES & ACCESS</u>

[1] Centers for Disease Control and Prevention. (2023). National health statistics reports: No. 191. Retrieved from https://www.cdc.gov/nchs/data/nhsr/nhsr191.pdf

[2] Rabin, R. C. (2023, May 1). Adolescents 'mental health hospitalizations are soaring. The New York Times. Retrieved from https://www.nytimes.com/2023/05/01/health/adolescents-mental-health-hospitals.html

[3] Bommersbach, T. J., McKean, A. J., Olfson, M., & Rhee, T. G. (2023). National Trends in Mental Health-Related Emergency Department Visits Among Youth, 2011-2020. *JAMA, 329*(17), 1469–1477. https://doi.org/10.1001/jama.2023.4809

[4] Leonard Davis Institute of Health Economics. (n.d.). Worsening faster than it's improving: The U.S. mental health care delivery system. Retrieved from https://ldi.upenn.edu/our-work/research-updates/worsening-faster-than-its-improving-the-us-mental-health-care-delivery-system/

[5] U.S. Department of Health and Human Services. (2021). Surgeon General's advisory: Protecting youth mental health. Retrieved from https://www.hhs.gov/sites/default/files/surgeon-general-youth-mental-health-advisory.pdf

[6] National Health Law Program. (2018). Navigating the challenges of Medi-Cal's mental health services in California: An examination of care coordination, referrals, and dispute resolution. Retrieved from https://healthlaw.org/resource/navigating-the-challenges-of-medi-cals-mental-health-services-in-california-an-examination-of-care-coordination-referrals-and-dispute-resolution/#:~:text=They%20are%20hampered%20by%20a,isresponsible%20for%20providing%20specialty%20mental

[7] California Department of Health Care Services. (2024). Medi-Cal specialty mental health services. Retrieved from https://www.dhcs.ca.gov/services/Pages/Medi-cal_SMHS.aspx

[8] Federal Trade Commission. (2023, March). FTC says online counseling service BetterHelp pushed people into handing over health information, broke the law. Retrieved from https://www.ftc.gov/business-guidance/blog/2023/03/ftc-says-online-counseling-service-betterhelp-pushed-people-handing-over-health-information-broke

[9] Coombs, N. C., Meriwether, W. E., Caringi, J., & Newcomer, S. R. (2021). Barriers to healthcare access among U.S. adults with mental health challenges: A population-based study. *SSM - population health, 15*, 100847. https://doi.org/10.1016/j.ssmph.2021.100847

---

[10] Kilbourne, A. M., Beck, K., Spaeth-Rublee, B., Ramanuj, P., O'Brien, R. W., Tomoyasu, N., & Pincus, H. A. (2018). Measuring and improving the quality of mental health care: a global perspective. *World psychiatry: official journal of the World Psychiatric Association (WPA), 17*(1), 30–38. https://doi.org/10.1002/wps.20482

[11] Psychology Today. (2023.). How much does therapy cost? Retrieved from https://www.psychologytoday.com/us/basics/therapy/how-much-does-therapy-cost#:~:text=Therapy%20sessions%20in%20the%20U.S.,to%20find%20lower%2Dpriced%20care

[12] Rowan, K., McAlpine, D. D., & Blewett, L. A. (2013). Access and cost barriers to mental health care, by insurance status, 1999-2010. *Health affairs (Project Hope), 32*(10), 1723–1730. https://doi.org/10.1377/hlthaff.2013.0133

[13] Walker, E. R., Cummings, J. R., Hockenberry, J. M., & Druss, B. G. (2015). Insurance status, use of mental health services, and unmet need for mental health care in the United States. *Psychiatric services (Washington, D.C.), 66*(6), 578–584. https://doi.org/10.1176/appi.ps.201400248

[14] https://www.foxbusiness.com/economy/nearly-70-percent-americans-struggling-pay-grocery-bills-survey-finds

[15] Modi H, Orgera K, Grover A. *Exploring Barriers to Mental Health Care in the U.S.* Washington, DC: AAMC; 2022. https://doi.org/10.15766/rai_a3ewcf9p

[16] Substance Abuse and Mental Health Services Administration. (2020). *Key substance use and mental health indicators in the United States: Results from the 2019 National Survey on Drug Use and Health* (HHS Publication No. PEP20-07-01-001, NSDUH Series H-55). Rockville, MD: Center for Behavioral Health Statistics and Quality, Substance Abuse and Mental Health Services Administration. Retrieved from https://www.samhsa.gov/data/

[17] Phantom Networks: Discrepancies Between Reported and Realized Mental Health Care Access In Oregon Medicaid Jane M. Zhu, Christina J. Charlesworth, Daniel Polsky, and K. John McConnell

[18] University of Michigan Behavioral Health Workforce Research Center.

[19] See University of Michigan Behavioral Health Workforce Research Center.

[20] https://www.commonwealthfund.org/publications/explainer/2023/may/understanding-us-behavioral-health-workforce-shortage

[21] Wyse, R., Hwang, WT., Ahmed, A.A. *et al.* Diversity by Race, Ethnicity, and Sex within the US Psychiatry Physician Workforce. *Acad Psychiatry,* 44, 523–530 (2020). https://doi.org/10.1007/s40596-020-01276-z

[22] National Alliance on Mental Illness. (n.d.). Types of mental health professionals. Retrieved from https://www.nami.org/About-Mental-Illness/Treatments/Types-of-Mental-Health-Professionals

[23] American Progress. (n.d.). The behavioral health care affordability problem. Retrieved from https://www.americanprogress.org/article/the-behavioral-health-care-affordability-problem/

[24] Commonwealth Fund. (2023, May). Understanding the U.S. behavioral health workforce shortage. Retrieved from https://www.commonwealthfund.org/publications/explainer/2023/may/understanding-us-behavioral-health-workforce-shortage

[25] Commonwealth Fund. (2023, May). Understanding the U.S. behavioral health workforce shortage. Retrieved from https://www.commonwealthfund.org/publications/explainer/2023/may/understanding-us-behavioral-health-workforce-shortage

[26] National Heart, Lung, and Blood Institute. (2014). Role of community health workers. Retrieved from https://www.nhlbi.nih.gov/health/educational/healthdisp/role-of-community-health-workers.htm

[27] Rural Health Information Hub. (2020). Grant funding for community health workers. Retrieved from https://www.ruralhealthinfo.org/toolkits/community-health-workers/6/grant-funding

[28] Blau, F. D., Koebe, J., & Meyerhofer, P. A. (2021). Who are the essential and frontline workers? *Business economics (Cleveland, Ohio)*, *56*(3), 168–178. https://doi.org/10.1057/s11369-021-00230-7

[29] https://www.hhs.gov/about/news/2022/01/20/biden-harris-administration-awards-103-million-american-rescue-plan-funds-reduce-burnout-promote-mental-health-wellness-among-health-care-workforce.html

[30] Han S, Shanafelt, TD, Sinsky CA, et al. Estimating the attributable cost of physician burnout in the United States. *Ann Intern Med*. 2019;170(11):784-790. doi:10.7326/M18-1422

[31] Khullar D. Burnout, Professionalism, and the Quality of US Health Care. *JAMA Health Forum*.2023;4(3):e230024. doi:10.1001/jamahealthforum.2023.0024

[32] Han, S, Shanafelt TD, Sinsky CA, et al. Estimating the attributable cost of physician burnout in the United States. *Ann Intern Med*. 2019;170(11):784-790. doi:10.7326/M18-1422

[33] BBC News. (2020, August 11). What's the difference between stress and burnout? Retrieved from https://www.bbc.com/news/health-53742121

[34] De Hert S. Burnout in healthcare workers: prevalence, impact and preventative strategies. *Local Reg Anesth*. 2020;13:171-183.

[35] Lockley SW, Barger LK, Ayas NT, Rothschild JM, Czeisler CA, Landrigan CP; Harvard Work Hours, Health and Safety Group. Effects of health care provider work hours and sleep deprivation on safety and performance. Jt Comm J Qual Patient Saf. 2007 Nov;33(11 Suppl):7-18. doi: 10.1016/s1553-7250(07)33109-7. PMID: 18173162.

[36] https://www.washingtonpost.com/lifestyle/2023/06/13/astrology-millennials-gen-z-science/

[37] Das A, Sharma MK, Kashyap H, Gupta S. Fixating on the future: An overview of increased astrology use. Int J Soc Psychiatry. 2022 Aug;68(5):925-932. doi: 10.1177/00207640221094155. Epub 2022 May 5. PMID: 35510634.

[38] Smith, HuffPost. (2019). Astrology and tarot cards: Can they affect your mental health? Retrieved from https://www.huffpost.com/entry/astrology-tarot-cards-mental-health_l_5df7b210e4b03aed50f25c30

[39] The University of California Berkeley. Astrology: Is It Scientific?, https://undsci.berkeley.edu/article/astrology_checklist#

[40] Lazar, Mona. Medium. (2022). The love and light gurus are ruining your life. Retrieved from https://medium.com/illumination/the-love-and-light-gurus-are-ruining-your-life-329aaf430f00

[41] Keen. (n.d.). How much is an astrology reading? Retrieved from https://www.keen.com/articles/astrology/how-much-is-an-astrology-reading

[42] Newport Institute. (n.d.). Manifesting change: Does it work for mental health? Retrieved from https://www.newportinstitute.com/resources/mental-health/manifesting-change/

[43] Why Now. (n.d.). Manifesting: The new materialistic cult with a dark side. Retrieved from https://whynow.co.uk/read/manifesting-the-new-materialistic-cult-with-a-dark-side

[44] Exploring Therapy. (2024). Is manifestation culture doing more harm than good? Retrieved from https://www.exploringtherapy.com/therapy-blog/is-manifestation-culture-doing-more-harm-than-good

[45] Psychology Today. (2024, January). The psychology of conspiracy theories. Retrieved from https://www.psychologytoday.com/us/blog/your-emotional-meter/202401/the-psychology-of-conspiracy-theories

[46] Gagliardi, L. (2023). The role of cognitive biases in conspiracy beliefs: A literature review. *Journal of Economic Surveys*, 1–34. https://doi.org/10.1111/joes.12604

CHAPTER 5: FAILURE IN EARLY INTERVENTION & MISDIAGNOSIS

[1] Solmi, M., Radua, J., Olivola, M. *et al.* Age at onset of mental disorders worldwide: large-scale meta-analysis of 192 epidemiological studies. *Mol Psychiatry* 27, 281–295 (2022). https://doi.org/10.1038/s41380-021-01161-7

[2] Singh, T., & Rajput, M. (2006). Misdiagnosis of bipolar disorder. *Psychiatry (Edgmont (Pa.: Township))*, *3*(10), 57–63.

[3] Singh, T., & Rajput, M. (2006). Misdiagnosis of bipolar disorder. *Psychiatry (Edgmont (Pa.: Township))*, *3*(10), 57–63.

[4] Novick, D. M., Swartz, H. A., & Frank, E. (2010). Suicide attempts in bipolar I and bipolar II disorder: a review and meta-analysis of the evidence. *Bipolar disorders*, *12*(1), 1–9. https://doi.org/10.1111/j.1399-5618.2009.00786.x

[5] Autism Speaks. (n.d.). Autism and bipolar disorder: Expert opinion. Retrieved from https://www.autismspeaks.org/expert-opinion/autism-bipolar#:~:text=Some%20studies%20have%20found%20that,diagnosed%20in%20those%20with%20autism

[6] Brittany Stahnke, A systematic review of misdiagnosis in those with obsessive-compulsive disorder, Journal of Affective Disorders Reports, Volume 6, 2021, 100231, ISSN 2666-9153, https://doi.org/10.1016/j.jadr.2021.100231.

[7] Brittany Stahnke, A systematic review of misdiagnosis in those with obsessive-compulsive disorder, Journal of Affective Disorders Reports, Volume 6, 2021, 100231, ISSN 2666-9153, https://doi.org/10.1016/j.jadr.2021.100231.

[8] Wakefield J. C. (2015). DSM-5, psychiatric epidemiology and the false positives problem. *Epidemiology and psychiatric sciences*, *24*(3), 188–196. https://doi.org/10.1017/S2045796015000116

[9] Wakefield J. C. (2015). DSM-5, psychiatric epidemiology and the false positives problem. *Epidemiology and psychiatric sciences*, *24*(3), 188–196. https://doi.org/10.1017/S2045796015000116

[10] National Institute of Mental Health. (n.d.). Chronic illness and mental health. Retrieved from https://www.nimh.nih.gov/health/publications/chronic-illness-mental-health#:~:text=Chronic%20illnesses%20such%20as%20cancer,chronic%20condition%20such%20as%20pain

[11] Slawson, N. The Guardian. (2019, December 18). Women have been woefully neglected: Does medical science have a gender problem? Retrieved from https://www.theguardian.com/education/2019/dec/18/women-have-been-woefully-neglected-does-medical-science-have-a-gender-problem

[12] Kate Manne's *Entitled,* goes into detail about (White) cis-male medical privilege and how that harms (non-White) women for further reading

[13] Kronzer, V. L., Bridges, S. L., Jr, & Davis, J. M., 3rd (2020). Why women have more autoimmune diseases than men: An evolutionary perspective. *Evolutionary applications*, *14*(3), 629–633. https://doi.org/10.1111/eva.13167

[14] American Psychiatric Association. (2017). Mental health facts for women. Retrieved from https://www.psychiatry.org/getmedia/aa325a61-5b60-4c71-80f1-dc80cf83c383/Mental-Health-Facts-for-Women.pdf

[15] Maserejian, N. N., Link, C. L., Lutfey, K. L., Marceau, L. D., & McKinlay, J. B. (2009). Disparities in physicians' interpretations of heart disease symptoms by patient gender: results of a video vignette factorial experiment. *Journal of women's health (2002)*, *18*(10), 1661–1667. https://doi.org/10.1089/jwh.2008.1007

CHAPTER 6: OVEREMPHASIS ON MEDICATION

[1] Ivanov, I., & Schwartz, J. M. (2021). Why Psychotropic Drugs Don't Cure Mental Illness-But Should They? *Frontiers in psychiatry*, *12*, 579566. https://doi.org/10.3389/fpsyt.2021.579566

[2] https://www.health.harvard.edu/blog/astounding-increase-in-antidepressant-use-by-americans-201110203624

[3] Kirsch, I. Placebo Effect in the Treatment of Depression and Anxiety. *Frontiers in Psychiatry*, VOL 10. (2019). https://www.frontiersin.org/journals/psychiatry/articles/10.3389/fpsyt.2019.00407, 10.3389/fpsyt.2019.00407, 1664-0640

[4] Jacob K. S. (2015). Recovery model of mental illness: a complementary approach to psychiatric care. *Indian journal of psychological medicine*, *37*(2), 117–119. https://doi.org/10.4103/0253-7176.155605

[5] https://www.apa.org/ptsd-guideline/patients-and-families/medication-or-therapy#:~:text=Research%20generally%20shows%20that%20psychotherapy,improve%20outcomes%20from%20psychotherapy%20alone.

[6] https://www.scientificamerican.com/article/has-the-drug-based-approach-to-mental-illness-failed/

[7] Brownlee, S., Chalkidou, K., Doust, J., Elshaug, A. G., Glasziou, P., Heath, I., Nagpal, S., Saini, V., Srivastava, D., Chalmers, K., & Korenstein, D. (2017). Evidence for overuse of medical services around the world. *Lancet (London, England)*, *390*(10090), 156–168. https://doi.org/10.1016/S0140-6736(16)32585-5

[8] Pharma News Intelligence. (n.d.). Senate report exposes Big Pharma's profiteering at Americans 'expense. Retrieved from https://pharmanewsintel.com/features/senate-report-exposes-big-pharmas-profiteering-at-americans-expense

[9] The Guardian. (2017, October 19). Big Pharma spends millions on lobbying to influence US opioid crisis. Retrieved from https://www.theguardian.com/us-news/2017/oct/19/big-pharma-money-lobbying-us-opioid-crisis

[10] The Washington Post. (2023, June 18). Foes of the Inflation Reduction Act race to repeal climate and drug pricing programs. Retrieved from https://www.washingtonpost.com/business/2023/06/18/foes-inflation-reduction-act-race-repeal-climate-drug-pricing-programs/

[11] Sanders, B. (n.d.). The greed of Big Pharma cannot continue. Retrieved from https://www.sanders.senate.gov/op-eds/the-greed-of-big-pharma-cannot-continue/

[12] Fierce Pharma. (n.d.). Pharma ad spending in just 1 year: The slow move away from TV and digital continues. Retrieved 1 from https://www.fiercepharma.com/marketing/pharma-ad-spending-just-1-year-slow-move-away-tv-and-digitalcontinues

[13] https://www.cms.gov/files/document/fact-sheet-medicare-drug-price-negotiation-program-ipay-2027-and-manufacturer-effectuation-mfp-2026.pdf

[14] Rashidian, A., Omidvari, A. H., Vali, Y., Sturm, H., & Oxman, A. D. (2015). Pharmaceutical policies: effects of financial incentives for prescribers. *The Cochrane database of systematic reviews*, *2015*(8), CD006731. https://doi.org/10.1002/14651858.CD006731.pub2

[15] https://www.madinamerica.com/2021/09/anatomy-industry-commerce-payments-psychiatrists-betrayal-public-good/

[16] Zarei, E., Ghaffari, A., Nikoobar, A., Bastami, S., & Hamdghaddari, H. (2023). Interaction between physicians and the pharmaceutical industry: A scoping review for developing a policy brief. *Frontiers in public health*, *10*, 1072708. https://doi.org/10.3389/fpubh.2022.1072708

---

[17] Pham-Kanter G. (2014). Act II of the Sunshine Act. *PLoS medicine, 11*(11), e1001754. https://doi.org/10.1371/journal.pmed.1001754

[18] https://www.madinamerica.com/2021/09/anatomy-industry-commerce-payments-psychiatrists-betrayal-public-good/

[19] https://www.madinamerica.com/2021/09/anatomy-industry-commerce-payments-psychiatrists-betrayal-public-good/

[20] https://www.madinamerica.com/2021/09/anatomy-industry-commerce-payments-psychiatrists-betrayal-public-good/

[21] https://www.madinamerica.com/2021/09/anatomy-industry-commerce-payments-psychiatrists-betrayal-public-good/

[22] https://www.madinamerica.com/2021/09/anatomy-industry-commerce-payments-psychiatrists-betrayal-public-good/

[23] https://www.madinamerica.com/2021/09/anatomy-industry-commerce-payments-psychiatrists-betrayal-public-good/

[24] https://www.madinamerica.com/2021/09/anatomy-industry-commerce-payments-psychiatrists-betrayal-public-good/

[25] https://www.madinamerica.com/2021/09/anatomy-industry-commerce-payments-psychiatrists-betrayal-public-good/

[26] https://www.madinamerica.com/2021/09/anatomy-industry-commerce-payments-psychiatrists-betrayal-public-good/

[27] https://www.madinamerica.com/2021/09/anatomy-industry-commerce-payments-psychiatrists-betrayal-public-good/

[28] https://www.cms.gov/priorities/key-initiatives/open-payments/data

[29] https://www.cms.gov/priorities/key-initiatives/open-payments/data

[30] Rhee, T. G., & Wilkinson, S. T. (2020). Exploring the Psychiatrist-Industry Financial Relationship: Insight from the Open Payment Data of Centers for Medicare and Medicaid Services. *Administration and policy in mental health, 47*(4), 526–530. https://doi.org/10.1007/s10488-020-01009-2

[31] Gøtzsche, P. C., Young, A. H., & Crace, J. (2015). Does long term use of psychiatric drugs cause more harm than good? *BMJ (Clinical research ed.), 350*, h2435. https://doi.org/10.1136/bmj.h2435

[32] Gaynes BN, Warden D, Trivedi MH, Wisniewski SR, Fava M, Rush AJ. What did STAR*D teach us? Results from a large-scale, practical, clinical trial for patients with depression. Psychiatr Serv. 2009 Nov;60(11):1439-45. doi: 10.1176/ps.2009.60.11.1439. PMID: 19880458.

[33] https://psychnews.psychiatryonline.org/doi/10.1176/appi.pn.2019.pp10a2

[34] Casagrande Tango R. (2003). Psychiatric side effects of medications prescribed in internal medicine. *Dialogues in clinical neuroscience, 5*(2), 155–165. https://doi.org/10.31887/DCNS.2003.5.2/rcasagrandetango

[35] Lakhan, S. E., & Hagger-Johnson, G. E. (2007). The impact of prescribed psychotropics on youth. *Clinical practice and epidemiology in mental health : CP & EMH, 3*, 21. https://doi.org/10.1186/1745-0179-3-21

[36] Murphy, A. L., Gardner, D. M., Cooke, C., Kisely, S., Hughes, J., & Kutcher, S. P. (2013). Prescribing trends of antipsychotics in youth receiving income assistance: results from a retrospective population database study. *BMC psychiatry, 13*, 198. https://doi.org/10.1186/1471-244X-13-198

[37] Simmel, C., Bowden, C. F., Neese-Todd, S., Hyde, J., & Crystal, S. (2021). Antipsychotic treatment for youth in foster care: Perspectives on improving youths' experiences in providing informed consent. *The American journal of orthopsychiatry, 91*(2), 258–270. https://doi.org/10.1037/ort0000532

[38] https://www.uptodate.com/contents/depression-treatment-options-for-children-and-adolescents-beyond-the-basics/print

CHAPTER 7: POLICING, PRISONS, AND HOSPITALS

[1] https://www-sup.stanford.edu/books/cite/?id=2147

[2] Rogers, MS, McNiel, DE, Binder, RL. *Journal of the American Academy of Psychiatry and the Law Online* Sep 2019, JAAPL.003863 19; DOI:10.29158/JAAPL.003863-19

[3] https://www.wbez.org/stories/mental-health-and-police-violence-how-crisis-intervention-teams-are-failing/bc032c4f-9f73-42e0-8141-ce72c994619d?utm_medium=url_copy

[4] Rogers, MS, McNiel, DE, Binder, RL. *Journal of the American Academy of Psychiatry and the Law Online* Sep 2019, JAAPL.003863 19; DOI:10.29158/JAAPL.003863-19

[5] https://www.vice.com/en/article/3azkeb/police-are-the-first-to-respond-to-mental-health-crises-they-shouldnt-be

[6] Mengual-Pujante, M., Morán-Sánchez, I., Luna-Ruiz Cabello, A., & Pérez-Cárceles, M. D. (2022). Attitudes of the police towards individuals with a known psychiatric diagnosis. *BMC psychiatry*, *22*(1), 614. https://doi.org/10.1186/s12888-022-04234-1

[7] Fuller, DA, Lamb, HR Biasotti, M, Snook, J. Overlooked and Undercounted

[8] Livingston, J.D. (2016) Contact Between Police and People with Mental Disorders: A Review of Rates. Psychiatric Services, 67:850–857.

[9] Chandler, R. K., Fletcher, B. W., & Volkow, N. D. (2009). Treating drug abuse and addiction in the criminal justice system: improving public health and safety. *JAMA*, *301*(2), 183–190. https://doi.org/10.1001/jama.2008.976

[10] https://bjs.ojp.gov/sites/g/files/xyckuh236/files/media/document/adutrpspi16st.pdf

[11] https://bjs.ojp.gov/library/publications/drug-use-dependence-and-abuse-among-state-prisoners-and-jail-inmates-2007-2009

[12] https://www.vera.org/news/the-united-states-criminalizes-people-who-need-health-care-and-housing

[13] https://www.prisonpolicy.org/blog/2024/01/30/punishing-drug-use/#:~:text=Most%20state%20and%20federal%20prisons,treatment%20program%2C%20professional%20counseling%2C%20detoxification

[14] Porter, C.N., Lee, R. The policing culture: an exploration into the mental health of former British police officers. Curr Psychol 43, 2214–2228 (2024). https://doi.org/10.1007/s12144-023-04365-y

[15] https://crsreports.congress.gov/product/pdf/LSB/LSB10492

[16] Behar, L., Friedman, R., Pinto, A., Katz-Leavy, J., & Jones, H. W. (2007). Protecting youth placed in unlicensed, unregulated residential "treatment" facilities. *Family Court Review, 45*(3).

[17] Lynch, S. E., Teich, J. L., & Smith, K. E. (2016). Psychiatric residential treatment centers for children and adolescents: Modeling variation in Facility Definition Type. *Journal of Child and Family Studies, 26*(4). doi:10.1007/s10826-016-0640-1

[18] https://www.unh.edu/inquiryjournal/blog/2022/04/troubled-teen-industry-its-effects-oral-history

[19] https://www.washingtonpost.com/opinions/2021/10/18/paris-hilton-child-care-facilities-abuse-reform/

[20] See https://www.washingtonpost.com/opinions/2021/10/18/paris-hilton-child-care-facilities-abuse-reform/

[21] See https://www.washingtonpost.com/opinions/2021/10/18/paris-hilton-child-care-facilities-abuse-reform/

[22] https://www.unsilenced.org/the-industry/

[23] https://www.unsilenced.org/the-industry/

[24] https://www.unsilenced.org/the-industry/

[25] https://www.proquest.com/openview/c00ead86d038c1e648b144b826c9047b/1?pq-origsite=gscholar&cbl=18750&diss=y

[26] https://www.unsilenced.org/the-industry/

[27] See https://www.unsilenced.org/the-industry/

[28] See https://www.unsilenced.org/the-industry/

[29] https://scholars.unh.edu/inquiry_spring_2022/8/

[30] Rauktis, Mary. (2015). "When You First Get There, You Wear Red": Youth Perceptions of Point and Level Systems in Group Home Care. Child and Adolescent Social Work Journal. 33. 10.1007/s10560-015-0406-4.

[31] https://www.unsilenced.org/the-industry/

[32] Lynch, S. E., Teich, J. L., & Smith, K. E. (2016). Psychiatric residential treatment centers for children and adolescents: Modeling variation in Facility Definition Type. *Journal of Child and Family Studies, 26*(4). doi:10.1007/s10826-016-0640-1

[33] https://web.archive.org/web/20210118072755/https://www.prisonlegalnews.org/news/2016/jun/3/scared-straight-programs-are-counterproductive/

[34] https://portal.cops.usdoj.gov/resourcecenter/ric/Publications/cops-p288-pub.pdf

[35] Petrosino A, Turpin-Petrosino C, Hollis-Peel M, Lavenberg JG. Scared Straight and Other Juvenile Awareness Programs for Preventing Juvenile Delinquency: A Systematic Review Campbell Systematic Reviews 2013:5

[36] https://www.aetv.com/shows/beyond-scared-straight

[1] https://www.hsph.harvard.edu/news/features/what-led-to-the-opioid-crisis-and-how-to-fix-it/

CHAPTER 8: THE DRUG EPIDEMIC

[2] https://www.cdc.gov/opioids/basics/epidemic.html#:~:text=The%20number%20of%20people%20who,in%202021%20involved%20an%20opioid.

[3] https://www.cdc.gov/drugoverdose/deaths/index.html

[4] https://www.jaacap.org/article/S0890-8567(24)00121-7/abstract#articleInformation

[5] https://www.uclahealth.org/news/release/about-22-high-school-age-adolescents-died-each-week

[6] https://www.dea.gov/sites/default/files/2020-06/Fentanyl-2020_0.pdf

[7] https://www.dea.gov/sites/default/files/2020-06/Fentanyl-2020_0.pdf

[8] https://www.thenationalcouncil.org/wp-content/uploads/2023/01/Fentanyl-Fact-Sheet-23.01.24-v1.pdf

[9] https://www.dea.gov/alert/sharp-increase-fake-prescription-pills-containing-fentanyl-and-meth

[10] https://childmind.org/article/teenagers-self-medicate/

[11] https://www.policeforum.org/assets/PolicingOpioidCrisis.pdf

[12] https://www.msn.com/en-us/health/medical/todays-marijuana-is-stronger-than-anything-your-parents-smoked-and-is-destroying-communities-expert-says/ar-BB1il6Jb

[13] https://www.nih.gov/news-events/news-releases/most-reported-substance-use-among-adolescents-held-steady-2022

[14] https://nap.nationalacademies.org/resource/24625/Cannabis_chapter_highlights.pdf

[15] https://www.nejm.org/doi/full/10.1056/NEJMoa1611618

[16] https://www.cdc.gov/cannabis/health-effects/brain-health.html#:~:text=Using%20cannabis%20before%20age%2018,to%20fully%20understand%20these%20effects.

[17] Miller, N. S., Ipeku, R., & Oberbarnscheidt, T. (2020). A Review of Cases of Marijuana and Violence. *International journal of environmental research and public health*, *17*(5), 1578. https://doi.org/10.3390/ijerph17051578

[18] https://www.cdc.gov/marijuana/health-effects/mental-health.html#:~:text=The%20association%20between%20marijuana%20and,%2C%20suicide%20attempts%2C%20and%20suicide.

[19] Vaillancourt, R., Gallagher, S., Cameron, J. D., & Dhalla, R. (2022). Cannabis use in patients with insomnia and sleep disorders: Retrospective chart review. *Canadian pharmacists journal : CPJ = Revue des pharmaciens du Canada : RPC*, *155*(3), 175–180. https://doi.org/10.1177/17151635221089617

[20] Chattu, V. K., Manzar, M. D., Kumary, S., Burman, D., Spence, D. W., & Pandi-Perumal, S. R. (2018). The Global Problem of Insufficient Sleep and Its Serious Public Health Implications. *Healthcare (Basel, Switzerland)*, *7*(1), 1. https://doi.org/10.3390/healthcare7010001

[21] https://nida.nih.gov/publications/research-reports/marijuana/marijuana-addictive#:~:text=People%20who%20begin%20using%20marijuana,marijuana%20use%20disorder%20than%20adults.&text=Marijuana%20use%20disorders%20are%20often,when%20not%20taking%20the%20drug.

[22] Sultan RS, Zhang AW, Olfson M, Kwizera MH, Levin FR. Nondisordered Cannabis Use Among US Adolescents. *JAMA Netw Open*. 2023;6(5):e2311294. doi:10.1001/jamanetworkopen.2023.11294

[23] Sultan RS, Zhang AW, Olfson M, Kwizera MH, Levin FR. Nondisordered Cannabis Use Among US Adolescents. *JAMA Netw Open*. 2023;6(5):e2311294. doi:10.1001/jamanetworkopen.2023.11294

[24] https://www.mentalhealth.org.uk/explore-mental-health/a-z-topics/drugs-and-mental-health

[25] https://www.bu.edu/sph/news/articles/2021/car-crash-deaths-involving-cannabis-on-the-rise/#:~:text=The%20percent%20of%20crash%20deaths,levels%20below%20the%20legal%20limit.

[26] Caputi, TL. 2020: The Medical Marijuana Industry and the Use of "Research as Marketing" American Journal of Public Health 110, 174_175,https://doi.org/10.2105/AJPH.2019.305477

[27] https://www.auroramedical.com/pages/blog

[28] https://www.cnn.com/2019/07/25/business/ufc-aurora-cannabis-cbd-study/index.html

[29] https://ajp.psychiatryonline.org/doi/abs/10.1176/appi.ajp.2021.21030320

[30] Caputi, TL. 2020: The Medical Marijuana Industry and the Use of "Research as Marketing" American Journal of Public Health 110, 174_175,https://doi.org/10.2105/AJPH.2019.305477

[31] https://www.cdc.gov/drugoverdose/deaths/index.html#:~:text=Opioids%E2%80%94mainly%20synthetic%20opioids%20(other,of%20all%20drug%20overdose%20deaths).

[32] https://www.uclahealth.org/news/release/about-22-high-school-age-adolescents-died-eachweek#:~:text=An%20average%20of%2022%20adolescents,counterfeit%20pills%2C%20new%20research%20finds.

CHAPTER 9: THE RISE OF AUTISM & ADHD

1 https://www.lifespan.org/lifespan-living/adhd-why-diagnosis-attention-deficit-hyperactivity-disorder-rising#:~:text=It%20is%20estimated%20that%2010.5,96%20percent.

[2] Hodges, H., Fealko, C., & Soares, N. (2020). Autism spectrum disorder: definition, epidemiology, causes, and clinical evaluation. *Translational pediatrics*, *9*(Suppl 1), S55–S65. https://doi.org/10.21037/tp.2019.09.09

[3] Hodges, H., Fealko, C., & Soares, N. (2020). Autism spectrum disorder: definition, epidemiology, causes, and clinical evaluation. *Translational pediatrics*, *9*(Suppl 1), S55–S65. https://doi.org/10.21037/tp.2019.09.09

[4] https://www.medicalnewstoday.com/articles/325106

[5] https://www.medicalnewstoday.com/articles/325106

[6] Hodges, H., Fealko, C., & Soares, N. (2020). Autism spectrum disorder: definition, epidemiology, causes, and clinical evaluation. *Translational pediatrics*, *9*(Suppl 1), S55–S65. https://doi.org/10.21037/tp.2019.09.09

[7] Kang-Yi, C. D., Grinker, R. R., Beidas, R., Agha, A., Russell, R., Shah, S. B., Shea, K., & Mandell, D. S. (2018). Influence of Community-Level Cultural Beliefs about Autism on Families' and Professionals' Care for Children. *Transcultural psychiatry*, *55*(5), 623–647. https://doi.org/10.1177/1363461518779831

[8] https://www.theatlantic.com/family/archive/2019/02/lack-services-adults-autism/582586/

[9] https://www.medicalnewstoday.com/articles/adhd-spectrum

[10] https://www.simplypsychology.org/signs-of-adhd.html

[11] https://www.nimh.nih.gov/health/topics/attention-deficit-hyperactivity-disorder-adhd#:~:text=Attention%2Ddeficit%2Fhyperactivity%20disorder%20(,interferes%20wit h%20functioning%20or%20development.

[12] https://www.medicalnewstoday.com/articles/high-functioning-adhd

[13] Substance Abuse and Mental Health Services Administration. DSM-5 Changes: Implications for Child Serious Emotional Disturbance. Rockville (MD): Substance Abuse and Mental Health Services Administration (US); 2016 Jun. Table 7, DSM-IV to DSM-5 Attention-Deficit/Hyperactivity Disorder Comparison. Available from: https://www.ncbi.nlm.nih.gov/books/NBK519712/table/ch3.t3/

[14] Substance Abuse and Mental Health Services Administration. DSM-5 Changes: Implications for Child Serious Emotional Disturbance. Rockville (MD): Substance Abuse and Mental Health Services Administration (US); 2016 Jun. Table 7, DSM-IV to DSM-5 Attention-Deficit/Hyperactivity Disorder Comparison. Available from: https://www.ncbi.nlm.nih.gov/books/NBK519712/table/ch3.t3/

[15] Substance Abuse and Mental Health Services Administration. DSM-5 Changes: Implications for Child Serious Emotional Disturbance. Rockville (MD): Substance Abuse and Mental Health Services Administration (US); 2016 Jun. Table 7, DSM-IV to DSM-5 Attention-Deficit/Hyperactivity Disorder Comparison. Available from: https://www.ncbi.nlm.nih.gov/books/NBK519712/table/ch3.t3/

[16] Substance Abuse and Mental Health Services Administration. DSM-5 Changes: Implications for Child Serious Emotional Disturbance. Rockville (MD): Substance Abuse and Mental Health Services Administration (US); 2016 Jun. Table 7, DSM-IV to DSM-5 Attention-Deficit/Hyperactivity Disorder Comparison. Available from: https://www.ncbi.nlm.nih.gov/books/NBK519712/table/ch3.t3/

[17] https://www.medicalnewstoday.com/articles/severe-adhd#is-it-a-disability

[18] https://www.medicalnewstoday.com/articles/severe-adhd#is-it-a-disability

[19] https://www.medicalnewstoday.com/articles/severe-adhd#is-it-a-disability

[20] https://www.medicalnewstoday.com/articles/severe-adhd#is-it-a-disability

[21] https://www.medicalnewstoday.com/articles/severe-adhd#is-it-a-disability

[22] https://mindfulcenter.org/an-intersectional-perspective-on-adhd/

[23] https://www.statnews.com/2024/04/15/adhd-is-often-overlooked-in-females-they-need-help-

[24] Hertz-Picciotto, I., & Delwiche, L. (2009). The rise in autism and the role of age at diagnosis. *Epidemiology (Cambridge, Mass.)*, *20*(1), 84–90. https://doi.org/10.1097/EDE.0b013e3181902d15

[25] Li Y, Yan X, Li Q, et al. Prevalence and Trends in Diagnosed ADHD Among US Children and Adolescents, 2017-2022. *JAMA Netw Open.* 2023;6(10):e2336872. doi:10.1001/jamanetworkopen.2023.36872

[26] https://www.cdc.gov/ncbddd/autism/data.html

[27] https://www.forbes.com/sites/jenniferpalumbo/2023/03/23/cdc-estimate-on-autism-prevalence-increases-to-1-in-36-children-in-us/?sh=2fac09996e7e

[28] https://www.verywellhealth.com/when-did-autism-start-to-rise-260133#:~:text=Since%201990%2C%20the%20incidence%20of,1%20in%2040%20in%202017.

[29] Abdelnour, E., Jansen, M. O., & Gold, J. A. (2022). ADHD Diagnostic Trends: Increased Recognition or Overdiagnosis?. Missouri medicine, 119(5), 467–473.

[30] Epstein, J. N., & Loren, R. E. (2013). Changes in the Definition of ADHD in DSM-5: Subtle but Important. Neuropsychiatry, 3(5), 455–458. https://doi.org/10.2217/npy.13.59

[31] Epstein, J. N., & Loren, R. E. (2013). Changes in the Definition of ADHD in DSM-5: Subtle but Important. Neuropsychiatry, 3(5), 455–458. https://doi.org/10.2217/npy.13.59

[32] https://www.aap.org/en/patient-care/autism/

[33] https://www.cdc.gov/ncbddd/actearly/screening.html#:~:text=The%20American%20Academy%20of%20Pediatrics,child%20visits%20at%20these%20ages%3A&text=9%20months,30%20months

[34] Kubota, T., & Mochizuki, K. (2016). Epigenetic Effect of Environmental Factors on Autism Spectrum Disorders. *International journal of environmental research and public health, 13*(5), 504. https://doi.org/10.3390/ijerph13050504

[35] Kubota, T., & Mochizuki, K. (2016). Epigenetic Effect of Environmental Factors on Autism Spectrum Disorders. *International journal of environmental research and public health, 13*(5), 504. https://doi.org/10.3390/ijerph13050504

[36] https://www.autismspeaks.org/science-news/identical-twins-autism-differ-significantly-severity-social-traits

[37] Hoxha, B., Hoxha, M., Domi, E., Gervasoni, J., Persichilli, S., Malaj, V., & Zappacosta, B. (2021). Folic Acid and Autism: A Systematic Review of the Current State of Knowledge. *Cells, 10*(8), 1976. https://doi.org

[38] Keil-Stietz, K., & Lein, P. J. (2023). Gene×environment interactions in autism spectrum disorders. *Current topics in developmental biology, 152*, 221–284. https://doi.org/10.1016/bs.ctdb.2022.11.001

[39] Rahman, M. M., Shu, Y. H., Chow, T., Lurmann, F. W., Yu, X., Martinez, M. P., Carter, S. A., Eckel, S. P., Chen, J. C., Chen, Z., Levitt, P., Schwartz, J., McConnell, R., & Xiang, A. H. (2022). Prenatal Exposure to Air Pollution and Autism Spectrum Disorder: Sensitive Windows of Exposure and Sex Differences. *Environmental health perspectives, 130*(1), 17008. https://doi.org/10.1289/EHP9509

[40] Fan, H. C., Chen, C. M., Tsai, J. D., Chiang, K. L., Tsai, S. C., Huang, C. Y., Lin, C. L., Hsu, C. Y., & Chang, K. H. (2022). Association between Exposure to Particulate Matter Air Pollution during Early Childhood and Risk of Attention-Deficit/Hyperactivity Disorder in Taiwan. *International journal of environmental research and public health, 19*(23), 16138. https://doi.org/10.3390/ijerph192316138

[41] Miani, A., Imbriani, G., De Filippis, G., De Giorgi, D., Peccarisi, L., Colangelo, M., Pulimeno, M., Castellone, M. D., Nicolardi, G., Logroscino, G., & Piscitelli, P. (2021). Autism Spectrum Disorder and Prenatal or Early Life Exposure to Pesticides: A Short Review. *International journal of environmental research and public health, 18*(20), 10991. https://doi.org/10.3390/ijerph182010991

[42] https://www.unmc.edu/newsroom/2023/08/31/researcher-studies-link-between-pesticide-use-and-

adhd/#:~:text=Exposure%20to%20pyrethroids%20when%20young,problems%20can%2
0persist%20into%20adulthood."

[43] https://www.ewg.org/research/how-toxic-pollutants-can-harm-future-unexposed-generations

[44] Nakamura K, Sekine Y, Ouchi Y, et al. Brain Serotonin and Dopamine Transporter Bindings in Adults with High-Functioning Autism. *Arch Gen Psychiatry.* 2010;67(1):59–68. doi:10.1001/archgenpsychiatry.2009.137

[45] Ames, J L., Burjak, M, Avalos, LA, Braun, JM, Bulka, CM, Croen, LA, Dunlop, AL, Ferrara, A, Fry, RC, Hedderson, MM, Karagas, MR, Liang, D, Lin, PD, Lyall, K, Moore, B, Morello-Frosch, R, O'Connor, TG, Oh, J, Padula, AM, Woodruff, TJ, Zhu, Y, Hamra, GB. Environmental influences on Child Health Outcomes. Prenatal Exposure to Per- and Polyfluoroalkyl Substances and Childhood Autism-related Outcomes. *Epidemiology* 34(3):p 450-459, May 2023. | DOI: 10.1097/EDE.0000000000001587

[46] https://www.cdc.gov/ncbddd/autism/features/autism-among-4-year-old-8-year-old-children-an-easy-read-summary.html

[47] https://www.bu.edu/articles/2022/why-many-autistic-girls-go-undiagnosed/

[48] Lockwood Estrin, G., Milner, V., Spain, D., Happé, F., & Colvert, E. (2021). Barriers to Autism Spectrum Disorder Diagnosis for Young Women and Girls: a Systematic Review. *Review journal of autism and developmental disorders*, 8(4), 454–470. https://doi.org/10.1007/s40489-020-00225-8

[49] Lockwood Estrin, G., Milner, V., Spain, D., Happé, F., & Colvert, E. (2021). Barriers to Autism Spectrum Disorder Diagnosis for Young Women and Girls: a Systematic Review. *Review journal of autism and developmental disorders*, 8(4), 454–470. https://doi.org/10.1007/s40489-020-00225-8

[50] Lockwood Estrin, G., Milner, V., Spain, D., Happé, F., & Colvert, E. (2021). Barriers to Autism Spectrum Disorder Diagnosis for Young Women and Girls: a Systematic Review. *Review journal of autism and developmental disorders*, 8(4), 454–470. https://doi.org/10.1007/s40489-020-00225-8

[51] https://childmind.org/article/autistic-girls-overlooked-undiagnosed-autism/#

[52] Lockwood Estrin, G., Milner, V., Spain, D., Happé, F., & Colvert, E. (2021). Barriers to Autism Spectrum Disorder Diagnosis for Young Women and Girls: a Systematic Review. *Review journal of autism and developmental disorders*, 8(4), 454–470. https://doi.org/10.1007/s40489-020-00225-8

[53] Lockwood E.G., Milner, V., Spain, D., Happé, F., & Colvert, E. (2021). Barriers to Autism Spectrum Disorder Diagnosis for Young Women and Girls: a Systematic Review. *Review journal of autism and developmental disorders*, 8(4), 454–470. https://doi.org/10.1007/s40489-020-00225-8

[54] https://www.healthline.com/health/adhd/adhd-symptoms-in-girls-and-boys#:~:text=ADHD%20and%20Gender,an%20ADHD%20diagnosis%20than%20girls.

[55] Young, S., Adamo, N., Ásgeirsdóttir, B. B., Branney, P., Beckett, M., Colley, W., Cubbin, S., Deeley, Q., Farrag, E., Gudjonsson, G., Hill, P., Hollingdale, J., Kilic, O., Lloyd, T., Mason, P., Paliokosta, E., Perecherla, S., Sedgwick, J., Skirrow, C., Tierney, K., ... Woodhouse, E. (2020). Females with ADHD: An expert consensus statement taking a lifespan approach providing guidance for the identification and treatment of attention-deficit/ hyperactivity disorder in girls and women. *BMC psychiatry*, 20(1), 404. https://doi.org/10.1186/s12888-020-02707-9

[56] Angold A, Erkanli A, Egger HL, Costello EJ. Stimulant treatment for children: a community perspective. *J Am Acad Child Adolesc Psychiatry.* 2000;39:975–984. doi: 10.1097/00004583-200008000-00009.

[57] Mowlem, F. D., Rosenqvist, M.A., Martin, J., Lichtenstein, P., Asherson, P., & Larsson, H. (2019). Sex differences in predicting ADHD clinical diagnosis and pharmacological

treatment. *European child & adolescent psychiatry*, *28*(4), 481–489.
https://doi.org/10.1007/s00787-018-1211-3

[58] https://add.org/adhd-
masking/#:~:text=Masking%20is%20when%20a%20person,who%20don't%20have%20
ADHD.

[59] See Childmind.org

[60] https://www.spectrumnews.org/news/girls-autism-high-risk-sexual-abuse-large-study-
says/

[61] https://www.spectrumnews.org/news/girls-autism-high-risk-sexual-abuse-large-study-
says/

CHAPTER 10: SYSTEMIC BIAS AND DISPARITIES

[1] https://www.ahrq.gov/topics/disparities.html#:~:text=Healthcare%20disparities%20are%2
0differences%20in,or%20gender%20and%20populations%20identified

[2] Office of the Surgeon General (US); Center for Mental Health Services (US); National
Institute of Mental Health (US). Mental Health: Culture, Race, and Ethnicity: A
Supplement to Mental Health: A Report of the Surgeon General. Rockville (MD):
Substance Abuse and Mental Health Services Administration (US); 2001 Aug. Available
from: https://www.ncbi.nlm.nih.gov/books/NBK44243/

[3] Office of the Surgeon General (US); Center for Mental Health Services (US); National
Institute of Mental Health (US). Mental Health: Culture, Race, and Ethnicity: A
Supplement to Mental Health: A Report of the Surgeon General. Rockville (MD):
Substance Abuse and Mental Health Services Administration (US); 2001 Aug. Available
from: https://www.ncbi.nlm.nih.gov/books/NBK44243/

[4] National Academies of Sciences, Engineering, and Medicine; Health and Medicine
Division; Board on Population Health and Public Health Practice; Committee on
Community-Based Solutions to Promote Health Equity in the United States; Baciu A,
Negussie Y, Geller A, et al., editors. Communities in Action: Pathways to Health Equity.
Washington (DC): National Academies Press (US); 2017 Jan 11. 3, The Root Causes of
Health Inequity. Available from: https://www.ncbi.nlm.nih.gov/books/NBK425845/

[5] McGuire, T. G., & Miranda, J. (2008). New evidence regarding racial and ethnic
disparities in mental health: policy implications. *Health affairs (Project Hope)*, *27*(2),
393–403. https://doi.org/10.1377/hlthaff.27.2.393

[6] McGuire TG, Alegria M, Cook BL, Wells KB, Zaslavsky AM. Implementing the Institute
of Medicine Definition of Disparities: An Application to Mental Health Care. *Health
Services Research*. 2006;41(5):1979–2005

[7] McGuire, T. G., & Miranda, J. (2008). New evidence regarding racial and ethnic
disparities in mental health: policy implications. *Health Affairs (Project Hope)*, *27*(2),
393–403. https://doi.org/10.1377/hlthaff.27.2.393

[8] McGuire, T. G., & Miranda, J. (2008). New evidence regarding racial and ethnic
disparities in mental health: policy implications. *Health affairs (Project Hope)*, *27*(2),
393–403. https://doi.org/10.1377/hlthaff.27.2.393

[9] US Census Bureau. (2015). American Community Survey 1-Year PUMS file. Retrieved
from www.census.gov/programs-surveys/acs/data/pums.html . "Other" racial/ethnic
groups included American Indian/Alaska Native, Native Hawaiian/Pacific Islander, and
people of two or more races. US doctorate holders included individuals in the workforce
with a doctoral/professional degree in any field. Total may not sum to 100 % due to
rounding.

[10] Burgess, D. J., Fu, S. S., & van Ryn, M. (2004). Why do providers contribute to
disparities and what can be done about it?. *Journal of general internal medicine*, *19*(11),
1154–1159. https://doi.org/10.1111/j.1525-1497.2004.30227.x

[11] Williams, D. R., & Rucker, T. D. (2000). Understanding and addressing racial disparities in healthcare. *Health care financing review*, *21*(4), 75–90.

[12] Williams, D. R., & Rucker, T. D. (2000). Understanding and addressing racial disparities in healthcare. *Health care financing review*, *21*(4), 75–90.

[13] Williams, D. R., & Rucker, T. D. (2000). Understanding and addressing racial disparities in healthcare. *Health care financing review*, *21*(4), 75–90.

[14] Williams, D. R., & Rucker, T. D. (2000). Understanding and addressing racial disparities in healthcare. *Health care financing review*, *21*(4), 75–90.

[15] Williams, D. R., & Rucker, T. D. (2000). Understanding and addressing racial disparities in healthcare. *Health care financing review*, *21*(4), 75–90.

[16] Cavalhieri, K. E., & Wilcox, M. M. (2022). The compounded effects of classism and racism on mental health outcomes for African Americans. *Journal of Counseling Psychology, 69*(1), 111–120. https://doi.org/10.1037/cou0000561

[17] Schouler-Ocak, M., Bhugra, D., Kastrup, M. C., Dom, G., Heinz, A., Küey, L., & Gorwood, P. (2021). Racism and mental health and the role of mental health professionals. *European psychiatry: the journal of the Association of European Psychiatrists, 64*(1), e42. https://doi.org/10.1192/j.eurpsy.2021.2216

[18] https://adata.org/factsheet/health#:~:text=The %20ADA %20defines %20disability %20as,workplace %20rights %20under %20the %20ADA.

[19] https://archive.ada.gov/hiv/index.html#:~:text=An %20individual %20is %20considered %20to,regarded %20as %20having %20such %20impairment.

[20] https://www.hr-brew.com/stories/2024/03/05/exclusive-25-of-disabled-workers-have-experienced-discrimination-during-the-job-interview-process-new-survey-finds

[21] Dammeyer, J., Chapman, M. A national survey on violence and discrimination among people with disabilities. *BMC Public Health* 18, 355 (2018). https://doi.org/10.1186/s12889-018-5277-0

[22] Williams, D. R., & Rucker, T. D. (2000). Understanding and addressing racial disparities in healthcare. *Health care financing review*, *21*(4), 75–90.

[23] https://www.aclu.org/news/racial-justice/why-access-to-education-is-key-to-systemic-equality

[24] Moagi, M. M., van Der Wath, A. E., Jiyane, P. M., & Rikhotso, R. S. (2021). Mental health challenges of lesbian, gay, bisexual and transgender people: An integrated literature review. *Health SA = SA Gesondheid, 26,* 1487. https://doi.org/10.4102/hsag.v26i0.1487

[25] Moagi, M. M., van Der Wath, A. E., Jiyane, P. M., & Rikhotso, R. S. (2021). Mental health challenges of lesbian, gay, bisexual and transgender people: An integrated literature review. *Health SA = SA Gesondheid, 26,* 1487. https://doi.org/10.4102/hsag.v26i0.1487

[26] Moagi, M. M., van Der Wath, A. E., Jiyane, P. M., & Rikhotso, R. S. (2021). Mental health challenges of lesbian, gay, bisexual and transgender people: An integrated literature review. *Health SA = SA Gesondheid, 26,* 1487. https://doi.org/10.4102/hsag.v26i0.1487

[27] Bass B, Nagy H. Cultural Competence in the Care of LGBTQ Patients. [Updated 2023 Nov 13]. In: StatPearls [Internet]. Treasure Island (FL): StatPearls Publishing; 2024 Jan-. Available from: https://www.ncbi.nlm.nih.gov/books/NBK563176/

[28] Gyamerah, A. O., Baguso, G., Santiago-Rodriguez, E., Sa'id, A., Arayasirikul, S., Lin, J., Turner, C. M., Taylor, K. D., McFarland, W., Wilson, E. C., & Wesson, P. (2021). Experiences and factors associated with transphobic hate crimes among transgender women in the San Francisco Bay Area: comparisons across race. *BMC public health, 21*(1), 1053. https://doi.org/10.1186/s12889-021-11107-x

[29] https://www.thetrevorproject.org/survey-2022/

CHAPTER 11: CAPITALISM'S FUEL TO THE FIRE

[1] Butler, S. The Impact of Advanced Capitalism on Well-being: an Evidence-Informed Model. *Hu Arenas* **2**, 200–227 (2019). https://doi.org/10.1007/s42087-018-0034-6

[2] Levy, J. Ages of American Capitalism: A History of the United States. New York: Random House, 2021. 944 pp. Illustrations, figures, notes, index. Paperback, $24.00. ISBN: 978-0-8129-8518-4.

[3] Lamoreaux NR. Ages of American Capitalism: A History of the United States. *Business History Review*. 2022;96(3):647-652. doi:10.1017/S0007680522000587

[4] Levy, J. Ages of American Capitalism: A History of the United States. New York: Random House, 2021. 944 pp. Illustrations, figures, notes, index. Paperback, $24.00. ISBN: 978-0-8129-8518-4.

[5] Levy, J. Ages of American Capitalism: A History of the United States. New York: Random House, 2021. 944 pp. Illustrations, figures, notes, index. Paperback, $24.00. ISBN: 978-0-8129-8518-4.

[6] Max Roser (2021) - "Extreme poverty: How far have we come, and how far do we still have to go?" Published online at OurWorldInData.org. Retrieved from: 'https://ourworldindata.org/extreme-poverty-in-brief'

[7] Steve Fraser, JONATHAN LEVY. *Ages of American Capitalism: A History of the United States.*, *The American Historical Review*, Volume 126, Issue 4, December 2021, Pages 1608–1611

[8] Plotnick, R., Smolensky, E., Evenhouse, E., & Reilly, S. (1998, July). *The twentieth century record of inequality and* ...Institute of Business and Economic Research of the University of California. https://www.irp.wisc.edu/publications/dps/pdfs/dp116698.pdf

[9] https://www.amnestyusa.org/updates/millennium-development-goals-are-failing-worlds-poorest-people/#:~:text=Unfortunately %2C %20the %20MDGs %20are %20failing,of %20100 %20million %20slum %20dwellers.

[10] https://sdgs.un.org/goals

[11] https://unstats.un.org/sdgs/report/2023/

[12] Zauzmer, J. (2017, August). Christians are more than twice as likely to blame a person's poverty on lack of effort- The Washington Post. Washington Post.https://www.washingtonpost.com/news/acts-of-faith/wp/2017

[13] Collier, P. (2007). *The Bottom Billion: Why the Poorest Countries are Failing and What Can Be Done About It.* Oxford University Press.

[14] https://www.census.gov/newsroom/stories/poverty-awareness-month.html#:~:text=The %20official %20poverty %20rate %20in,and %20Table %20A %2D1).

[15] https://www.census.gov/data/tables/time-series/demo/income-poverty/historical-poverty-thresholds.html

[16] https://www.statista.com/statistics/1219286/average-studio-apartment-rent-usa-by-state/

[17] https://www.census.gov/data/tables/time-series/demo/income-poverty/historical-poverty-thresholds.html

[18] https://www.cnbc.com/2023/08/29/the-salary-a-single-person-needs-to-get-by-in-every-us-state.html

[19] Knifton, L., & Inglis, G. (2020). Poverty and mental health: policy, practice and research implications. *BJPsych bulletin*, *44*(5), 193–196. https://doi.org/10.1192/bjb.2020.78

[20] https://www.samhsa.gov/data/sites/default/files/report_2720/Spotlight-2720.html

[21] Sinclair, U. (1990). The jungle. New York, New American Library.

[22] Sinclair, U. (1990). The jungle. New York, New American Library.

[23] Sinclair, U. (1990). The jungle. New York, New American Library.

[24] Pew Research Center. (2021, March 16). *Many Americans continue to experience mental health difficulties as pandemic enters second year.* Pew Research Center. Retrieved

December 1, 2021, from https://www.pewresearch.org/fact-tank/2021/03/16/many-americans-continue-to-experience-mental-health-difficulties-as-pandemic-enters-second-year/

[25] Ferraro, K. F., & Nuriddin, T. A. (2006). Psychological distress and mortality: are women more vulnerable?. *Journal of health and social behavior*, *47*(3), 227–241. https://doi.org/10.1177/002214650604700303

[26] Dow WH, Godøy A, Lowenstein C, Reich M. Can Labor Market Policies Reduce Deaths of Despair? J Health Econ. 2020 Dec;74:102372. doi: 10.1016/j.jhealeco.2020.102372. Epub 2020 Sep 13. PMID: 33038779; PMCID: PMC8403492.

[27] Gertner AK, Rotter JS, Shafer PR. Association Between State Minimum Wages and Suicide Rates in the US Am J Prev Med. 2019 May;56(5):648-654. doi: 10.1016/j.amepre.2018.12.008. Epub 2019 Mar 21. PMID: 30905484.

[28] https://www.dol.gov/general/topic/wages/minimumwage

[29] https://www.dir.ca.gov/DIRNews/2023/2023-66.html#:~:text=Oakland %E2 %80 %94California's %20minimum %20wage %20will,be %20paid %20the %20minimum %20wage.

[30] https://www.cbsnews.com/news/college-grads-jobs-underemployed/

[31] https://crsreports.congress.gov/product/pdf/R/R46723

[32] Rotz, C.A. 2023. Impact of Beef Cattle on the Environment[abstract]. American Dairy Science Association Proceedings. p. 1.

[33] https://sealevelrise.org/#:~:text=Although %20the %20sea %20level %20has,flooding %20across %20the %20United %20States.

[34] https://earthly.org/en-US/how-many-species-are-extinct-due-to-climate-change

[35] Viana, C.M., Freire, D., Abrantes, P., Rocha, J., & Pereira, P. Agricultural land systems importance for supporting food security and sustainable development goals: A systematic review. *Science of The Total Environment, Volume 806, Part 3,* 1 February 2022, 150718

[36] https://www.pewresearch.org/short-reads/2023/08/09/what-the-data-says-about-americans-views-of-climate-change/#:~:text=Overall %2C %20a %20majority %20of %20US,to %20the %20country's %20well %2Dbeing.

[37] https://yaleclimateconnections.org/2022/01/un-report-the-worlds-farms-stretched-to-a-breaking-point/

[38] Lawrence, EL, Thompson, R., Newberry Le Vay, J, Page, L, Jennings, N. The Impact of Climate Change on Mental Health and Emotional Wellbeing: A Narrative Review of Current Evidence, and its Implications. *Int Rev Psychiatry*. 2022 Aug;34(5):443-498. doi: 10.1080/09540261.2022.2128725. Erratum in: Int Rev Psychiatry. 2022 Aug;34(5):iii. doi: 10.1080/09540261.2022.2161567. PMID: 36165756.

[39] Padhy, S. K., Sarkar, S., Panigrahi, M., & Paul, S. (2015). Mental health effects of climate change. *Indian journal of occupational and environmental medicine*, *19*(1), 3–7. https://doi.org/10.4103/0019-5278.156997

[40] Segovia-Mendoza, M., Palacios-Arreola, M. I., Pavón, L., Becerril, L. E., Nava-Castro, K. E., Amador-Muñoz, O., & Morales-Montor, J. (2022). Environmental Pollution to Blame for Depressive Disorder?. *International journal of environmental research and public health*, *19*(3), 1737. https://doi.org/10.3390/ijerph19031737

[41] https://education.nationalgeographic.org/resource/light-pollution/

[42] https://darksky.org/news/5-appalling-facts-about-light-pollution/#:~:text=In %20an %20average %20year %20in,of %20that %20light %20is %20wasted.

[43] https://darksky.org/news/5-appalling-facts-about-light-pollution/#:~:text=In %20an %20average %20year %20in,of %20that %20light %20is %20wasted.

[44] https://www.cnn.com/2020/07/08/health/night-light-pollution-disrupt-sleep-wellness/index.html#:~:text=A %20new %20study %2C %20published %20Wednesday,low %20levels %20of %20outdoor %20light.

45 Al-Abri M. A. (2015). Sleep Deprivation and Depression: A bi-directional association. *Sultan Qaboos University medical journal, 15*(1), e4–e6.

46 Chattu, V. K., Manzar, M. D., Kumary, S., Burman, D., Spence, D. W., & Pandi-Perumal, S. R. (2018). The Global Problem of Insufficient Sleep and Its Serious Public Health Implications. *Healthcare (Basel, Switzerland), 7*(1), 1. https://doi.org/10.3390/healthcare7010001

<u>CHAPTER 12: PARENTING OF GEN Z</u>

1 Kumari V. (2020). Emotional abuse and neglect: time to focus on prevention and mental health consequences. *The British journal of psychiatry: the journal of mental science, 217*(5), 597–599. https://doi.org/10.1192/bjp.2020.154

2 Committee on Child Maltreatment Research, Policy, and Practice for the Next Decade: Phase II; Board on Children, Youth, and Families; Committee on Law and Justice; Institute of Medicine; National Research Council; Petersen AC, Joseph J, Feit M, editors. Washington (DC): National Academies Press (US); 2014 Mar 25.

3 https://www.goodtherapy.org/blog/how-to-recognize-overcome-childhood-emotional-neglect-0218165#:~:text=Emotional%20neglect%20can%20take%20many,begins%20to%20feel%20self%2Ddoubt.

4 Chris, Phillipson. (2008). Understanding the Baby Boom Generation: Comparative Perspectives. International Journal of Ageing and Later Life. 2. 10.3384/ijal.1652-8670.07227.

5 https://medium.com/@andreaswagner_68972/baby-boomers-and-millenials-how-trauma-is-informing-the-generational-conflict-d970e689107b

6 Fingerman, K. L., Pillemer, K. A., Silverstein, M., & Suitor, J. J. (2012). The Baby Boomers' intergenerational relationships. *The Gerontologist, 52*(2), 199–209. https://doi.org/10.1093/geront/gnr139

7 https://www.linkedin.com/pulse/lifes-fair-so-suck-up-gen-x-trying-work-out-millennial-david-berry

8 Glickman, E. A., Choi, K. W., Lussier, A. A., Smith, B. J., & Dunn, E. C. (2021). Childhood Emotional Neglect and Adolescent Depression: Assessing the Protective Role of Peer Social Support in a Longitudinal Birth Cohort. *Frontiers in psychiatry, 12*, 681176. https://doi.org/10.3389/fpsyt.2021.681176

9 Shelley A. Riggs (2010) Childhood Emotional Abuse and the Attachment System Across the Life Cycle: What Theory and Research Tell Us, Journal of Aggression, Maltreatment & Trauma, 19:1, 5-51, DOI: 10.1080/10926770903475968

10 Marici, M., Clipa, O., Runcan, R., & Pîrghie, L. (2023). Is Rejection, Parental Abandonment or Neglect a Trigger for Higher Perceived Shame and Guilt in Adolescents? *Healthcare (Basel, Switzerland), 11*(12), 1724.

11 Ami Rokach, Shauna Clayton, Chapter 9 - The various ways of child neglect, Editor(s): Ami Rokach, Shauna Clayton, Adverse Childhood Experiences and their Life-Long Impact, Academic Press, 2023, Pages 181-206, ISBN 9780323858533, https://doi.org/10.1016/B978-0-323-85853-3.00014-8.

12 https://www.healthline.com/health/mental-health/childhood-emotional-neglect

13 Lippard, E. T. C., & Nemeroff, C. B. (2020). The Devastating Clinical Consequences of Child Abuse and Neglect: Increased Disease Vulnerability and Poor Treatment Response in Mood Disorders. *The American journal of psychiatry, 177*(1), 20–36. https://doi.org/10.1176/appi.ajp.2019.19010020

14 https://www.healthline.com/health/mental-health/childhood-emotional-neglect#symptoms-in-children

---

[15] Lippard, E. T. C., & Nemeroff, C. B. (2020). The Devastating Clinical Consequences of Child Abuse and Neglect: Increased Disease Vulnerability and Poor Treatment Response in Mood Disorders. *The American journal of psychiatry, 177*(1), 20–36. https://doi.org/10.1176/appi.ajp.2019.19010020

[16] Lippard, E. T. C., & Nemeroff, C. B. (2020). The Devastating Clinical Consequences of Child Abuse and Neglect: Increased Disease Vulnerability and Poor Treatment Response in Mood Disorders. *The American journal of psychiatry, 177*(1), 20–36. https://doi.org/10.1176/appi.ajp.2019.19010020

[17] Stephen Ludwig, Anthony Rostain, Chapter 10 - Family Function And Dysfunction, Editor(s): William B. Carey, Allen C. Crocker, William L. Coleman, Ellen Roy Elias, Heidi M. Feldman, Developmental-Behavioral Pediatrics (Fourth Edition), W.B. Saunders, 2009, Pages 103-118, ISBN 9781416033707, https://doi.org/10.1016/B978-1-4160-3370-7.00010-9.

[18] Lippard, E. T. C., & Nemeroff, C. B. (2020). The Devastating Clinical Consequences of Child Abuse and Neglect: Increased Disease Vulnerability and Poor Treatment Response in Mood Disorders. *The American journal of psychiatry, 177*(1), 20–36. https://doi.org/10.1176/appi.ajp.2019.19010020

[19] https://laurissa.org/breaking-the-cycle-childhood-emotional-neglect

[20] https://thunderbird.asu.edu/thought-leadership/insights/why-generation-z-so-depressed-overprotective-parents

[21] https://www.theatlantic.com/technology/archive/2024/03/teen-childhood-smartphone-use-mental-health-effects/677722/

[22] https://www.theatlantic.com/technology/archive/2024/03/teen-childhood-smartphone-use-mental-health-effects/677722/

[23] Flynn, R.M., Shaman, N.J. and Redleaf, D.L. (2023), The Unintended Consequences of "Lack of Supervision" Child Neglect Laws: How Developmental Science Can Inform Policies about Childhood Independence and Child Protection. Social Policy Report, 36: 1-38. https://doi.org/10.1002/sop2.27

[24] Flynn, R.M., Shaman, N.J. and Redleaf, D.L. (2023), The Unintended Consequences of "Lack of Supervision" Child Neglect Laws: How Developmental Science Can Inform Policies about Childhood Independence and Child Protection. Social Policy Report, 36: 1-38. https://doi.org/10.1002/sop2.27

[25] https://childsafety.losangelescriminallawyer.pro/missing-and-abducted-children.html

[26] https://www.cdc.gov/violenceprevention/communicationresources/infographics/CAN.html

[27] Flynn, R.M., Shaman, N.J. and Redleaf, D.L. (2023), The Unintended Consequences of "Lack of Supervision" Child Neglect Laws: How Developmental Science Can Inform Policies about Childhood Independence and Child Protection. Social Policy Report, 36: 1-38. https://doi.org/10.1002/sop2.27

[28] https://www.psychologytoday.com/us/blog/the-age-of-overindulgence/202311/does-overparenting-contribute-to-loneliness-and-anxiety-in#:~:text=There %20are %2068.5 %20million %20emerging,regulation %20issues %20In %20emerging %20adults.

[29] Minson, JA., Dorison, CA. Why is exposure to opposing views aversive? Reconciling three theoretical perspectives, Current Opinion in Psychology, Volume 47, 2022, 101435, ISSN 2352-250X, https://doi.org/10.1016/j.copsyc.2022.101435.

[30] https://newrepublic.com/article/175311/america-polarized-traumatized-trump-violence

[31] https://www.pewresearch.org/short-reads/2019/07/22/key-findings-about-americans-declining-trust-in-government-and-each-other/

[32] Henry E. Brady, Thomas B. Kent; Fifty Years of Declining Confidence & Increasing Polarization in Trust in American Institutions. *Daedalus* 2022; 151 (4): 43–66. doi: https://doi.org/10.1162/daed_a_01943

33 https://www.pewresearch.org/social-trends/2023/01/24/parenting-in-america-today/

34 https://bpr.studentorg.berkeley.edu/2019/04/16/overprotective-parents-and-a-new-generation-of-american-children/

35 Benoit A K., Silk, J. S., Meller, S., Tan, P. Z., Ladouceur, C. D., Sheeber, L. B., Forbes, E. E., Dahl, R. E., Siegle, G. J., McMakin, D. L., & Ryan, N. D. (2016). Parental autonomy granting and child perceived control: effects on the everyday emotional experience of anxious youth. *Journal of child psychology and psychiatry, and allied disciplines, 57*(7), 835–842. https://doi.org/10.1111/jcpp.12482

36 Johnson, S. B., Riley, A. W., Granger, D. A., & Riis, J. (2013). The science of early life toxic stress for pediatric practice and advocacy. *Pediatrics, 131*(2), 319–327. https://doi.org/10.1542/peds.2012-0469

37 Marconi, A. M., Myers, U. S., Hanson, B., Nolan, S., & Sarrouf, E. B. (2023). Psychiatric medication prescriptions increasing for college students above and beyond the COVID-19 pandemic. *Scientific reports, 13*(1), 19063. https://doi.org/10.1038/s41598-023-46303-9

38 Marconi, A. M., Myers, U. S., Hanson, B., Nolan, S., & Sarrouf, E. B. (2023). Psychiatric medication prescriptions increasing for college students above and beyond the COVID-19 pandemic. *Scientific reports, 13*(1), 19063. https://doi.org/10.1038/s41598-023-46303-9

39 Varma, P., Junge, M., Meaklim, H., & Jackson, M. L. (2021). Younger people are more vulnerable to stress, anxiety and depression during COVID-19 pandemic: A global cross-sectional survey. *Progress in neuro-psychopharmacology & biological psychiatry, 109*, 110236. https://doi.org/10.1016/j.pnpbp.2020.110236

CHAPTER 13: THE LONELINESS EPIDEMIC

1 https://www.usatoday.com/story/news/health/2023/12/24/loneliness-epidemic-u-s-surgeon-general-solution/71971896007/#

2 https://static1.squarespace.com/static/5b7c56e255b02c683659fe43/t/6021776bdd04957c45 57c212/1612805995893/Loneliness+in+America+2021_02_08_FINAL.pdf

3 https://www.vivekmurthy.com/together-book

4 https://www.hhs.gov/sites/default/files/surgeon-general-social-connection-advisory.pdf

5 https://www.hhs.gov/sites/default/files/surgeon-general-social-connection-advisory.pdf

6 https://www.hhs.gov/sites/default/files/surgeon-general-social-connection-advisory.pdf

7 https://www.lyrics.com/lyric/819417/The+Beatles/Eleanor+Rigby

8 Franklin, A., & Tranter, B. (2021). Loneliness and the cultural, spatial, temporal and generational bases of belonging. *Australian Journal of Psychology, 73*(1), 57–69. https://doi.org/10.1080/00049530.2020.1837007

9 Franklin, A., & Tranter, B. (2021). Loneliness and the cultural, spatial, temporal and generational bases of belonging. *Australian Journal of Psychology, 73*(1), 57–69. https://doi.org/10.1080/00049530.2020.1837007

10 Mushtaq, R., Shoib, S., Shah, T., & Mushtaq, S. (2014). Relationship between loneliness, psychiatric disorders and physical health? A review on the psychological aspects of loneliness. *Journal of clinical and diagnostic research: JCDR, 8*(9), WE01–WE4. https://doi.org/10.7860/JCDR/2014/10077.4828

11 Veazie S, Gilbert J, Winchell K, et al. Rockville (MD): Agency for Healthcare Research and Quality (US); 2019 Feb.

12 https://www.hhs.gov/sites/default/files/surgeon-general-social-connection-advisory.pdf

13 https://www.hhs.gov/sites/default/files/surgeon-general-social-connection-advisory.pdf

14 https://www.hhs.gov/sites/default/files/surgeon-general-social-connection-advisory.pdf

15 https://www.hhs.gov/sites/default/files/surgeon-general-social-connection-advisory.pdf

16 Ruben, M. A., Stosic, M. D., Correale, J., & Blanch-Hartigan, D. (2021). Is Technology Enhancing or Hindering Interpersonal Communication? A Framework and Preliminary Results to Examine the Relationship Between Technology Use and Nonverbal Decoding Skill. *Frontiers in psychology*, *11*, 611670. https://doi.org/10.3389/fpsyg.2020.611670

17 https://datareportal.com/reports/digital-2024-deep-dive-the-time-we-spend-on-social-media

18 https://news.gallup.com/poll/512576/teens-spend-average-hours-social-media-per-day.aspx

19 Primack, B. A., Shensa, A., Sidani, J. E., Whaite, E. O., Lin, L. Y., Rosen, D., Colditz, J. B., Radovic, A., & Miller, E. (2017). Social Media Use and Perceived Social Isolation Among Young Adults in the US American journal of preventive medicine, 53(1), 1–8. https://doi.org/10.1016/j.amepre.2017.01.010

20 Adler, I. (2013 January 17). How our digital devices are affecting our personal relationships. WBUR. Retrieved from http://www.wbur.org/2013/01/17/digital-lives-i

21 Dwyer, Ryan & Kushlev, Kostadin & Dunn, Elizabeth. (2017). Smartphone use undermines enjoyment of face-to-face social interactions. Journal of Experimental Social Psychology. 78. 10.1016/j.jesp.2017.10.007.

22 Nixon C. L. (2014). Current perspectives: the impact of cyberbullying on adolescent health. *Adolescent health, medicine and therapeutics*, *5*, 143–158. https://doi.org/10.2147/AHMT.S36456

23 https://www.hhs.gov/sites/default/files/surgeon-general-social-connection-advisory.pdf

24 https://www.hhs.gov/sites/default/files/surgeon-general-social-connection-advisory.pdf

25 https://www.pewresearch.org/religion/2022/09/13/how-u-s-religious-composition-has-changed-in-recent-decades/

26 https://www.pewresearch.org/religion/2022/09/13/how-u-s-religious-composition-has-changed-in-recent-decades/

27 https://www.forbes.com/sites/roberthart/2021/03/29/poll-american-church-membership-drops-below-50-for-first-time/?sh=182336d82d18

28 https://cms.childtrends.org/wp-content/uploads/2002/01/Child_Trends-2002_01_01_FR_ReligionSpiritAdol.pdf

29 McCallum, S. M., Calear, A. L., Cherbuin, N., Farrer, L. M., Gulliver, A., Shou, Y., Dawel, A., & Batterham, P. J. (2021). Associations of loneliness, belongingness and health behaviors with psychological distress and wellbeing during COVID-19. Journal of affective disorders reports, 6, 100214.

30 https://www.nationalreview.com/corner/are-americans-losing-their-sense-of-belonging/

31 https://www.americanimmigrationcouncil.org/research/the-belonging-barometer

32 Franklin, A., & Tranter, B. (2021). Loneliness and the cultural, spatial, temporal and generational bases of belonging. Australian Journal of Psychology, 73(1), 57–69. https://doi.org/10.1080/00049530.2020.1837007

33 https://www.latimes.com/california/newsletter/2023-07-11/more-than-anything-the-key-to-feeling-ok-is-belonging-group-therapy

34 https://www.theguardian.com/sustainable-business/2016/jun/30/america-working-hours-minimum-wage-overworked

35 https://www.pbs.org/newshour/show/why-americans-are-lonelier-and-its-effects-on-our-health

36 https://qz.com/1344501/americans-now-spend-11-hours-with-media-in-an-average-day-study

37 https://www.nytimes.com/2023/04/18/opinion/ezra-klein-podcast-sheila-liming.html

38 https://worldhappiness.report/ed/2020/cities-and-happiness-a-global-ranking-and-analysis/

[39] Baobeid, Abdulla & Koç, Muammer & Al-Ghamdi, Sami G.. (2021). Walkability and Its Relationships With Health, Sustainability, and Livability: Elements of Physical Environment and Evaluation Frameworks. Frontiers in Built Environment. 7. 10.3389/fbuil.2021.721218.

[40] Baobeid, Abdulla & Koç, Muammer & Al-Ghamdi, Sami G.. (2021). Walkability and Its Relationships With Health, Sustainability, and Livability: Elements of Physical Environment and Evaluation Frameworks. Frontiers in Built Environment. 7. 10.3389/fbuil.2021.721218.

[41] https://www.un.org/development/desa/en/news/population/2018-revision-of-world-urbanization-prospects.html#:~:text=News-,68 %25 %20of %20the %20world %20population %20projected %20to %20live %20in,areas %20by %202050 %2C %20says %20UN&text=Today %2C %2055 %25 %20of %20the %20world's,increase %20to %2068 %25 %20by %202050.

[42] https://www.congress.gov/bill/105th-congress/house-bill/2400

[43] Southworth, Michael. "Designing the Walkable City." *Journal of Urban Planning and Development*, vol. 131, no. 4, Dec. 2005, pp. 246–257, https://doi.org/10.1061/(asce)0733-9488(2005)131:4(246).

[44] https://slate.com/business/2023/01/real-estate-walkable-home-prices-rent-smart-growth-america-report.html

[45] https://insights.grcglobalgroup.com/the-impact-of-pedestrian-friendly-urban-planning-on-communities/#:~:text=Social %20Impact,in %20other %20communities %20(Mask).

[46] Mask, R L. "What Is Social Capital and Why Is It so Important?" Www.snhu.edu, 19 Nov. 2019, www.snhu.edu/about-us/newsroom/business/what-is-social-capital#:~:text=Simply %20put %2C %20social %20capital %20is.

[47] Leyden, KM. "Social Capital and the Built Environment: The Importance of Walkable Neighborhoods." *American Journal of Public Health*, vol. 93, no. 9, Sept. 2003, pp. 1546–1551, https://doi.org/10.2105/ajph.93.9.1546.

[48] Zhu, X., Lu, Z., Yu, C. Y., Lee, C., & Mann, G. (2013). Walkable communities: Impacts on residents' physical and social health: Researchers from Texas A&M University studied residents in a newly developed 'walkable community' in Austin, Texas to see how it changed their habits for physical activity and whether it increased social interaction and cohesion in the community. *World health design*, 6(3), 68–75.

[49] https://www.thegoodtrade.com/features/third-place-community-spaces/

[50] https://ilsr.org/affordable-space/

[51] Brandt, L., Liu, S., Heim, C., & Heinz, A. (2022). The effects of social isolation stress and discrimination on mental health. *Translational psychiatry*, 12(1), 398. https://doi.org/10.1038/s41398-022-02178-4

[52] Weiss, I., Paxton, P., Velasco, K., & Ressler, R. W. (2019). Revisiting Declines in Social Capital: Evidence from a New Measure. *Social indicators research*, 142(3), 1015–1029. https://doi.org/10.1007/s11205-018-1956-6

[53] Finlay, J., Esposito, M., Kim, M. H., Gomez-Lopez, I., & Clarke, P. (2019). Closure of 'third places'? Exploring potential consequences for collective health and wellbeing. Health & place, 60, 102225. https://doi.org/10.1016/j.healthplace.2019.102225

[54] National Academies of Sciences, Engineering, and Medicine; Division of Behavioral and Social Sciences and Education; Health and Medicine Division; Board on Behavioral, Cognitive, and Sensory Sciences; Board on Health Sciences Policy; Committee on the Health and Medical Dimensions of Social Isolation and Loneliness in Older Adults. Washington (DC): National Academies Press (US); 2020 Feb 27.

[55] Mann, F., Wang, J., Pearce, E., Ma, R., Schlief, M., Lloyd-Evans, B., Ikhtabi, S., & Johnson, S. (2022). Loneliness and the onset of new mental health problems in the general population. Social psychiatry and psychiatric epidemiology, 57(11), 2161–2178. https://doi.org/10.1007/s00127-022-02261-7

56 Loades, M. E., Chatburn, E., Higson-Sweeney, N., Reynolds, S., Shafran, R., Brigden, A., Linney, C., McManus, M. N., Borwick, C., & Crawley, E. (2020). Rapid Systematic Review: The Impact of Social Isolation and Loneliness on the Mental Health of Children and Adolescents in the Context of COVID-19. *Journal of the American Academy of Child and Adolescent Psychiatry, 59*(11), 1218–1239.e3. https://doi.org/10.1016/j.jaac.2020.05.009

57 Brinker, J., & Cheruvu, V. K. (2016). Social and emotional support as a protective factor against current depression among individuals with adverse childhood experiences. *Preventive medicine reports, 5*, 127–133. https://doi.org/10.1016/j.pmedr.2016.11.018

58 Van Orden, K. A., Witte, T. K., Cukrowicz, K. C., Braithwaite, S. R., Selby, E. A., & Joiner, T. E., Jr (2010). The interpersonal theory of suicide. *Psychological review, 117*(2), 575–600. https://doi.org/10.1037/a0018697

59 Jones, F., Verity, L., Panayiotou, M., & Qualter, P. A review of evidence on the link between masculinity, loneliness, and suicide as observed in social media discussions, Current Research in Behavioral Sciences, Volume 5, 2023, 100129, ISSN 2666-5182, https://doi.org/10.1016/j.crbeha.2023.100129.

CHAPTER 14: NUTRITION AND EXERCISE CRISIS

1 https://www.theguardian.com/global/article/2024/jun/27/ultra-processed-foods-need-tobacco-style-warnings-says-scientist

2 https://globalwellnessinstitute.org/global-wellness-institute-blog/2023/08/29/physical-inactivity-for-kids-is-out-of-control-policymakers-are-taking-action/#:~:text=The%20World%20Health%20Organization%20recently,vs%2078%25%20of%20boys).

3 Selvaraj, R., Selvamani, T. Y., Zahra, A., Malla, J., Dhanoa, R. K., Venugopal, S., Shoukrie, S. I., Hamouda, R. K., & Hamid, P. (2022). Association Between Dietary Habits and Depression: A Systematic Review. Cureus, 14(12), e32359. https://doi.org/10.7759/cureus.32359

4 Patangia, D. V., Anthony Ryan, C., Dempsey, E., Paul Ross, R., & Stanton, C. (2022). Impact of antibiotics on the human microbiome and consequences for host health. *MicrobiologyOpen, 11*(1), e1260. https://doi.org/10.1002/mbo3.1260

5 Ursell, L. K., Metcalf, J. L., Parfrey, L. W., & Knight, R. (2012). Defining the human microbiome. Nutrition reviews, 70 Suppl 1(Suppl 1), S38–S44. https://doi.org/10.1111/j.1753-4887.2012.00493.x

6 Bull, M. J., & Plummer, N. T. (2014). Part 1: The Human Gut Microbiome in Health and Disease. *Integrative medicine (Encinitas, Calif.), 13*(6), 17–22.

7 Chaudhry, T. S., Senapati, S. G., Gadam, S., Mannam, H. P. S. S., Voruganti, H. V., Abbasi, Z., Abhinav, T., Challa, A. B., Pallipamu, N., Bheemisetty, N., & Arunachalam, S. P. (2023). The Impact of Microbiota on the Gut-Brain Axis: Examining the Complex Interplay and Implications. *Journal of clinical medicine, 12*(16), 5231. https://doi.org/10.3390/jcm12165231

8 Appleton J. (2018). The Gut-Brain Axis: Influence of Microbiota on Mood and Mental Health. Integrative medicine (Encinitas, Calif.), 17(4), 28–32.

9 Limbana, T., Khan, F., & Eskander, N. (2020). Gut Microbiome and Depression: How Microbes Affect the Way We Think. Cureus, 12(8), e9966. https://doi.org/10.7759/cureus.9966

10 Appleton J. (2018). The Gut-Brain Axis: Influence of Microbiota on Mood and Mental Health. *Integrative medicine (Encinitas, Calif.), 17*(4), 28–32.

11 Belkaid, Y., & Hand, T. W. (2014). Role of the microbiota in immunity and inflammation. *Cell, 157*(1), 121–141. https://doi.org/10.1016/j.cell.2014.03.011

[12] Jeyakumar, T., Beauchemin, N., & Gros, P. Impact of the Microbiome on the Human Genome, Trends in Parasitology, Volume 35, Issue 10, 2019, Pages 809-821, ISSN 1471-4922

[13] Zhang, Y. J., Li, S., Gan, R. Y., Zhou, T., Xu, D. P., & Li, H. B. (2015). Impacts of gut bacteria on human health and diseases. *International journal of molecular sciences, 16*(4), 7493–7519. https://doi.org/10.3390/ijms16047493

[14] Clapp, M., Aurora, N., Herrera, L., Bhatia, M., Wilen, E., & Wakefield, S. (2017). Gut microbiota's effect on mental health: The gut-brain axis. Clinics and practice, 7(4), 987. https://doi.org/10.4081/cp.2017.987

[15] Clapp, M., Aurora, N., Herrera, L., Bhatia, M., Wilen, E., & Wakefield, S. (2017). Gut microbiota's effect on mental health: The gut-brain axis. *Clinics and practice, 7*(4), 987. https://doi.org/10.4081/cp.2017.987

[16] Safadi, J. M., Quinton, A. M. G., Lennox, B. R., Burnet, P. W. J., & Minichino, A. (2022). Gut dysbiosis in severe mental illness and chronic fatigue: a novel trans-diagnostic construct? A systematic review and meta-analysis. *Molecular psychiatry, 27*(1), 141–153. https://doi.org/10.1038/s41380-021-01032-1

[17] Di Vincenzo, F., Del Gaudio, A., Petito, V. *et al.* Gut microbiota, intestinal permeability, and systemic inflammation: a narrative review. *Intern Emerg Med* **19**, 275–293 (2024). https://doi.org/10.1007/s11739-023-03374-w

[18] Di Vincenzo, F., Del Gaudio, A., Petito, V. *et al.* Gut microbiota, intestinal permeability, and systemic inflammation: a narrative review. *Intern Emerg Med* **19**, 275–293 (2024). https://doi.org/10.1007/s11739-023-03374-w

[19] Di Vincenzo, F., Del Gaudio, A., Petito, V. *et al.* Gut microbiota, intestinal permeability, and systemic inflammation: a narrative review. *Intern Emerg Med* **19**, 275–293 (2024). https://doi.org/10.1007/s11739-023-03374-w

[20] Li, Q., Han, Y., Dy, A. B. C., & Hagerman, R. J. (2017). The Gut Microbiota and Autism Spectrum Disorders. *Frontiers in cellular neuroscience, 11*, 120. https://doi.org/10.3389/fncel.2017.00120

[21] Li, Q., Han, Y., Dy, A. B. C., & Hagerman, R. J. (2017). The Gut Microbiota and Autism Spectrum Disorders. *Frontiers in cellular neuroscience, 11*, 120. https://doi.org/10.3389/fncel.2017.00120

[22] Mehra, A., Arora, G., Sahni, G., Kaur, M., Singh, H., Singh, B., & Kaur, S. (2022). Gut microbiota and Autism Spectrum Disorder: From pathogenesis to potential therapeutic perspectives. *Journal of traditional and complementary medicine, 13*(2), 135–149. https://doi.org/10.1016/j.jtcme.2022.03.001

[23] Mehra, A., Arora, G., Sahni, G., Kaur, M., Singh, H., Singh, B., & Kaur, S. (2022). Gut microbiota and Autism Spectrum Disorder: From pathogenesis to potential therapeutic perspectives. *Journal of traditional and complementary medicine, 13*(2), 135–149. https://doi.org/10.1016/j.jtcme.2022.03.001

[24] Elmira, A., Zatollah, A., Reza, D.K., Fereshteh, B., Ebrahim, K., Reza, T.O., & Ali, H.G., Salami Mahmoud, S. Effect of Probiotic Supplementation on Cognitive Function and Metabolic Status in Alzheimer's Disease: A Randomized, Double-Blind and Controlled Trial, Frontiers in Aging Neuroscience VOL 8, 2016, https://www.frontiersin.org/articles/10.3389/fnagi.2016.00256, 10.3389/fnagi.2016.00256, 663-4365

[25] Bistas, K. G., & Tabet, J. P. (2023). The Benefits of Prebiotics and Probiotics on Mental Health. *Cureus, 15*(8), e43217. https://doi.org/10.7759/cureus.43217

[26] Tillisch, K., Labus, J., Kilpatrick, L., Jiang, Z., Stains, J., Ebrat, B., Guyonnet, D., Legrain-Raspaud, S., Trotin, B., Naliboff, B., & Mayer, E. A. (2013). Consumption of fermented milk product with probiotic modulates brain activity. *Gastroenterology, 144*(7), 1394–1401.e14014. https://doi.org/10.1053/j.gastro.2013.02.043

[27] Tillisch, K., Labus, J., Kilpatrick, L., Jiang, Z., Stains, J., Ebrat, B., Guyonnet, D., Legrain-Raspaud, S., Trotin, B., Naliboff, B., & Mayer, E. A. (2013). Consumption of fermented milk product with probiotic modulates brain activity. *Gastroenterology, 144*(7), 1394–1401.e14014. https://doi.org/10.1053/j.gastro.2013.02.043

[28] Di Vincenzo, F., Del Gaudio, A., Petito, V. *et al.* Gut microbiota, intestinal permeability, and systemic inflammation: a narrative review. *Intern Emerg Med* **19**, 275–293 (2024). https://doi.org/10.1007/s11739-023-03374-w

[29] Di Vincenzo, F., Del Gaudio, A., Petito, V. *et al.* Gut microbiota, intestinal permeability, and systemic inflammation: a narrative review. *Intern Emerg Med* **19**, 275–293 (2024). https://doi.org/10.1007/s11739-023-03374-w

[30] Wallace, C. J. K., & Milev, R. (2017). The effects of probiotics on depressive symptoms in humans: a systematic review. *Annals of general psychiatry, 16*, 14. https://doi.org/10.1186/s12991-017-0138-2

[31] Masters, A., Pandi-Perumal, S. R., Seixas, A., Girardin, J. L., & McFarlane, S. I. (2014). Melatonin, the Hormone of Darkness: From Sleep Promotion to Ebola Treatment. *Brain disorders & therapy, 4*(1), 1000151. https://doi.org/10.4172/2168-975X.1000151

[32] Masters, A., Pandi-Perumal, S. R., Seixas, A., Girardin, J. L., & McFarlane, S. I. (2014). Melatonin, the Hormone of Darkness: From Sleep Promotion to Ebola Treatment. *Brain disorders & therapy, 4*(1), 1000151. https://doi.org/10.4172/2168-975X.1000151

[33] Rathod, R., Kale, A., & Joshi, S. (2016). Novel insights into the effect of vitamin B_{12} and omega-3 fatty acids on brain function. *Journal of biomedical science, 23*, 17. https://doi.org/10.1186/s12929-016-0241-8

[34] Rathod, R., Kale, A., & Joshi, S. (2016). Novel insights into the effect of vitamin B_{12} and omega-3 fatty acids on brain function. *Journal of biomedical science, 23*, 17. https://doi.org/10.1186/s12929-016-0241-8

[35] Calderón-Ospina, C. A., & Nava-Mesa, M. O. (2020). B Vitamins in the nervous system: Current knowledge of the biochemical modes of action and synergies of thiamine, pyridoxine, and cobalamin. *CNS neuroscience & therapeutics, 26*(1), 5–13. https://doi.org/10.1111/cns.13207

[36] Harrison, F. E., & May, J. M. (2009). Vitamin C function in the brain: vital role of the ascorbate transporter SVCT2. *Free radical biology & medicine, 46*(6), 719–730. https://doi.org/10.1016/j.freeradbiomed.2008.12.018

[37] Akpınar, Ş., & Karadağ, M. G. (2022). Is Vitamin D Important in Anxiety or Depression? What Is the Truth?. *Current nutrition reports, 11*(4), 675–681. https://doi.org/10.1007/s13668-022-00441-0

[38] Böhm V. (2018). Vitamin E. *Antioxidants (Basel, Switzerland), 7*(3), 44. https://doi.org/10.3390/antiox7030044

[39] Maier, J. A. M., Locatelli, L., Fedele, G., Cazzaniga, A., & Mazur, A. (2022). Magnesium and the Brain: A Focus on Neuroinflammation and Neurodegeneration. *International journal of molecular sciences, 24*(1), 223.

[40] Song, Y., Leonard, S. W., Traber, M. G., & Ho, E. (2009). Zinc deficiency affects DNA damage, oxidative stress, antioxidant defenses, and DNA repair in rats. *The Journal of nutrition, 139*(9), 1626–1631. https://doi.org/10.3945/jn.109.106369

[41] Udensi, U. K., & Tchounwou, P. B. (2017). Potassium Homeostasis, Oxidative Stress, and Human Disease. *International journal of clinical and experimental physiology, 4*(3), 111–122. https://doi.org/10.4103/ijcep.ijcep_43_17

[42] Wani, A. L., Bhat, S. A., & Ara, A. (2015). Omega-3 fatty acids and the treatment of depression: a review of scientific evidence. *Integrative medicine research, 4*(3), 132–141. https://doi.org/10.1016/j.imr.2015.07.003

[43] Wani, A. L., Bhat, S. A., & Ara, A. (2015). Omega-3 fatty acids and the treatment of depression: a review of scientific evidence. *Integrative medicine research, 4*(3), 132–141. https://doi.org/10.1016/j.imr.2015.07.003

[44] Norwitz, N.G. , Naidoo U. Nutrition as Metabolic Treatment for Anxiety, Frontiers in Psychiatry, Vol 12, 2021, https://www.frontiersin.org/journals/psychiatry/articles/10.3389/fpsyt.2021.598119, 10.3389/fpsyt.2021.598119, 1664-0640

[45] Villagomez A., Cross M., & Ranjbar N. Broad spectrum micronutrients: a potential key player to address emotional dysregulation, Frontiers in Child and Adolescent Psychiatry, VOL 2, 2023, https://www.frontiersin.org/articles/10.3389/frcha.2023.1295635, 10.3389/frcha.2023.1295635, 2813-4540

[46] Li Y, Lv MR, Wei YJ, Sun L, Zhang JX, Zhang HG, Li B. Dietary patterns and depression risk: A meta-analysis. Psychiatry Res. 2017 Jul;253:373-382. doi: 10.1016/j.psychres.2017.04.020. Epub 2017 Apr 11. PMID: 28431261.

[47] Zielińska, M., Łuszczki, E., Michońska, I., & Dereń, K. (2022). The Mediterranean Diet and the Western Diet in Adolescent Depression-Current Reports. *Nutrients, 14*(20), 4390. https://doi.org/10.3390/nu14204390

[48] https://www.nimhd.nih.gov/resources/understanding-health-disparities/food-accessibility-insecurity-and-health-outcomes.html

[49] Jernigan, V. B. B., Huyser, K. R., Valdes, J., & Simonds, V. W. (2017). Food Insecurity among American Indians and Alaska Natives: A National Profile using the Current Population Survey-Food Security Supplement. *Journal of hunger & environmental nutrition, 12*(1), 1–10. https://doi.org/10.1080/19320248.2016.1227750

[50] Dutko, P., Ploeg, M.V., & Farrigan, T. Characteristics and Influential Factors of Food Deserts, ERR-140, US Department of Agriculture, Economic Research Service, August 2012.

[51] Cooksey-Stowers, K., Schwartz, M. B., & Brownell, K. D. (2017). Food Swamps Predict Obesity Rates Better Than Food Deserts in the United States. *International journal of environmental research and public health, 14*(11), 1366. https://doi.org/10.3390/ijerph14111366

[52] Cooksey-Stowers, K., Schwartz, M. B., & Brownell, K. D. (2017). Food Swamps Predict Obesity Rates Better Than Food Deserts in the United States. *International journal of environmental research and public health, 14*(11), 1366. https://doi.org/10.3390/ijerph14111366

[53] Cooksey-Stowers, K., Schwartz, M. B., & Brownell, K. D. (2017). Food Swamps Predict Obesity Rates Better Than Food Deserts in the United States. *International journal of environmental research and public health, 14*(11), 1366. https://doi.org/10.3390/ijerph14111366

[54] Kern, D. M., Auchincloss, A. H., Stehr, M. F., Roux, A. V. D., Moore, L. V., Kanter, G. P., & Robinson, L. F. (2017). Neighborhood Prices of Healthier and Unhealthier Foods and Associations with Diet Quality: Evidence from the Multi-Ethnic Study of Atherosclerosis. *International journal of environmental research and public health, 14*(11), 1394. https://doi.org/10.3390/ijerph14111394

[55] Lewis, M., Herron, L. M., Chatfield, M. D., Tan, R. C., Dale, A., Nash, S., & Lee, A. J. (2023). Healthy Food Prices Increased More Than the Prices of Unhealthy Options during the COVID-19 Pandemic and Concurrent Challenges to the Food System. *International journal of environmental research and public health, 20*(4), 3146. https://doi.org/10.3390/ijerph20043146

[56] https://en.wikipedia.org/wiki/Wilbur_Olin_Atwater

[57] https://www.eatingwell.com/article/8019040/eat-less-move-more-doesnt-work-for-weight-loss-new-study/

[58] https://www.bbc.com/future/bespoke/follow-the-food/why-modern-food-lost-its-nutrients/

[59] National Academies of Sciences, Engineering, and Medicine; Division on Earth and Life Studies; Board on Agriculture and Natural Resources; Committee on Genetically

[60] Engineered Crops: Past Experience and Future Prospects. Washington (DC): National Academies Press (US); 2016 May 17.

[60] https://ourworldindata.org/grapher/land-use-vs-yield-change-in-cereal-production

[61] Weffort, V.R.S., & Lamounier, J.A. (2024). Hidden hunger - a narrative review. *Jornal de pediatria, 100 Suppl 1*(Suppl 1), S10–S17. https://doi.org/10.1016/j.jped.2023.08.009

[62] Bird, J. K., Murphy, R. A., Ciappio, E. D., & McBurney, M. I. (2017). Risk of Deficiency in Multiple Concurrent Micronutrients in Children and Adults in the United States. *Nutrients, 9*(7), 655. https://doi.org/10.3390/nu9070655

[63] Bhardwaj, R.L., Parashar, A., Parewa, H.P., & Vyas, L. 2024. "An Alarming Decline in the Nutritional Quality of Foods: The Biggest Challenge for Future Generations' Health" *Foods* 13, no. 6: 877. https://doi.org/10.3390/foods13060877

[64] Crinnion, W.J. Organic foods contain higher levels of certain nutrients, lower levels of pesticides, and may provide health benefits for the consumer. Altern Med Rev. 2010 Apr;15(1):4-12. PMID: 20359265.

[65] https://www.who.int/news/item/19-10-2022-who-highlights-high-cost-of-physical-inactivity-in-first-ever-global-report

[66] https://www.who.int/publications/i/item/9789240059153

[67] Bull, F. C., Al-Ansari, S. S., Biddle, S., Borodulin, K., Buman, M. P., Cardon, G., Carty, C., Chaput, J. P., Chastin, S., Chou, R., Dempsey, P. C., DiPietro, L., Ekelund, U., Firth, J., Friedenreich, C. M., Garcia, L., Gichu, M., Jago, R., Katzmarzyk, P. T., Lambert, E., … Willumsen, J. F. (2020). World Health Organization 2020 guidelines on physical activity and sedentary behaviour. British journal of sports medicine, 54(24), 1451–1462. https://doi.org/10.1136/bjsports-2020-102955

[68] https://www.who.int/news-room/fact-sheets/detail/physical-activity

[69] https://www.weforum.org/agenda/2022/12/lack-exercise-inactivity-preventable-diseases/

[70] World Health Organization. (2020). *Physical activity.* https://www.who.int/news-room/fact-sheets/detail/physical-activity

[71] Craft, L.L., & Perna, F.M. (2004). The Benefits of Exercise for the Clinically Depressed. *The Primary Care Companion to The Journal of Clinical Psychiatry*, 6(3), 104-111. https://www.ncbi.nlm.nih.gov/pmc/articles/PMC474733/

[72] https://www.health.harvard.edu/staying-healthy/exercising-to-relax#:~:text=Exercise%20reduces%20levels%20of%20the,natural%20painkillers%20and%20mood%20elevators.

[73] Rebar, A.L., Stanton, R., Geard, D., Short, C., Duncan, M.J., & Vandelanotte, C. (2015). A meta-meta-analysis of the effect of physical activity on depression and anxiety in non-clinical adult populations. *Health Psychology Review*, 9(3), 366-378. DOI: 10.1080/17437199.2015.1022901

[74] Ghrouz, A.K, Noohu, M.M, Manzer, M.D., Spence D.W., BaHammam A.S., Pandi-Perumal S.R. Physical activity and sleep quality in relation to mental health among college students. *Sleep Breath.* 2019;23:627–634

[75] Lederman, O, Ward, PB, Firth, J, et al. Does exercise improve sleep quality in individuals with mental illness? A systematic review and meta-analysis. *J Psychiatr Res.* 2019;109:96–106.

CHAPTER 15: SOCIAL MEDIA DILEMMA

[1] https://www.webkinz.com/

[2] Zubair, U., Khan, M. K., & Albashari, M. (2023). Link between excessive social media use and psychiatric disorders. *Annals of medicine and surgery (2012)*, 85(4), 875–878. https://doi.org/10.1097/MS9.0000000000000112

[3] https://collider.com/best-teen-shows-2000s/

[4] https://www.ranker.com/list/best-teen-shows-2000s/ranker-tv

[5] https://medium.com/write-a-catalyst/book-summary-the-anxious-generation-how-the-great-rewiring-of-childhood-is-causing-an-epidemic-of-4ffbb1ace5fc

[6] Arias E. How Does Media Influence Social Norms? Experimental Evidence on the Role of Common Knowledge. Political Science Research and Methods. 2019;7(3):561-578. doi:10.1017/psrm.2018.1

[7] Arias E. How Does Media Influence Social Norms? Experimental Evidence on the Role of Common Knowledge. Political Science Research and Methods. 2019;7(3):561-578. doi:10.1017/psrm.2018.1

[8] https://www.washingtonpost.com/style/of-interest/2024/02/14/ozempic-body-positivity-influencers-weight-loss-drugs/

[9] https://www.npr.org/2023/04/01/1166781510/ozempic-weight-loss-drug-big-business

[10] https://www.tiktok.com/tag/ozempic?lang=en

[11] https://www.modernsalon.com/1089023/top-10-states-using-ozempic-the-most

[12] https://knowledge.wharton.upenn.edu/article/the-marketing-psychology-behind-celebrity-endorsements/

[13] https://knowledge.wharton.upenn.edu/article/the-marketing-psychology-behind-celebrity-endorsements/

[14] https://now.org/now-foundation/love-your-body/love-your-body-whats-it-all-about/get-the-facts/

[15] https://now.org/now-foundation/love-your-body/love-your-body-whats-it-all-about/get-the-facts/

[16] https://bmcpediatr.biomedcentral.com/articles/10.1186/s12887-020-1993-6

[17] https://www.huffpost.com/entry/body-image-boys-eating-disorders_n_624e231ce4b068157f800861

[18] Mundell, E. (2002). Sitcoms, videos make even fifth-graders feel fat. *Reuters Health.*

[19] Tiggemann, M., and Pickering, A. S. (1996). Role of television in adolescent women's body dissatisfaction and drive for thinness. *International Journal of Eating Disorders*, 20, 199-203. *USA Today*, (1996, August 12). (p. 1)

[20] Eisend, M., Möller, J. The influence of TV viewing on consumers' body images and related consumption behavior. Market Lett 18, 101–116 (2007). https://doi.org/10.1007/s11002-006-9004-8

[21] Eisend, M., Möller, J. The influence of TV viewing on consumers' body images and related consumption behavior. Market Lett 18, 101–116 (2007). https://doi.org/10.1007/s11002-006-9004-8

[22] https://citeseerx.ist.psu.edu/document?repid=rep1&type=pdf&doi=a311e4c92fc99cbbf25be8b6b65c65a3211d2693

[23] Santos, R.M.S., Mendes, C.G., Sen Bressani, G. *et al.* The associations between screen time and mental health in adolescents: a systematic review. *BMC Psychol* 11, 127 (2023). https://doi.org/10.1186/s40359-023-01166-7

[24] https://www.envisionkindness.org/wp-content/uploads/2016/06/Johnston-and-Davey-1997-Psychological-Impact-of-Negative-TV-News.pdf

[25] Ayers JW, Althouse BM, Leas EC, et al. (2017) Internet searches for suicide following the release of 13 Reasons Why. *JAMA Internal Medicine* 177(10): 1527–1529.

[26] https://www.stat.cmu.edu/~joel/JAACAP#:~:text=Conclusion%3A%20The%20release%20of%2013,to%20the%20series%20is%20warranted.

[27] NASP (2017) *13 Reasons Why* Netflix Series: Considerations for Educators. Available at: https://www.nasponline.org/resources-and-publications/resources/school-safety-and-crisis/preventing-youth-suicide/13-reasons-why-netflix-series-considerations-for-educators/13-reasons-why-netflix-series-considerations-for-educators

[28] NASP (2017) *13 Reasons Why* Netflix Series: Considerations for Educators. Available at: https://www.nasponline.org/resources-and-publications/resources/school-safety-and-

crisis/preventing-youth-suicide/13-reasons-why-netflix-series-considerations-for-educators/13-reasons-why-netflix-series-considerations-for-educators

[29] https://www.thecrimson.com/article/2004/2/9/hundreds-register-for-new-facebook-website/

[30] https://www.statista.com/statistics/346167/facebook-global-dau/#:~:text=Facebook %3A %20number %20of %20daily %20active %20users %20worldwide %202011 %2D2023&text=During %20the %20fourth %20quarter %20of,increase %20on %20the %20previous %20quarter.

[31] https://www.thoughtco.com/who-invented-facebook-1991791

[32] https://www.thecrimson.com/article/2003/11/19/facemash-creator-survives-ad-board-the/

[33] https://www.washingtonpost.com/news/the-switch/wp/2018/04/11/channeling-the-social-network-lawmaker-grills-zuckerberg-on-his-notorious-beginnings/

[34] https://www.cdc.gov/nchs/products/databriefs/db352.htm#:~:text=The %20suicide %20rate %20among %20persons,2013 %20(3 %25 %20annually).

[35] https://www.hhs.gov/sites/default/files/sg-youth-mental-health-social-media-advisory.pdf

[36] Riehm KE, Feder KA, Tormohlen KN, et al. Associations Between Time Spent Using Social Media and Internalizing and Externalizing Problems Among US Youth. *JAMA Psychiatry*. 2019;76(12):1266–1273. doi:10.1001/jamapsychiatry.2019.2325

[37] https://mcgillbusinessreview.com/articles/fake-personalities-real-impact-the-rise-of-virtual-influencers

[38] Ortega-Barón, J. Machimbarrena, J.M. Calvete, E. Orue, I. Pereda, N. González-Cabrera, Epidemiology of online sexual solicitation and interaction of minors with adults: A longitudinal study. *Child Abuse Negl*. 2022 Sep:131:105759. doi: 10.1016/j.chiabu.2022.105759. Epub 2022 Jun 24.

[39] Ortega-Barón, J. Machimbarrena, J.M. Calvete, E. Orue, I. Pereda, N. González-Cabrera, Epidemiology of online sexual solicitation and interaction of minors with adults: A longitudinal study. *Child Abuse Negl*. 2022 Sep:131:105759. doi: 10.1016/j.chiabu.2022.105759. Epub 2022 Jun 24.

[40] Hitcham, L., Jackson, H., & James, R.J.E. The relationship between smartphone use and smartphone addiction: An examination of logged and self-reported behavior in a pre-registered, two-wave sample,Computers in Human Behavior, Volume 146, 2023, 107822, ISSN 0747-5632, https://doi.org/10.1016/j.chb.2023.107822.

[41] Wacks, Y., & Weinstein, A. M. (2021). Excessive Smartphone Use Is Associated With Health Problems in Adolescents and Young Adults. *Frontiers in psychiatry*, *12*, 669042. https://doi.org/10.3389/fpsyt.2021.669042

[42] Wacks, Y., & Weinstein, A. M. (2021). Excessive Smartphone Use Is Associated With Health Problems in Adolescents and Young Adults. *Frontiers in psychiatry*, *12*, 669042. https://doi.org/10.3389/fpsyt.2021.669042

[43] Beyari H. (2023). The Relationship between Social Media and the Increase in Mental Health Problems. *International journal of environmental research and public health*, *20*(3), 2383. https://doi.org/10.3390/ijerph20032383

[44] Beyari H. (2023). The Relationship between Social Media and the Increase in Mental Health Problems. *International journal of environmental research and public health*, *20*(3), 2383. https://doi.org/10.3390/ijerph20032383

[45] Beyari H. (2023). The Relationship between Social Media and the Increase in Mental Health Problems. *International journal of environmental research and public health*, *20*(3), 2383. https://doi.org/10.3390/ijerph20032383

[46] Jiotsa, B., Naccache, B., Duval, M., Rocher, B., & Grall-Bronnec, M. (2021). Social Media Use and Body Image Disorders: Association between Frequency of Comparing One's Own Physical Appearance to That of People Being Followed on Social Media and Body Dissatisfaction and Drive for Thinness. International journal of environmental research and public health, 18(6), 2880. https://doi.org/10.3390/ijerph18062880

[47] Vuong, A. T., Jarman, H. K., Doley, J. R., & McLean, S. A. (2021). Social Media Use and Body Dissatisfaction in Adolescents: The Moderating Role of Thin- and Muscular-Ideal Internalisation. International journal of environmental research and public health, 18(24), 13222. https://doi.org/10.3390/ijerph182413222

[48] Castellanos Silva Raquel , Steins Gisela, "Social media and body dissatisfaction in young adults: An experimental investigation of the effects of different image content and influencing constructs," *Frontiers in Psychology*, 14, 2023, https://www.frontiersin.org/journals/psychology/articles/10.3389/fpsyg.2023.1037932, 10.3389/fpsyg.2023.1037932, ISSN 1664-1078

[49] Nixon C. L. (2014). Current perspectives: the impact of cyberbullying on adolescent health. Adolescent health, medicine and therapeutics, 5, 143–158. https://doi.org/10.2147/AHMT.S36456

[50] Nixon C. L. (2014). Current perspectives: the impact of cyberbullying on adolescent health. *Adolescent health, medicine and therapeutics*, 5, 143–158. https://doi.org/10.2147/AHMT.S36456

[51] Nixon C. L. (2014). Current perspectives: the impact of cyberbullying on adolescent health. *Adolescent health, medicine and therapeutics*, 5, 143–158. https://doi.org/10.2147/AHMT.S36456

[52] Jiotsa, B., Naccache, B., Duval, M., Rocher, B., & Grall-Bronnec, M. (2021). Social Media Use and Body Image Disorders: Association between Frequency of Comparing One's Own Physical Appearance to That of People Being Followed on Social Media and Body Dissatisfaction and Drive for Thinness. *International journal of environmental research and public health*, 18(6), 2880. https://doi.org/10.3390/ijerph18062880

[53] Ramphul, K., & Mejias, S. G. (2018). Is "Snapchat Dysmorphia" a Real Issue?. *Cureus*, 10(3), e2263. https://doi.org/10.7759/cureus.2263

[54] Ramphul, K., & Mejias, S. G. (2018). Is "Snapchat Dysmorphia" a Real Issue?. *Cureus*, 10(3), e2263. https://doi.org/10.7759/cureus.2263

[55] https://www.apa.org/news/press/releases/2023/02/social-media-body-image

[56] Lee J. K. (2022). The effects of social comparison orientation on psychological wellbeing in social networking sites: Serial mediation of perceived social support and self-esteem. *Current psychology (New Brunswick, N.J.)*, 41(9), 6247–6259. https://doi.org/10.1007/s12144-020-01114-3

[57] Lee J. K. (2022). The effects of social comparison orientation on psychological wellbeing in social networking sites: Serial mediation of perceived social support and self-esteem. *Current psychology (New Brunswick, N.J.)*, 41(9), 6247–6259. https://doi.org/10.1007/s12144-020-01114-3

[58] Ozimek, P., Brandenberg, G., Rohmann, E., & Bierhoff, H. W. (2023). The Impact of Social Comparisons More Related to Ability vs. More Related to Opinion on Well-being: An Instagram Study. *Behavioral sciences (Basel, Switzerland)*, 13(10), 850. https://doi.org/10.3390/bs13100850

[59] https://dictionary.apa.org/social-comparison-theory

[60] Wang, J. L., Wang, H. Z., Gaskin, J., & Hawk, S. (2017). The Mediating Roles of Upward Social Comparison and Self-esteem and the Moderating Role of Social Comparison Orientation in the Association between Social Networking Site Usage and Subjective Well-being. *Frontiers in psychology*, 8, 771. https://doi.org/10.3389/fpsyg.2017.00771

[61] https://www.pewresearch.org/internet/2023/12/11/teens-social-media-and-technology-2023/

[62] Nesi, J., & Prinstein, M. J. (2015). Using Social Media for Social Comparison and Feedback-Seeking: Gender and Popularity Moderate Associations with Depressive Symptoms. *Journal of abnormal child psychology*, 43(8), 1427–1438. https://doi.org/10.1007/s10802-015-0020-0

[63] https://en.wikipedia.org/wiki/The_Social_Dilemma

[64] https://www.jeffersonhealth.org/your-health/living-well/the-addictiveness-of-social-media-how-teens-get-hooked

[65] Jafar, Z., Quick, J. D., Larson, H. J., Venegas-Vera, V., Napoli, P., Musuka, G., Dzinamarira, T., Meena, K. S., Kanmani, T. R., & Rimányi, E. (2023). Social media for public health: Reaping the benefits, mitigating the harms. *Health promotion perspectives, 13*(2), 105–112. https://doi.org/10.34172/hpp.2023.13

[66] https://www.jeffersonhealth.org/your-health/living-well/the-addictiveness-of-social-media-how-teens-get-hooked

[67] Torous J, Chan SR, Yee-Marie Tan S, Behrens J, Mathew I, Conrad EJ, Hinton L, Yellowlees P, Keshavan M. Patient Smartphone Ownership and Interest in Mobile Apps to Monitor Symptoms of Mental Health Conditions: A Survey in Four Geographically Distinct Psychiatric Clinics. JMIR Ment Health. 2014 Dec 23;1(1):e5. doi: 10.2196/mental.4004. PMID: 26543905; PMCID: PMC4607390.

[68] Miller, B. J., Stewart, A., Schrimsher, J., Peeples, D., & Buckley, P. F. (2015). How connected are people with schizophrenia? Cell phone, computer, email, and social media use. *Psychiatry Research, 225*(3), 458–463.

[69] Berger, M., Wagner, T. H., & Baker, L. C. (2005). Internet use and stigmatized illness. *Social Science & Medicine, 61*(8), 1821–1827.

[70] Spinzy, Y., Nitzan, U., Becker, G., Bloch, Y., & Fennig, S. (2012). Does the Internet offer social opportunities for individuals with schizophrenia? A cross-sectional pilot study. *Psychiatry Research, 198*(2), 319–320.

[71] Gowen, K., Deschaine, M., Gruttadara, D., & Markey, D. (2012). Young adults with mental health conditions and social networking websites: seeking tools to build community. *Psychiatric Rehabilitation Journal, 35*(3), 245–250.

[72] Giacco, D., Palumbo, C., Strappelli, N., Catapano, F., & Priebe, S. (2016). Social contacts and loneliness in people with psychotic and mood disorders. *Comprehensive Psychiatry, 66*, 59–66.

[73] Brusilovskiy, E., Townley, G., Snethen, G., & Salzer, M. S. (2016). Social media use, community participation and psychological wellbeing among individuals with serious mental illnesses. *Computers in Human Behavior, 65*, 232–240.

[74] Brusilovskiy, E., Townley, G., Snethen, G., & Salzer, M. S. (2016). Social media use, community participation and psychological wellbeing among individuals with serious mental illnesses. *Computers in Human Behavior, 65*, 232–240.

[75] Brusilovskiy, E., Townley, G., Snethen, G., & Salzer, M. S. (2016). Social media use, community participation and psychological wellbeing among individuals with serious mental illnesses. *Computers in Human Behavior, 65*, 232–240.

[76] Lal, S., Nguyen, V., & Theriault, J. (2018). Seeking mental health information and support online: experiences and perspectives of young people receiving treatment for first-episode psychosis. *Early Intervention in Psychiatry, 12*(3), 324–330.

[77] Biagianti, B., Quraishi, S. H., & Schlosser, D. A. (2018). Potential benefits of incorporating peer-to-peer interactions into digital interventions for psychotic disorders: a systematic review. *Psychiatric Services, 69*(4), 377–388.

[78] Alvarez-Jimenez, M., Bendall, S., Lederman, R., Wadley, G., Chinnery, G., Vargas, S., Larkin, M., Killackey, E., McGorry, P., & Gleeson, J. F. (2013). On the HORYZON: moderated online social therapy for long-term recovery in first episode psychosis. *Schizophrenia Research, 143*(1), 143–149.

[79] Schlosser, D. A., Campellone, T., Kim, D., Truong, B., Vergani, S., Ward, C., & Vinogradov, S. (2016). Feasibility of PRIME: a cognitive neuroscience-informed mobile app intervention to enhance motivated behavior and improve quality of life in recent onset schizophrenia. *JMIR Research Protocols, 5*(2).

[80] https://www.pornhub.com/insights/tech-review

260

[81] Maitland, D. W. M., & Neilson, E. C. (2023). Associations Between Pornography Consumption Patterns, Pornography Consumption Motives, and Social Wellbeing among US College Students: A Latent Profile Analysis with a Primarily Female Sample. *Journal of sex & marital therapy*, *49*(7), 739–754. https://doi.org/10.1080/0092623X.2023.2193182

[82] Privara, M., & Bob, P. (2023). Pornography Consumption and Cognitive-Affective Distress. The Journal of nervous and mental disease, 211(8), 641–646. https://doi.org/10.1097/NMD.0000000000001669

[83] Camilleri, C., Perry, J. T., & Sammut, S. (2021). Compulsive Internet Pornography Use and Mental Health: A Cross-Sectional Study in a Sample of University Students in the United States. Frontiers in psychology, 11, 613244. https://doi.org/10.3389/fpsyg.2020.613244

[84] https://www.cnbc.com/2018/02/13/youtube-is-causing-stress-and-sexualization-in-young-children.html

[85] Martinez GM, Abma JC. Sexual activity and contraceptive use among teenagers aged 15–19 in the United States, 2015–2017. NCHS Data Brief, no 366. Hyattsville, MD: National Center for Health Statistics. 2020.

[86] https://sundial.csun.edu/168783/print-editions/this-generation-loves-porn-how-is-it-affecting-their-perception-of-intimacy/

[87] https://www.latimes.com/california/story/2023-08-03/young-adults-less-sex-gen-z-millennials-generations-parents-grandparents

[88] https://www.bbc.com/worklife/article/20220831-situationships-why-gen-z-are-embracing-the-grey-area

[89] https://lisa-wade.com/american-hookup/

[90] https://www.psychologytoday.com/us/blog/fulfillment-any-age/201303/how-casual-sex-can-affect-our-mental-health

[91] https://sundial.csun.edu/168783/print-editions/this-generation-loves-porn-how-is-it-affecting-their-perception-of-intimacy/

[92] https://slate.com/podcasts/icymi

[93] https://www.latimes.com/california/story/2023-11-19/california-commits-to-media-literacy-classes

CHAPTER 16: TOXINS ARE EVERYWHERE

[1] https://www.acs.org/education/whatischemistry/landmarks/rachel-carson-silent-spring.html

[2] https://www.acs.org/education/whatischemistry/landmarks/rachel-carson-silent-spring.html

[3] https://www.hsph.harvard.edu/news/hsph-in-the-news/pfas-health-risks-underestimated/

[4] https://www.hsph.harvard.edu/prc/2022/10/03/lead-concentrations-in-us-school-drinking-water-testing-programs-prevalence-and-policy-opportunities-2016-2018/

[5] https://www.theguardian.com/environment/2023/sep/13/us-environmental-protection-agency-failed-policy-consumer-chemicals

[6] https://www.theguardian.com/environment/2023/sep/13/us-environmental-protection-agency-failed-policy-consumer-chemicals

[7] https://www.gao.gov/products/gao-09-428t#:~:text=Highlights-,Highlights,determines%20pose%20an%20unreasonable%20risk.

[8] Mitro, S. D., Johnson, T., & Zota, A. R. (2015). Cumulative Chemical Exposures During Pregnancy and Early Development. *Current environmental health reports*, *2*(4), 367–378. https://doi.org/10.1007/s40572-015-0064-x

[9] Cecil, K. M., Brubaker, C. J., Adler, C. M., Dietrich, K. N., Altaye, M., Egelhoff, J. C., Wessel, S., Elangovan, I., Hornung, R., Jarvis, K., & Lanphear, B. P. (2008). Decreased brain volume in adults with childhood lead exposure. *PLoS medicine, 5*(5), e112. https://doi.org/10.1371/journal.pmed.0050112

[10] Hlisníková, H., Petrovičová, I., Kolena, B., Šidlovská, M., & Sirotkin, A. (2020). Effects and Mechanisms of Phthalates' Action on Reproductive Processes and Reproductive Health: A Literature Review. *International journal of environmental research and public health, 17*(18), 6811. https://doi.org/10.3390/ijerph17186811

[11] Hlisníková, H., Petrovičová, I., Kolena, B., Šidlovská, M., & Sirotkin, A. (2020). Effects and Mechanisms of Phthalates' Action on Reproductive Processes and Reproductive Health: A Literature Review. *International journal of environmental research and public health, 17*(18), 6811. https://doi.org/10.3390/ijerph17186811

[12] Blake, B. E., & Fenton, S. E. (2020). Early life exposure to per- and polyfluoroalkyl substances (PFAS) and latent health outcomes: A review including the placenta as a target tissue and possible driver of peri- and postnatal effects. *Toxicology, 443*, 152565. https://doi.org/10.1016/j.tox.2020.152565

[13] Blake, B. E., & Fenton, S. E. (2020). Early life exposure to per- and polyfluoroalkyl substances (PFAS) and latent health outcomes: A review including the placenta as a target tissue and possible driver of peri- and postnatal effects. *Toxicology, 443*, 152565. https://doi.org/10.1016/j.tox.2020.152565

[14] Blake, B. E., & Fenton, S. E. (2020). Early life exposure to per- and polyfluoroalkyl substances (PFAS) and latent health outcomes: A review including the placenta as a target tissue and possible driver of peri- and postnatal effects. *Toxicology, 443*, 152565. https://doi.org/10.1016/j.tox.2020.152565

[15] https://www.fda.gov/food/food-packaging-other-substances-come-contact-food-information-consumers/bisphenol-bpa-use-food-contact-application#:~:text=BPA%20has%20been%20used%20in,can%20be%20consumed%20with%20it.

[16] Manikkam, M., Guerrero-Bosagna, C., Tracey, R., Haque, M. M., & Skinner, M. K. (2012). Transgenerational actions of environmental compounds on reproductive disease and identification of epigenetic biomarkers of ancestral exposures. *PloS one, 7*(2), e31901. https://doi.org/10.1371/journal.pone.0031901

[17] Manikkam, M., Guerrero-Bosagna, C., Tracey, R., Haque, M. M., & Skinner, M. K. (2012). Transgenerational actions of environmental compounds on reproductive disease and identification of epigenetic biomarkers of ancestral exposures. *PloS one, 7*(2), e31901. https://doi.org/10.1371/journal.pone.0031901

[18] La Merrill, M. A., Krigbaum, N. Y., Cirillo, P. M., & Cohn, B. A. (2020). Association between maternal exposure to the pesticide dichlorodiphenyltrichloroethane (DDT) and risk of obesity in middle age. *International journal of obesity (2005), 44*(8), 1723–1732. https://doi.org/10.1038/s41366-020-0586-7

[19] La Merrill, M. A., Krigbaum, N. Y., Cirillo, P. M., & Cohn, B. A. (2020). Association between maternal exposure to the pesticide dichlorodiphenyltrichloroethane (DDT) and risk of obesity in middle age. *International journal of obesity (2005), 44*(8), 1723–1732. https://doi.org/10.1038/s41366-020-0586-7

[20] Fenton, S. E., Ducatman, A., Boobis, A., DeWitt, J. C., Lau, C., Ng, C., Smith, J. S., & Roberts, S. M. (2021). Per- and Polyfluoroalkyl Substance Toxicity and Human Health Review: Current State of Knowledge and Strategies for Informing Future Research. *Environmental toxicology and chemistry, 40*(3), 606–630. https://doi.org/10.1002/etc.4890

[21] Nielsen, C., & Jöud, A. (2021). Susceptibility to COVID-19 after High Exposure to Perfluoroalkyl Substances from Contaminated Drinking Water: An Ecological Study

from Ronneby, Sweden. *International journal of environmental research and public health*, *18*(20), 10702. https://doi.org/10.3390/ijerph182010702

[22] Balali-Mood Mahdi , Naseri Kobra , Tahergorabi Zoya , Khazdair Mohammad Reza , Sadeghi Mahmood Toxic Mechanisms of Five Heavy Metals: Mercury, Lead, Chromium, Cadmium, and Arsenic Frontiers in Pharmacology VOL 12 2021 https://www.frontiersin.org/journals/pharmacology/articles/10.3389/fphar.2021.643972 10.3389/fphar.2021.643972 1663-9812

[23] https://blogs.loc.gov/law/2022/04/the-history-of-the-elimination-of-leaded-gasoline/#:~:text=In %20the %20US %2C %20the %20Environmental,gram %20per %20gallon %20by %201986.

[24] Braun, J. M., Kahn, R. S., Froehlich, T., Auinger, P., & Lanphear, B. P. (2006). Exposures to environmental toxicants and attention deficit hyperactivity disorder in US children. *Environmental health perspectives*, *114*(12), 1904–1909. https://doi.org/10.1289/ehp.9478

[25] Braun, J. M., Kahn, R. S., Froehlich, T., Auinger, P., & Lanphear, B. P. (2006). Exposures to environmental toxicants and attention deficit hyperactivity disorder in US children. *Environmental health perspectives*, *114*(12), 1904–1909. https://doi.org/10.1289/ehp.9478

[26] Cecil, K. M., Brubaker, C. J., Adler, C. M., Dietrich, K. N., Altaye, M., Egelhoff, J. C., Wessel, S., Elangovan, I., Hornung, R., Jarvis, K., & Lanphear, B. P. (2008). Decreased brain volume in adults with childhood lead exposure. *PLoS medicine*, *5*(5), e112. https://doi.org/10.1371/journal.pmed.0050112

[27] https://www.atsdr.cdc.gov/pfas/health effects/index.html#: :text=These %20animal %20studies %20have %20found,newborn %20deaths %20in %20lab %20animals.

[28] https://www.healthandenvironment.org/uploads-old/MentalHealth.pdf

[29] https://www.niehs.nih.gov/health/topics/agents/endocrine

[30] Beard, J. D., Umbach, D. M., Hoppin, J. A., Richards, M., Alavanja, M. C., Blair, A., Sandler, D. P., & Kamel, F. (2014). Pesticide exposure and depression among male private pesticide applicators in t he agricultural health study. Environmental health perspectives, 122(9), 984–991. https://doi.org/10.1289/ehp.1307450

<u>CHAPTER 17: THE PROBLEM WITH COLLEGE</u>

[1] https://twitter.com/BarackObama/status/360093742532788224

[2] https://blog.massmutual.com/planning/college-admissions-counselors#:~:text=The%20IECA%20reported%20that%20the,the%20%244%2C000%2D%246%2C000%20range.&text=For%20families%20on%20a%20tight,fees%20or%20waive%20them%20altogether.

[3] https://www.aplu.org/our-work/4-policy-and-advocacy/publicuvalues/employment-earnings/

[4] https://sites.ed.gov/naciqi/files/2018/05/Complete-History-Series.pdf

[5] https://www.chronicle.com/article/how-the-gi-bill-changed-higher-education/

[6] https://www.history.com/news/gi-bill-black-wwii-veterans-benefits

[7] https://www.chronicle.com/article/how-the-gi-bill-changed-higher-education/

[8] https://www.chronicle.com/article/how-the-gi-bill-changed-higher-education/

[9] https://www.chronicle.com/article/how-the-gi-bill-changed-higher-education/

[10] https://www.npr.org/2014/03/18/290868013/how-the-cost-of-college-went-from-affordable-to-sky-high

[11] https://www.npr.org/2014/03/18/290868013/how-the-cost-of-college-went-from-affordable-to-sky-high

[12] https://www.npr.org/2014/03/18/290868013/how-the-cost-of-college-went-from-affordable-to-sky-high

[13] https://www.npr.org/2014/03/18/290868013/how-the-cost-of-college-went-from-affordable-to-sky-high

[14] https://www.npr.org/2014/03/18/290868013/how-the-cost-of-college-went-from-affordable-to-sky-high

[15] https://www.chronicle.com/article/the-new-order

[16] https://www.abc10.com/article/news/local/what-happened-to-californias-free-tuition-a-history-of-fees-and-budget-issues/103-465128027

[17] https://www.nytimes.com/1982/11/14/education/reagan-record-in-education-mixed-results.html

[18] https://www.dissentmagazine.org/article/from-master-plan-to-no-plan-the-slow-death-of-public-higher-education/

[19] https://www.dissentmagazine.org/article/from-master-plan-to-no-plan-the-slow-death-of-public-higher-education/

[20] https://www.dissentmagazine.org/article/from-master-plan-to-no-plan-the-slow-death-of-public-higher-education/

[21] https://www.nytimes.com/2023/06/30/briefing/affirmative-action-supreme-court-decision.html

[22] https://www.gse.harvard.edu/ideas/usable-knowledge/18/07/case-affirmative-action#:~:text=The%20purpose%20of%20affirmative%20action,thinking%20on%20issues%20of%20race.

[23] https://soeonline.american.edu/blog/inequality-in-public-school-funding/

[24] Smedley BD, Stith AY, Colburn L, et al.; Institute of Medicine (US). The Right Thing to Do, The Smart Thing to Do: Enhancing Diversity in the Health Professions: Summary of the Symposium on Diversity in Health Professions in Honor of Herbert W. Nickens, M.D. Washington (DC): National Academies Press (US); 2001. *Inequality in Teaching and Schooling: How Opportunity Is Rationed to Students of Color in America*. Available from: https://www.ncbi.nlm.nih.gov/books/NBK223640/

[25] https://www.theguardian.com/us-news/2019/jan/23/elite-schools-ivy-league-legacy-admissions-harvard-wealthier-whiter

[26] https://talkpoverty.org/2016/05/02/why-student-loan-debt-harms-low-income-students-the-most/index.html

[27] https://ballardbrief.byu.edu/issue-briefs/educational-disparities-among-racial-and-ethnic-minority-youth-in-the-united-states

[28] Alam, A., & Mohanty, A. (2023). Cultural beliefs and equity in educational institutions: exploring the social and philosophical notions of ability groupings in teaching and learning of mathematics. *International Journal of Adolescence and Youth, 28*(1). https://doi.org/10.1080/02673843.2023.2270662

[29] https://www.ed.gov/news/press-releases/us-department-education-releases-report-state-school-diversity-announces-new-grant-opportunity#:~:text=Schools%20that%20are%20isolated%20along,to%20grow%20and%20excel%20academically.

[30] https://cew.georgetown.edu/cew-reports/the-college-payoff/

[31] https://www.highereddatastories.com/2019/08/changes-in-educational-attainment-1940.html

[32] https://www.statista.com/statistics/184260/educational-attainment-in-the-

[33] https://bpr.studentorg.berkeley.edu/2021/01/30/no-more-lies-the-truth-about-raising-the-minimum-wage/#:~:text=The%20slow%20growth%20of%20wages,in%20the%20same%20time%20period.

[34] https://www.bestcolleges.com/research/college-costs-over-time/#:~:text=Across%20all%20types%20of%20schools,times%2C%20between%20196

3%20and%202021.&text=Compared%20to%20other%20school%20types,to%20just%2
0under%20%2422%2C000%20annually.

[35] https://educationdata.org/college-dropout-
rates#:~:text=College%20dropout%20rates%20indicate%20that,up%20to%2040%25%2
0drop%20out.

[36] https://www.bls.gov/careeroutlook/2023/data-on-display/education-pays.htm

[37] https://www.ihep.org/press/most-colleges-lead-to-a-return-on-investment-for-students/

[38] https://static1.squarespace.com/static/6197797102be715f55c0e0a1/t/64192bd965e9974c7
81cd025/1679371227418/Making+The+Bachelor%27s+Degree+More+Valuable.pdf

[39] https://static1.squarespace.com/static/6197797102be715f55c0e0a1/t/64192bd965e9974c7
81cd025/1679371227418/Making+The+Bachelor%27s+Degree+More+Valuable.pdf

[40] https://www.wsj.com/lifestyle/careers/college-degree-jobs-unused-440b2abd

[41] https://www.bls.gov/opub/mlr/1990/article/1980s-a-decade-of-job-growth-and-industry-
shifts.htm

[42] https://www.edweek.org/teaching-learning/gen-z-lacks-job-readiness-skills-survey-
shows/2023/12

[43] https://www.foxbusiness.com/lifestyle/college-grads-struggling-land-jobs-lack-
preparedness-study-finds#

[44] https://www.voanews.com/a/forty-percent-of-employers-avoid-hiring-gen-z-workers-
survey-says-/7425325.html#

[45] https://www.business.com/hiring/new-graduates-job-search-experiment/

[46] https://www.business.com/hiring/new-graduates-job-search-experiment/

[47] https://www.bls.gov/news.release/empsit.nr0.htm

[48] https://www.forbes.com/sites/karadennison/2023/11/27/how-ghost-job-postings-are-
creating-a-false-sense-of-hope/?sh=56b8e86a7dc0

[49] https://www.forbes.com/sites/karadennison/2023/11/27/how-ghost-job-postings-are-
creating-a-false-sense-of-hope/?sh=56b8e86a7dc0

[50] https://www.cbsnews.com/news/ai-job-losses-artificial-intelligence-challenger-report/

[51] https://seo.ai/blog/ai-replacing-jobs-statistics

[52] https://www.mckinsey.com/featured-insights/future-of-work/ai-automation-and-the-
future-of-work-ten-things-to-solve-for

[53] https://www.apa.org/monitor/2023/07/psychologists-preventing-teen-suicide

[54] Martinez-Ales, G., Hernandez-Calle, D., Khauli, N., & Keyes, K. M. (2020). Why Are
Suicide Rates Increasing in the United States? Towards a Multilevel Reimagination of
Suicide Prevention. Current topics in behavioral neurosciences, 46, 1–23.
https://doi.org/10.1007/7854_2020_158

[55] Jiang, M. M., Gao, K., Wu, Z. Y., & Guo, P. P. (2022). The influence of academic
pressure on adolescents' problem behavior: Chain mediating effects of self-control,
parent-child conflict, and subjective well-being. *Frontiers in psychology*, *13*, 954330.
https://doi.org/10.3389/fpsyg.2022.954330

[56] https://pacificteentreatment.com/mental-health/what-are-the-effects-of-academic-
pressure/

[57] https://pacificteentreatment.com/mental-health/what-are-the-effects-of-academic-
pressure/

[58] https://pacificteentreatment.com/mental-health/what-are-the-effects-of-academic-
pressure/

[59] https://pacificteentreatment.com/mental-health/what-are-the-effects-of-academic-
pressure/

[60] https://pacificteentreatment.com/mental-health/what-are-the-effects-of-academic-
pressure/

[61] Alhamed A. A. (2023). The link among academic stress, sleep disturbances, depressive symptoms, academic performance, and the moderating role of resourcefulness in health professions students during COVID-19 pandemic. *Journal of professional nursing: official journal of the American Association of Colleges of Nursing, 46*, 83–91. https://doi.org/10.1016/j.profnurs.2023.02.010

[62] https://www.ucl.ac.uk/news/2023/aug/link-found-between-academic-pressure-and-mental-health-problems-adolescence

[63] Zhang, C., Shi, L., Tian, T., Zhou, Z., Peng, X., Shen, Y., Li, Y., & Ou, J. (2022). Associations Between Academic Stress and Depressive Symptoms Mediated by Anxiety Symptoms and Hopelessness Among Chinese College Students. *Psychology research and behavior management, 15*, 547–556. https://doi.org/10.2147/PRBM.S353778

[64] Wu, Q., Qi, T., Wei, J., & Shaw, A. (2023). Relationship between psychological detachment from work and depressive symptoms: indirect role of emotional exhaustion and moderating role of self-compassion. *BMC psychology, 11*(1), 344. https://doi.org/10.1186/s40359-023-01384-z

[65] Thomas Steare, Carolina Gutiérrez Muñoz, Alice Sullivan, Gemma Lewis, The association between academic pressure and adolescent mental health problems: A systematic review, Journal of Affective Disorders, Volume 339, 2023, Pages 302-317, ISSN 0165-0327, https://doi.org/10.1016/j.jad.2023.07.028.

[66] Jiang, M. M., Gao, K., Wu, Z. Y., & Guo, P. P. (2022). The influence of academic pressure on adolescents' problem behavior: Chain mediating effects of self-control, parent-child conflict, and subjective well-being. *Frontiers in psychology, 13*, 954330. https://doi.org/10.3389/fpsyg.2022.954330

[67] https://www.npr.org/2021/10/07/1043737586/college-degree-high-school-diploma-high-paying-trade-jobs

[68] https://www.npr.org/2021/10/07/1043737586/college-degree-high-school-diploma-high-paying-trade-jobs

CHAPTER 18: THE CULT OF GUNS IN AMERICA

[1] https://www.law.cornell.edu/wex/second_amendment

[2] https://www.sandyhookpromise.org/blog/gun-violence/facts-about-gun-violence-and-school-shootings/

[3] https://www.sandyhookpromise.org/blog/gun-violence/facts-about-gun-violence-and-school-shootings/

[4] https://www.washingtonpost.com/education/interactive/school-shootings-database/

[5] https://www.statista.com/statistics/971544/number-k-12-school-shootings-us-age-shooter/

[6] https://www.statesman.com/story/news/politics/politifact/2022/05/27/fact-check-most-mass-shooters-ages-18-19-texas-school-shooting-uvalde-robb-elementary/9933032002/

[7] https://pewrsr.ch/448q4hU

[8] Stuart H. (2003). Violence and mental illness: an overview. *World psychiatry : official journal of the World Psychiatric Association (WPA), 2*(2), 121–124.

[9] https://www.cdc.gov/vitalsigns/firearm-deaths/index.html

[10] https://www.cdc.gov/vitalsigns/firearm-deaths/index.html

[11] https://siepr.stanford.edu/publications/health/surviving-school-shooting-impacts-mental-health-education-and-earnings-american

[12] https://siepr.stanford.edu/publications/health/surviving-school-shooting-impacts-mental-health-education-and-earnings-american

[13] https://siepr.stanford.edu/publications/health/surviving-school-shooting-impacts-mental-health-education-and-earnings-american

[14] https://siepr.stanford.edu/publications/health/surviving-school-shooting-impacts-mental-health-education-and-earnings-american

[15] Cabral, Marika, Bokyung Kim, Maya Rossin-Slater, Molly Schnell, and Hannes Schwandt, "Trauma at School: The Impacts of Shootings on Students' Human Capital and Economic Outcomes," No. w28311, National Bureau of Economic Research, 2021.

[16] https://siepr.stanford.edu/publications/health/surviving-school-shooting-impacts-mental-health-education-and-earnings-american

[17] Rossin-Slater, Maya, Molly Schnell, Hannes Schwandt, Sam Trejo, and Lindsey Uniat, "Local exposure to school shootings and youth antidepressant use," *Proceedings of the National Academy of Sciences*, 2020, 117 (38), 23484–23489.

[18] Levine, Phillip B., and Robin McKnight, "Exposure to a School Shooting and Subsequent Well-Being," Working Paper w28307, *National Bureau of Economic Research*, 2020.

[19] Lowe, Sarah R., and Sandro Galea, "The mental health consequences of mass shootings," *Trauma, Violence, & Abuse*, 2017, 18 (1), 62–82.

[20] Smith, M.E., Sharpe, T.L., Richardson, J., Pahwa, R., Smith, D., & DeVylder, J. The impact of exposure to gun violence fatality on mental health outcomes in four urban U.S. settings. *Soc Sci Med*. 2020. Feb:246:112587. doi: 10.1016/j.socscimed.2019.112587. Epub 2019 Oct 4.

[21] Smith, M.E., Sharpe, T.L., Richardson, J., Pahwa, R., Smith, D., & DeVylder, J. The impact of exposure to gun violence fatality on mental health outcomes in four urban U.S. settings. *Soc Sci Med*. 2020. Feb:246:112587. doi: 10.1016/j.socscimed.2019.112587. Epub 2019 Oct 4.

[22] https://constitution.congress.gov

[23] https://www.fmprc.gov.cn/eng/wjdt_665385/2649_665393/202302/t20230216_11025874.html#:~:text=The%20United%20States%20is%20the,of%20global%20civilian%20gun%20ownership.

[24] https://www.healthdata.org/news-events/insights-blog/acting-data/gun-violence-united-states-outlier

[25] https://www.hoplofobia.info/wp-content/uploads/2015/08/MGLC-3rd-Edition.pdf

[26] https://www.scientificamerican.com/article/more-guns-do-not-stop-more-crimes-evidence-shows/

[27] https://med.stanford.edu/news/all-news/2020/06/handgun-ownership-associated-with-much-higher-suicide-risk.html

[28] https://www.bbc.com/news/world-us-canada-35261394#:~:text=The%20association%20claimed%20that%20membership,at%20closer%20to%20three%20million.&text=Current%20NRA%20members%20include%20former,Tom%20Selleck%20and%20Whoopi%20Goldberg.

[29] https://www.cnn.com/2018/02/21/politics/trump-listening-sessions-parkland-students/index.html#:~:text="If%20you%20had%20a%20teacher,may%20try%20and%20attack%20them.

[30] https://www.npr.org/2022/05/29/1101994074/nra-convention-houston-ends#:~:text=Science-,After%20the%20Uvalde%20shooting%2C%20the%20NRA%20convention%20went%20on%20as,advocating%20for%20gun%20control%20legislation.

[31] https://news.gallup.com/poll/513623/majority-continues-favor-stricter-gun-laws.aspx

[32] https://elections.bradyunited.org/take-action/nra-donations-116th-congress-senators

[33] https://nrawatch.org/news/nra-membership-dues-and-spending-continue-to-shrink-report-shows/

[34] https://www.statista.com/statistics/249398/lobbying-expenditures-of-the-national-rifle-associaction-in-the-united-states/

[35] https://tigermedianet.com/?p=39228

[36] https://www.americanprogress.org/article/guns-lies-fear/

[37] https://www.bu.edu/articles/2022/the-long-failed-history-of-gun-control-legislation/

[38] https://www.bradyunited.org/take-action/sign-a-petition/dissolve-the-nra

[39] https://news.gallup.com/poll/513623/majority-continues-favor-stricter-gun-laws.aspx

[40] https://news.gallup.com/poll/513623/majority-continues-favor-stricter-gun-laws.aspx

[41] https://www.americanprogress.org/article/debunking-the-guns-make-us-safer-myth/

[42] Katherine Schaeffer, "Key facts about Americans and guns," Pew Research Center, September 13, 2023, available at https://www.pewresearch.org/short-reads/2023/09/13/key-facts-about-americans-and-guns/

[43] https://www.americanprogress.org/article/debunking-the-guns-make-us-safer-myth/

[44] Laura Kurtzman, "Access to Guns Increases Risk of Suicide, Homicide," University of California, San Francisco, January 21, 2014, available at https://www.ucsf.edu/news/2014/01/111286/access-guns-increases-risk-suicide-homicide.

[45] https://www.americanprogress.org/article/debunking-the-guns-make-us-safer-myth/

[46] https://www.reuters.com/world/us/number-us-children-killed-by-guns-hit-record-high-2021-study-2023-08-22/

CHAPTER 19: THE PROBLEM WITH INDIVIDUALISM

[1] https://hls.harvard.edu/today/the-business-ethics-of-elon-musk-tesla-twitter-and-the-tech-industry/

[2] https://www.cnbc.com/2020/08/05/how-bill-gates-mother-influenced-the-success-of-microsoft.html

[3] https://www.census.gov/programs-surveys/ces/data/analysis-visualization-tools/opportunity-atlas.html

[4] Bloome D. (2017). Childhood Family Structure and Intergenerational Income Mobility in the United States. *Demography*, *54*(2), 541–569. https://doi.org/10.1007/s13524-017-0564-4

[5] https://www.wsj.com/articles/BL-REB-35714

[6] https://liberalarts.tamu.edu/blog/2020/05/15/why-was-germany-more-effective-at-containing-covid-19/

[7] https://www.youtube.com/watch?v=jW6wdS2murg

[8] https://www.simplypsychology.org/what-areindividualisticcultures.html

[9] Hofstede, G. (1980). Culture and Organizations. *International Studies of Management & Organization*, *10*(4), 15–41. http://www.jstor.org/stable/40396875

[10] Schwartz, Shalom. (1990). Individualism-Collectivism Critique and Proposed Refinements. Journal of Cross-Cultural Psychology. 21. 139-157. 10.1177/0022022190212001.

[11] Hampton, R.S., Varnum, M.E.W. (2020). Individualism-Collectivism. In: Zeigler-Hill, V., Shackelford, T.K. (eds) Encyclopedia of Personality and Individual Differences. Springer, Cham. https://doi.org/10.1007/978-3-319-24612-3_2023

[12] Svoray, T., Dorman, M., Abu-Kaf, S. et al. Nature and happiness in an individualist and a collectivist culture. Sci Rep 12, 7701 (2022). https://doi.org/10.1038/s41598-022-11619-5

[13] https://www.simplypsychology.org/what-are-individualistic-cultures.html

[14] https://www.simplypsychology.org/what-are-individualistic-cultures.html

[15] https://morganlatif.com/insight/how-does-empathy-vary-across-different-cultures/#:~:text=In%20contrast%2C%20cultures%20that%20are,and%20valuing%20their%20self%2Dexpression.

[16] Eckersley, R. A New Narrative of Young People's Health and Wellbeing. *J. Youth Stud.* **2011**, *14*, 627–638.

[17] Scott, G., Ciarrochi, J. and Deane, F.P. (2004), Disadvantages of being an individualist in an individualistic culture: Idiocentrism, emotional competence, stress, and mental health. Australian Psychologist, 39: 143-154. https://doi.org/10.1080/00050060410001701861

[18] Humphrey, A., & Bliuc, A. 2022. "Western Individualism and the Psychological Wellbeing of Young People: A Systematic Review of Their Associations" *Youth* 2, no. 1: 1-11. https://doi.org/10.3390/youth2010001

[19] Eskin M, Tran US, Carta MG, Poyrazli S, Flood C, Mechri A, Shaheen A, Janghorbani M, Khader Y, Yoshimasu K, Sun JM, Kujan O, Abuidhail J, Aidoudi K, Bakhshi S, Harlak H, Moro MF, Phillips L, Hamdan M, Aburderman A, Tsuno K, Voracek M. Is Individualism Suicidogenic? Findings From a Multinational Study of Young Adults From 12 Countries. Front Psychiatry. 2020 Apr 3;11:259. doi: 10.3389/fpsyt.2020.00259. PMID: 32308634; PMCID: PMC7145967.

[20] Bettencourt, B.A.; Dorr, N. Collective self esteem as a mediator of the relationship between allocentrism and subjective well-being. *Personal. Soc. Psychol. Bull.* **1997**, *23*, 955–964.

[21] https://www.bbc.com/worklife/article/20220218-are-younger-generations-truly-weaker-than-older-ones

[22] https://leaderchat.org/2019/02/01/the-importance-of-self-awareness-with-tasha-eurich/#:~:text="Our%20data%20reveals%20that%2095,%2Dawareness%3A%20internal%20and%20external.

[23] https://time.com/6271915/self-love-loneliness/

[24] https://theholisticpsychologist.com

[25] https://www.amazon.com/Self-Love-Experiment-Principles-Compassionate-Accepting/dp/0143130692

[26] https://drdansiegel.com/book/intraconnected-mwe-me-we-as-the-integration-of-self-identity-and-belonging/

[27] https://drdansiegel.com/book/intraconnected-mwe-me-we-as-the-integration-of-self-identity-and-belonging/

[28] https://www.goodtherapy.org/blog/how-advertisements-targeting-women-undermine-body-image-0708137

[29] https://www.forbes.com/sites/traversmark/2022/11/13/a-psychologist-tells-you-why-you-need-to-escape-the-toxic-world-of-self-help/?sh=6db5eb2d3785

[30] https://www.sbs.com.au/news/the-feed/article/the-industry-rakes-in-billions-each-year-but-does-self-help-actually-work/n1mhgtywi

[31] https://www.mentalhelp.net/blogs/when-self-focus-becomes-a-hazard/

[32] https://citeseerx.ist.psu.edu/document?repid=rep1&type=pdf&doi=7c868e877f24b7c3d2f181022ea66d197479ff59

[33] https://www.npr.org/sections/health-shots/2015/11/29/457255876/loneliness-may-warp-our-genes-and-our-immune-systems

[34] https://www.ama-assn.org/delivering-care/public-health/what-doctors-wish-patients-knew-about-loneliness-and-health

[35] Raymond, C., Marin, M. F., Hand, A., Sindi, S., Juster, R. P., & Lupien, S. J. (2016). Salivary Cortisol Levels and Depressive Symptomatology in Consumers and Nonconsumers of Self-Help Books: A Pilot Study. *Neural plasticity, 2016*, 3136743. https://doi.org/10.1155/2016/3136743

[36] Labouliere, C. D., Kleinman, M., & Gould, M. S. (2015). When self-reliance is not safe: associations between reduced help-seeking and subsequent mental health symptoms in suicidal adolescents. *International journal of environmental research and public health, 12*(4), 3741–3755. https://doi.org/10.3390/ijerph120403741

[37] https://www.pewresearch.org/short-reads/2019/07/22/key-findings-about-americans-declining-trust-in-government-and-each-other/

CHAPTER 20: THE PATH TOWARDS SYSTEMIC CHANGE

[1] https://nlihc.org/sites/default/files/oor/2021/Out-of-Reach_2021.pdf

[2] https://info.primarycare.hms.harvard.edu/perspectives/articles/mental-health-unaffordable

[3] Baicker K, Chandra A, Shepard M. A Different Framework to Achieve Universal Coverage in the US. JAMA Health Forum. 2023;4(2):e230187. doi:10.1001/jamahealthforum.2023.0187

(220 medical debt)https://www.healthsystemtracker.org/brief/the-burden-of-medical-debt-in-the-united-states/

[4] Baicker K, Chandra A, Shepard M. A Different Framework to Achieve Universal Coverage in the US. JAMA Health Forum. 2023;4(2):e230187. doi:10.1001/jamahealthforum.2023.0187

[5] https://www.brookings.edu/articles/designing-us-health-insurance-from-scratch-a-proposal-for-universal-basic-coverage/

[6]https://www.internationalinsurance.com/health/systems/sweden.php#:~:text=Public%20healthcare%20in%20Sweden%20is,now%20carry%20private%20health%20insurance.

[7] https://www.health.org.uk/publications/long-reads/nine-major-challenges-facing-health-and-care-in-england#:~:text=The%20main%20reasons%20people%20gave,supporters%20of%20different%20political%20parties.

[8] https://www.politico.com/story/2019/04/15/pete-buttigieg-national-service-program-1277274

[9] https://www.cnbc.com/2019/07/03/pete-buttigieg-calls-for-national-service-plan-with-student-debt-relief.html

[10] https://www.cnbc.com/2019/07/03/pete-buttigieg-calls-for-national-service-plan-with-student-debt-relief.html

[11] https://www.democracyinaction.us/2020/buttigieg/buttigiegpolicy070319service.html

[12] https://www.democracyinaction.us/2020/buttigieg/buttigiegpolicy070319service.html

[13] https://www.democracyinaction.us/2020/buttigieg/buttigiegpolicy070319service.html

[14] https://www.cato.org/commentary/mandatory-national-service-bad-idea-wont-die

[15] https://research.com/universities-colleges/college-dropout-rates#:~:text=What%20percentage%20of%20people%20drop,%5BEDI%5D%2C%202020 21).

[16] Bower, M., Kent, J., Patulny, R., Green, O., McGrath, L., Teesson, L., Jamalishahni, T., Sandison, H., & Rugel, E. The impact of the built environment on loneliness: A systematic review and narrative synthesis, Health & Place, Volume 79, 2023, 102962, ISSN 1353-8292, https://doi.org/10.1016/j.healthplace.2022.102962.

[17] Navarrete-Hernandez, P., & Laffan, K. A greener urban environment: Designing green infrastructure interventions to promote citizens' subjective wellbeing, Landscape and Urban Planning, Volume 191, 2019, 103618, ISSN 0169-2046, https://doi.org/10.1016/j.landurbplan.2019.103618.

[18] Moore, G., Fardghassemi, S., & Joffe, H. Wellbeing in the city: Young adults' sense of loneliness and social connection in deprived urban neighbourhoods, Wellbeing, Space and Society, Volume 5, 2023, 100172, ISSN 2666-5581,https://doi.org/10.1016/j.wss.2023.100172.

[19] https://insights.grcglobalgroup.com/the-impact-of-pedestrian-friendly-urban-planning-on-communities/

[20] Finlay, J., Esposito, M., Kim, M. H., Gomez-Lopez, I., & Clarke, P. (2019). Closure of 'third places'? Exploring potential consequences for collective health and wellbeing. *Health & place*, *60*, 102225. https://doi.org/10.1016/j.healthplace.2019.102225

[21] Swaminathan, S. & Schellenberg, E.. (2014). Arts education, academic achievement, and cognitive ability. 10.1017/CBO9781139207058.018.

[22] https://calmatters.org/commentary/2022/02/arts-education-is-woefully-underfunded-in-california-schools/

[23] https://www.cde.ca.gov/eo/in/prop28artsandmusicedfunding.asp#:~:text=On%20November%208%2C%202022%2C%20California,schools%20beginning%20in%202023%E2%80%9324.

[24] https://greatergood.berkeley.edu/article/item/how_to_combat_americas_creativity_crisis

[25] https://www.wm.edu/news/stories/2016/the-cure-for-the-creativity-crisis.php

[26] https://www.wm.edu/news/stories/2016/the-cure-for-the-creativity-crisis.php

[27] https://www.csun.edu/~vcpsy00h/creativity/define.htm

[28] https://www.igi-global.com/dictionary/creativity/6166

[29] https://kemlaurin.medium.com/our-outdated-educational-system-is-failing-todays-students-b062ef668257

[30] https://www.americansforthearts.org/by-program/reports-and-data/legislation-policy/what-is-arts-policy/national-arts-policy-history-timeline

[31] Edyta Swider-Cios, Anouk Vermeij, Margriet M. Sitskoorn, Young children and screen-based media: The impact on cognitive and socioemotional development and the importance of parental mediation, Cognitive Development, Volume 66, 2023, 101319, ISSN 0885-2014, https://doi.org/10.1016/j.cogdev.2023.101319.

[32] https://care-clinics.com/therapeutic-benefits-of-art-and-expression/#:~:text=Engaging%20in%20creative%20activities%20can%20reduce%20stress%2C%20foster%20mindfulness%2C%20and,healing%20and%20finding%20inner%20strength.

[33] https://greatergood.berkeley.edu/article/item/how_to_combat_americas_creativity_crisis

[34] https://greatergood.berkeley.edu/article/item/how_to_combat_americas_creativity_crisis

[35] https://www.forbes.com/sites/forbesbusinesscouncil/2023/08/16/the-power-of-diversity-and-inclusion-driving-innovation-and-success/?sh=209d004c2505

[36] https://www.consizos.com/strategy/adhocracy-culture/

[37] https://breakthroughcolab.com/empowering-teams-through-collaborative-leadership/

[38] https://en.wikipedia.org/wiki/Rwandan_genocide#:~:text=The%20most%20widely%20accepted%20scholarly,500%2C000%20to%20800%2C000%20Tutsi%20deaths.

[39] https://open.maricopa.edu/twowatersreviewvolumeone/chapter/ashley-clark-how-ordinary-people-become-perpetrators-of-genocide-a-look-at-the-psychological-factors/

[40] https://www.burmalibrary.org/docs23/Dutton-The-Psychology-of-Genocide-Massacres-and-Extreme-Violence-red.pdf

[41] Williams, T. "The Complexity of Evil: A Multi-Faceted Approach to Genocide Perpetration." *Zeitschrift Für Friedens- Und Konfliktforschung* 3, no. 1 (2014): 71–98. https://www.jstor.org/stable/48518906.

42 https://www.hrw.org/legacy/backgrounder/africa/rwanda0406/

43 https://www.hrw.org/legacy/backgrounder/africa/rwanda0406/

44 https://en.wikipedia.org/wiki/January_6_United_States_Capitol_attack

45 https://www.adl.org/january-6-effect-evolution-hate-and-extremism

46 https://abcnews.go.com/US/republicans-false-pedophilia-claims-attack-democrats-lgbtq-people/story?id=84344687

47 Jiang, J., Ren, X., & Ferrara, E. (2021). Social Media Polarization and Echo Chambers in the Context of COVID-19: Case Study. *JMIRx med*, *2*(3), e29570. https://doi.org/10.2196/29570

48 https://greatergood.berkeley.edu/article/item/when_is_political_polariz ation_good_and_when_does_it_go_bad

49 https://en.wikipedia.org/wiki/Democratic_backsliding_in_the_United_ States

50 https://www.queensu.ca/gazette/stories/political-polarization-affecting-mental-health

51 Smith K. B. (2022). Politics is making us sick: The negative impact of political engagement on public health during the Trump administration. PloS one, 17(1), e0262022. https://doi.org/10.1371/journal.pone.0262022

52 https://www.sciencedaily.com/releases/2019/09/190926073348.htm

53 https://www.apa.org/monitor/2022/03/career-navigating-therapy

54 https://www.fec.gov/legal-resources/court-cases/citizens-united-v-fec/#:~:text=On%20January%2021%2C%202010%2C%20the,the%20part%20of%20McConnell%20v.

55 https://campaignlegal.org/update/how-does-citizens-united-decision-still-affect-us-2024

56 https://www.fec.gov/press/resources-journalists/political-action-committees-pacs/

57 https://campaignlegal.org/update/super-pacs-are-continuing-hide-secret-money-wealthy-special-interests-heres-how

58 https://www.justice.gov/opa/pr/johnson-johnson-pay-more-22-billion-resolve-criminal-and-civil-investigations#:~:text=Until%20late%202006%2C%20Risperdal%20was,to%20write%20prescriptions%20for%20Risperdal.

59 https://www.lexology.com/library/detail.aspx?g=bac4e90d-6b80-4329-bd9f-aa2b251f789e

60 https://www.pbs.org/newshour/show/what-is-christian-nationalism-and-why-it-raises-concerns-about-threats-to-democracy

61 https://isps.yale.edu/news/blog/2022/10/understanding-white-christian-nationalism

62 https://isps.yale.edu/news/blog/2022/10/understanding-white-christian-nationalism

63 Müller, Veronika, 'Right, Left, and Religious Ideologies: Their Need-Serving Capacities and Potential for Conflicts', *Ideology and the Microfoundations of Conflict: From Human Needs to Intergroup Violence*(New York, 2024; online edn, Oxford Academic, 22 Feb. 2024), https://doi.org/10.1093/oso/9780197670187.003.0007, accessed 18 Apr. 2024.

64 https://www.timesofisrael.com/in-documentary-god-and-country-rob-reiner-shines-a-light-on-christian-nationalism/

65 https://www.americanprogress.org/article/nondiscrimination-protections-for-lgbtq-communities/

66 Misra, S., Kwon, S. C., Abraído-Lanza, A. F., Chebli, P., Trinh-Shevrin, C., & Yi, S. S. (2021). Structural Racism and Immigrant Health in the United States. *Health education & behavior : the official publication of the Society for Public Health Education*, 48(3), 332–341. https://doi.org/10.1177/10901981211010676

[67] Williams, D. R., Lawrence, J. A., Davis, B. A., & Vu, C. (2019). Understanding how discrimination can affect health. *Health services research, 54 Suppl 2*(Suppl 2), 1374–1388. https://doi.org/10.1111/1475-6773.13222

[68] Pascoe, E. A., & Smart Richman, L. (2009). Perceived discrimination and health: a meta-analytic review. *Psychological bulletin, 135*(4), 531–554. https://doi.org/10.1037/a0016059

[69] Pascoe, E. A., & Smart Richman, L. (2009). Perceived discrimination and health: a meta-analytic review. *Psychological bulletin, 135*(4), 531–554. https://doi.org/10.1037/a0016059

[70] https://2020.yang2020.com/what-is-freedom-dividend-faq/

[71] https://thereader.mitpress.mit.edu/the-deep-and-enduring-history-of-universal-basic-income/

[72] Naomi Wilson, Shari McDaid, The mental health effects of a Universal Basic Income: A synthesis of the evidence from previous pilots, Social Science & Medicine, Volume 287, 2021, 114374, ISSN 0277-9536, https://doi.org/10.1016/j.socscimed.2021.114374.

[73] https://psych.ubc.ca/news/cash-transfers-to-people-experiencing-homelessness/

[74] https://basicincome.stanford.edu/news/lab-updates/global-map-of-ubi-experiments-where-have-we-been-where-are-we-now-and-where-are-we-going/

[75] Frasquilho, D., Matos, M., Salonna, F. *et al.* Mental health outcomes in times of economic recession: a systematic literature review. *BMC Public Health* 16, 115 (2015). https://doi.org/10.1186/s12889-016-2720-y

[76] https://www.procon.org/headlines/universal-basic-income-top-3-pros-and-cons/

[77] Aceytuno-Pérez, M.T. & De Paz Báñez, M.A. & Sánchez-López, C. (2023). Assessing the Impact of the Implementation of Universal Basic Income on Entrepreneurship. Basic Income Studies. 18. 10.1515/bis-2022-0022.

[78] Francese & Prady, "Universal Basic Income: Debate and Impact Assessment" International Monetary Fund December 2018://www.cbpp.org › poverty-and-opportunity › com

[79] https://rooseveltinstitute.org/publications/macroeconomic-effects-universal-basic-income-ubi/

[80] https://www.vox.com/policy-and-politics/2017/8/30/16220134/universal-basic-income-roosevelt-institute-economic-growth

[81] https://www.pandemicoversight.gov/data-interactive-tools/data-stories/update-three-rounds-stimulus-checks-see-how-many-went-out-and#:~:text=More%20than%20476%20million%20payments,dependents%2C%20like%20a%20relative).

[82] https://sites.fordschool.umich.edu/poverty2021/files/2022/11/Material-Hardship-PB-final.pdf

[83] https://sites.fordschool.umich.edu/poverty2021/files/2022/11/Material-Hardship-PB-final.pdf

[84] https://medium.com/thoughts-economics-politics-sustainability/pros-and-cons-of-universal-basic-income-d7bd11b5864f

[85] https://www.factcheck.org/2022/06/stimulus-spending-a-factor-but-far-from-whole-story-on-inflation/

[86] Cunha, J.M. "Testing Paternalism: Cash versus In-Kind Transfers." *American Economic Journal: Applied Economics* 6, no. 2 (2014): 195–230. http://www.jstor.org/stable/43189483.

[87] Cunha, J.M. "Testing Paternalism: Cash versus In-Kind Transfers." *American Economic Journal: Applied Economics* 6, no. 2 (2014): 195–230. http://www.jstor.org/stable/43189483.

[88] https://www.census.gov/library/stories/2020/06/how-are-americans-using-their-stimulus-payments.html

89 https://www.census.gov/library/stories/2020/06/how-are-americans-using-their-stimulus-payments.html

90 https://www.foxbusiness.com/economy/nearly-70-percent-americans-struggling-pay-grocery-bills-survey-finds

91 https://www.imf.org/en/Publications/fandd/issues/Series/Back-to-Basics/Fiscal-Policy

92 https://www.nimh.nih.gov/news/science-news/2023/youth-suicide-rates-increased-during-the-covid-19-pandemic

CHAPTER 21: WHAT YOU CAN DO

1 Stroh, D. 2015, *Systems Thinking for Social Change.* p. 32

2 https://www.pulse.ng/lifestyle/sociologist-knows-why-gen-zs-are-emotionally-immature/pftp5mm

3 https://www.news.week.com/companies-avoid-hiring-gen-z-workplace-1884613

4 https://www.tiktok.com/discover/gen-z-needs-to-stop-being-judgemental

5 https://www.pewresearch.org/social-trends/2020/05/14/on-the-cusp-of-adulthood-and-facing-an-uncertain-future-what-we-know-about-gen-z-so-far-2/

6 https://www.amadorvalleytoday.org/9884/news/are-we-the-most-tolerant-or-intolerant-generation-in-history/

7 https://www.mentalhelp.net/depression/judgmental-thinking-and-anxiety/

8 https://www.mentalhelp.net/depression/judgmental-thinking-and-anxiety/

9 https://www.apa.org/topics/resilience/building-your-resilience

10 https://rightasrain.uwmedicine.org/life/parenthood/active-listening-skills

11 https://www.health.harvard.edu/blog/the-art-of-a-heartfelt-apology-20210413222366#:~:text=Aaron%20Lazare%2C%20an%20apology%20expert,your%20behavior%20was%20not%20acceptable.

12 https://connectedpreside.com/the-art-of-a-heartfelt-apology/

13 https://connectedpreside.com/the-art-of-a-heartfelt-apology/

14 https://www.apa.org/gradpsych/2010/09/culturally-competent

15https://www.forbes.com/sites/forbeshumanresourcescouncil/2024/02/05/the-impact-of-gen-z-in-the-workplace/

16 https://www.verdict.co.uk/gen-z-hybrid-working-futute-of-work/#:~:text=Gen%20Z%20is%20demanding%20workplace,uncertainty%20and%20enforced%20remote%20working.

17 https://www.deskbird.com/blog/generation-z-communication-preferences

18 https://moodle.com/us/news/gen-z-workplace-training/#:~:text=In%20workplace%20settings%2C%20Generation%20Z,at%204.89%20out%20of%205.

19 https://hbr.org/2023/09/research-consumers-sustainability-demands-are-rising

EPILOGUE

1 Heifetz, R. A., Grashow, A., & Linsky, M. (2009). The practice of adaptive leadership: Tools and tactics for changing your organization and the world. Harvard Business Review Press. https://www.amazon.com/Practice-Adaptive-Leadership-Changing-Organization/dp/1422105768